The Ethics c

MW01156516

The Ethics of Development: An Introduction systematically and comprehensively examines the ethical issues surrounding the concept of development. The book addresses important questions such as:

- What does development mean?
- Is there a human right to development?
- If we aim for sustainable development in an age of global climate change, should developed nations sacrifice economic growth for the sake of allowing developing countries to catch up?
- Should eradication of poverty or diminution of radical inequality be the principal focus of developmental policy?
- What are the macroeconomic theories of development? And how have they informed development policy?
- How does development work in practice?

Featuring case studies throughout, this textbook provides a philosophical introduction to an incredibly topical issue studied by students within the fields of applied ethics, global justice, economics, politics, sociology, and public policy.

David Ingram is Professor of Philosophy at Loyola University Chicago, USA. His most recent book is *World Crisis and Underdevelopment: A Critical Theory of Poverty, Agency, and Coercion.*

Thomas Derdak is Lecturer in Philosophy at Loyola University Chicago, USA. He has over 20 years of experience in the field of international development and is the executive director of Global Alliance for Africa, an NGO with programs in East Africa.

The Ethics of . . .

Series page URL: https://www.routledge.com/The-Ethics-of-/book-series/ETHICSOF

When is it right to go to war? What are the causes of poverty? Are human intelligence and machine intelligence the same? What is cyber-terrorism? Do races exist? What makes a person a refugee?

Each engaging textbook from *The Ethics of . . .* series focuses on a significant ethical issue and provides a clear and stimulating explanation of the surrounding philosophical discussions. Focusing on moral debates at the forefront of contemporary society, they have been designed for use by students studying philosophy, applied ethics, global ethics and related subjects such as politics, international relations and sociology. Features to aid study include chapter summaries, study questions, annotated further reading and glossaries.

The Ethics of War and Peace: An Introduction
Second Edition
Helen Frowe

The Ethics of Global Poverty: An Introduction
Scott Wisor

The Ethics of Surveillance: An Introduction
Kevin Macnish

The Ethics of Climate Change: An Introduction
Byron Williston

The Ethics of Development: An Introduction
David Ingram and Thomas Derdak

The Ethics of Development

An Introduction

David Ingram and Thomas Derdak

Routledge
Taylor & Francis Group

LONDON AND NEW YORK

First published 2019
by Routledge
2 Park Square, Milton Park, Abingdon, Oxon OX14 4RN

and by Routledge
52 Vanderbilt Avenue, New York, NY 10017

Routledge is an imprint of the Taylor & Francis Group, an informa business

© 2019 David Ingram and Thomas Derdak

British Library Cataloguing-in-Publication Data
A catalogue record for this book is available from the British Library

Library of Congress Cataloging-in-Publication Data
Names: Ingram, David, 1952– author. | Derdak, Thomas, 1952– author.
Title: The ethics of development : an introduction / David Ingram and
    Thomas Derdak.
Description: Abingdon, Oxon ; New York, NY : Routledge, 2019. |
    Series: The ethics of | Includes bibliographical references and index.
Identifiers: LCCN 2018028024 (print) | LCCN 2018031697 (ebook) |
    ISBN 9780429433085 (eBook) | ISBN 9781138203433
    (hardback : alk. paper) | ISBN 9781138203440 (pbk. : alk. paper)
Subjects: LCSH: Economic development—Moral and ethical aspects.
Classification: LCC HD82 (ebook) | LCC HD82 .I34146 2019 (print) |
    DDC 174/.4—dc23
LC record available at https://lccn.loc.gov/2018028024

ISBN: 978-1-138-20343-3 (hbk)
ISBN: 978-1-138-20344-0 (pbk)
ISBN: 978-0-429-43308-5 (ebk)

Typeset in Times New Roman
by Apex CoVantage, LLC

To:
Those who have loved us
And those who have sacrificed so that others can live better

Contents

Foreword

Development studies today finds practitioners within three major fields of studies: economics, social philosophy, and cultural anthropology. Each of these disciplines addresses development from its own perspective: the efficient growth and distribution of income; the values, norms, duties, and rights intrinsic to conceptions of goodness and justice; and the contingent, historical forces revolving around power and culture that shape our thinking about the human and planetary condition, in general. We have written this book principally from a social philosophical perspective. At the same time, we have sought to include the balancing perspectives of economics (Chapter 5) and cultural anthropology (Chapter 1). Although we discuss issues raised by critical race and post- (and de-) colonial theory, feminism, and indigenous cultural studies, we recommend turning to David Ingram's *World Crisis and Human Development* for a more in-depth and advanced treatment of them. Although graduate students and professional philosophers will hopefully profit from its use, our textbook has been designed specifically to meet the needs of undergraduates at all levels who are not yet proficient in technical social philosophy. Importantly, and uniquely, it also addresses the needs of development practitioners and experts outside of philosophy, proper.

David Ingram
August 15, 2018

Acknowledgments

The authors wish to thank Alec Stubbs for helping with the preparation of this manuscript. We also thank Don Sillers, former staff economist for the U.S. Agency for International Development (USAID) for granting us permission to reprint a table on reducing poverty through economic transfers (Table 1) that he personally prepared for us, along with a detailed explanation of its contents. David Ingram thanks Cambridge University Press for granting permission to reprint portions of his book, *World Crisis and Underdevelopment: A Critical Theory of Poverty, Agency, and Coercion.* Finally, we thank our editor, Gabrielle Coakeley, Sheri Sipka, and the production staff at Routledge and Apex CoVantage for making this project possible.

Introduction

We live in a world of kaleidoscopic diversity, marked by cultural richness as well as economic destitution. These two facts – one a source of wonder, the other a cause for despair – are difficult to separate. Perhaps this explains why we are hesitant to label as backward any society that is culturally different from ours just because we judge its standard of living to be deficient in comparison to our own. If an aborigine living in some remote area does not complain about her lack of material comforts and opportunities for learning computational skills, why should we? Hasn't the so-called developed world caused enough mischief in carrying out its global civilizing mission to warrant skepticism regarding its own claim to superiority? Can't the oppression of the poor be reduced without their being "developed"?

One purpose of this book is to explore possible responses to these questions. The ethics of development cannot skirt the most basic of philosophical queries: Is there anything universal in the human condition that enables us to talk about desirable levels of individual and societal functioning which "development" (however conceived) can help attain?

This book does not offer a definitive answer to this question. Instead it charts several ways in which we might speak of social and individual development without presuming, to use a familiar metaphor, that "one size fits all." Once we have opened the door to development as an ethical project worthy of serious discussion, we can then explore the ethics of development across a wide range of issues.

One issue is sustainable development. The idea of sustainable development has become an increasingly urgent issue as we enter the twenty-first century. Most people today agree that improving people's standard of living is a good thing. They agree, too, that limiting forms of growth that cause global climate change and environmental damage is also a good thing. Hence the question: What if improving people's standard of living required increasing levels of consumption that contribute to climate change and environmental damage?

This book examines a range of responses to this question, including the response held by some economists that we can "have our cake and eat it too." Yet it is sufficiently skeptical of prospects for reconciling unlimited growth *and* environmental salvation to ask these questions of basic justice: Do developed societies have a duty to slow their growth so that developing nations can "catch up" to them? If the goal of sustainable development is not to make developing countries carbon copies of developed countries (pun intended) but to enable them to meet a threshold of well-being through an alternative form of development, what would this threshold look like? Conversely, should already developed countries "scale down" their levels of consumption and production in convergence toward some happy mean of development that everyone can live with?

These justice questions are urgent. People are dying now from the effects of poverty and global climate change. Furthermore they raise concerns about global inequality, both within and between countries. Moral philosophy suggests different ethical approaches one might take in addressing them. One is *utilitarianism*, or the approach that privileges policies that maximize overall well-being. Developmental theorists schooled in neoclassical economics tend to favor this approach, which focuses more on how to grow well-being (typically equated with income) than on how to distribute it. It is also the approach favored by governments. In general, what I call the domain of *public morality* focuses mainly on the duty that governments and international organizations have toward increasing global well-being in all its varieties. These duties – which moral philosophers call *positive* duties – are more familiarly known as duties of beneficence (or duties to help others).

Governments, of course, have other duties besides positive duties to improve welfare. They have duties to act justly toward their own citizens and toward each other. These duties of justice are explained by moral philosophers using different approaches. The *social contract* approach focuses on fairly distributing the burdens and benefits of mutual cooperation. This theory finds exemplary application in the public morality of international relations, in which (for instance) developed and developing nations negotiate fair terms of trade and cooperation. It also prescribes compensating those who were made poor and "underdeveloped" due to unjust forms of *coercive* cooperation extending back in time to the heyday of colonialism.

Another approach to thinking about the public morality of justice focuses on the basic duties governments owe to individuals as bearers of *human rights*, quite apart from their role as participants in any particular cooperative venture. If needy individuals have a human right to develop a life of dignity which their own society denies them, then distantly related persons might have a duty to protect them in attaining it to the extent that they can.

Human rights are often understood as claims that individuals bring against their communities. However, communities, too, can be the bearer of human rights (such as a right to development). The ethical theory that best explains our duties to communities is *communitarianism*. Communitarianism reminds us that stable communities are the precondition for caring relationships in which persons' moral dispositions and identities are constituted. A poorly developed community lacking in shared cultural meanings and values will produce poorly developed individuals.

The approaches discussed above find ample application in almost any area of ethical concern. Their application to the ethics of development is most obvious in reference to public morality, or the duties that pertain to creating equitable, large-scale economic and social structures that frame development. Such duties fall within the province of developmental policies promoted by governments and international institutions. It is important, however, not to lose sight of ethical duties of a personal nature that make up *private morality*. Each of us individually, apart from our role as citizen or public office holder, has a duty to act justly toward others by not harming them. We also have private duties to improve others' well-being. These duties are generally thought to be stronger when directed toward family, friends, and members of our local community whose lives can be directly and greatly improved by our individual actions.

Governments command much greater resources than each of us taken in isolation. They are better positioned to improve the lives of others *distant* from us. Therefore, assuming that the strength and extent of our duties depend on our capacities, our private duty to improve the lives of distant others is limited. Perhaps this should not trouble our moral conscience too much. Failure to make persons better off is generally thought to be less wrong than acting unjustly toward them. By contrast, if we harm others, we violate a strong duty of justice (what moral philosophers call a *negative* duty). As it turns out, although our private (positive) duties to help distant others might be limited, our private (negative) duties to refrain from harming them might be unlimited. As we shall see in Chapter 5, our contributing to the production of seriously harmful greenhouse gases violates a negative duty toward those who are harmed that requires compensation.

Because governments are the main agents for engineering sustainable development, this book will mainly focus on the public morality of beneficence and justice. However, not to be ignored are the public and private duties that fall on businesses and development agencies. Moral dilemmas arise in the everyday conduct of doing business in developing countries and in the delivery of development assistance that cannot be resolved by applying the formulaic ethical approaches discussed above. How far should businesses and development agencies accommodate corrupt governments? How far should they accommodate local customs that discriminate against women? How should they respond to the unequal power they leverage within the communities they seek to help?

Our discussion of public and private morality has neglected to mention any duties we might have to non-humans and our surrounding environment. These duties raise an additional question: What spiritual traditions can move us beyond *anthropocentric* concerns to care for the well-being and development of the planet and all the beings that constitute it? Religion, rather than philosophical ethics, is best positioned to answer this question. As authors of this textbook, our sole claim to expertise lies in analyzing empirical and conceptual arguments, not in speculating about divine purposes. Authorship of each chapter correlates with our personal expertise; Tom Derdak has drawn from his extensive background as philosopher and founder/CEO of a non-profit development organization in presenting the arguments contained in Chapters 4, 7, 8, and 9, while David Ingram has used his knowledge of development theory in presenting the arguments contained in other chapters. Most of the arguments we will be examining in this book are inconclusive. We do not claim to know better than average persons what the truth is. The meanings and criteria of knowledge are socially and historically constructed and, as such, reflect particular if widely accepted standpoints. However, we believe that awareness of the arguments and complexities surrounding the ethics of development will help citizens perform their democratic duty to deliberate together on good and just policies for humanity as whole.

Some facts about underdevelopment

We have touched on philosophical and ethical concerns that motivated our writing this book. But what are the facts that compel us to think about development in the first place?

The World Bank's Poverty Data for 2015 estimates that over 700 million persons in the world (about 10% of the world's population) live in extreme poverty, surviving on an income of less than $1.90 per day.[1] A child living on that appallingly low income has between a 1 in 6 and 1 in 12 chance of dying before the age of five, in comparison to the 1 in 140 chance that a child in the developed world has. In fact, it has been estimated that 18 million of the world's poorest die prematurely from poverty-related causes every year, one-third of all deaths, and from 2000 to 2014, more than the deaths caused by all the wars and genocides of the twentieth century combined. The daily toll from poverty-related deaths is 50,000, 29,000 of them children under the age of five.

Income levels reveal only the tip of the iceberg. Data for 2010 showed that 100 million lacked access to safe water, 2.6 billion lacked access to basic sanitation, 1 billion lacked access to adequate housing, 2 billion lacked access to essential drugs, 774 million couldn't read or write, 218 million children were forced to work for their subsistence, and 72 million elementary school–age children attended no school. Altogether, one in nine persons inhabiting the planet (805 million) remain chronically undernourished.

World Bank calculations show that the percentage of people living in poverty is diminishing and that the number of chronically undernourished people declined by 100 million over the last decade. So the Millennium Development Goals (MDGs) pledged by 186 nations who attended the 1996 World Food Summit in Rome to reduce by one-half the number of hungry people by 2015 may have been achieved (although this claim is disputed). But the major gains have been concentrated in China (627M), India (35M), and Southeast Asia (123M), with only a handful of developing countries halving their poor during this period. Some countries, such as Haiti, saw their poor population grow from 4.4 million to 5.3 million from 2012 to 2015. Most disturbing of all is the rapidly growing number of poor in sub-Saharan Africa, which has increased by 182 million, adding to a growing scourge of global poverty that, in its less extreme but still severe manifestations (based on an average daily per capita income of $3.00 per day), still afflicts 3 billion of the world's inhabitants. Given the current state of global civil unrest and economic volatility, it is hard to imagine how the new Sustainable Development Goals (SDGs) for eliminating extreme poverty by 2030 will be achievable.

The persistence of poverty appears especially glaring in light of global inequality. In 2005 the income ratio between the top and bottom tenths was 273:1; the corresponding wealth ratio was 2,730:1. The top 1% possessed 40% of global wealth; the top 10% possessed 85%. Today, average per capita consumption in high-income countries is 30 times greater than that in low-income countries, with the poorest 40% of the world's population accounting for just 1.7% of all household consumption in comparison to the top 15%, who account for 81%.[2] According to the World Bank's 2018 Report, "The Changing Wealth of Nations," from 1995 to 2014 global . . . wealth – here calculated in terms of productive capital (buildings, machinery, etc.), natural capital (land, minerals, etc.), human capital (employable skills, cultural assets, etc.), and foreign capital (foreign investments, assistance, etc.) – increased by 66%, from $690 trillion to $1,143 trillion in constant 2014 US dollars at market prices, but per capita wealth declined or stagnated in 25 countries in various income brackets, most of them African. In 2017 Oxfam reported that the eight wealthiest persons' combined assets, totaling over $420 billion, exceeded the $409 billion held by the world's poorest 3.6 billion.

Global climate change is quickly eclipsing global inequality as the latest affront to the poor. World Bank President Jim Yong Kim noted that, despite our best efforts to moderate global warming, "we could witness the rolling back of decades of development gains and force tens of millions more to live in poverty."[3] Absent more effective efforts, poverty will increase even more dramatically, unleashing new waves of migration. Rising temperatures are predicted to slash rice and corn yields, creating food insecurity for hundreds of millions of people.[4] Drought, rising sea levels, and extreme weather events also affect the poor disproportionately, with developing countries suffering 98% of deaths and 90% of financial losses.[5] Water and other resource scarcities, in turn, give rise to military conflicts, such as the current civil war in Syria. Meanwhile carbon emissions exacerbate the acidification of the world's oceans, wreaking havoc on marine life and the food chain.

Persons in high-income countries bear a disproportionate responsibility for driving climate change. The World Bank estimates that OECD member countries generate an average of 10.2 metric tons of CO_2 per capita, while the least developed countries emit 0.3 metric tons of CO_2 per capita (World Bank Data).[6] In fact, the world's governments continue to encourage the production of fossil fuels through direct and indirect subsidies that amount to $1.9 trillion per year. It remains to be seen whether the recently ratified Paris Agreement under the UN Framework Convention on Climate Change will result in effective carbon reduction legislation.

What is being done?

Radical global inequities in living standards cannot be adequately addressed by ad hoc delivery of emergency aid alone. Both the MDGs and SDGs concede that eliminating these inequities requires long-term development policy. Limiting the impact of climate change only indirectly supports such a policy. One policy that directly targets development is Official Development Assistance (ODA). As defined by the Development Assistance Committee (DAC) of the Organization for Economic Cooperation and Development (OECD), ODA provides loans and grants from governments specifically targeting the welfare and development of the neediest countries. Approximately $149 billion was spent on ODA in 2013, a 69% increase since 2000, but far short of the $450 billion annually that the OECD itself has determined is necessary to help developing countries to develop while adapting to climate change. Altogether, it is estimated that implementing the SDGs will cost $2.5 trillion per year – more than twice the private and public investment in today's developing world.[7]

Are developing nations giving enough? In 2005 the Millennium Project estimated that its goal for poverty reduction would require all high-income countries to donate .7% of their GNP. The current level hovers around .2%. The biggest donor of ODA, and the wealthiest country in the world, the United States (at $31.5 billion), gave just .19% of its GNP to ODA in 2015, one-sixteenth of what it spent on military defense that year. The amount of ODA that actually targets low-income countries has barely risen to 57%, with only a fraction of that percentage – about 14% – meeting basic social services.

Although less evident than it was during the heyday of the Cold War, politics plays a role in "tying" aid to conditions that render it less efficient. For example, in 2014 the Obama administration determined that it could feed 4 million more people at a savings of $500 million if it could use $1.4 billion earmarked for the program to buy food vouchers for the needy to purchase food grown locally in poor countries, thereby bypassing costs associated with transporting 1.44 million tons of basic foodstuffs and other bulk commodities across the Atlantic. This new policy had the added benefit of not driving local farmers out of business by "dumping" underpriced US agricultural goods in local markets. Opposition from the American Farm Bureau Federation, maritime associations, and other lobbying groups, who argued that vouchers invited corruption and would result in the loss of Americans jobs, ended in the passage of a diluted bill. That policy sets aside only 20% of the money earmarked for food relief to be spent on vouchers serving 3.4 million fewer starving people than what had been projected under the original proposal.

It is estimated that reforming tax codes could more than compensate for shortfalls in needed ODA. Closing tax havens, which account for $32 trillion – one-quarter of the world's wealth – could free up $189 billion alone. Unfortunately, governments are doing little to address this loss in revenue, with the recent trend favoring more regressive tax policies that favor the rich and exacerbate domestic and global inequality. Alternatively, further gains in "aid" could be accomplished by forgiving the huge debts to lending institutions in the developed world that governments of developing countries are obligated to service – during the peak of the debt crisis in the mid-1990s, for every $1 that was given in aid, $9 was taken back through debt repayments. Gains could also be made by reducing licensing fees that poor countries have to pay to pharmaceutical and other transnational corporations in order to access value-added goods and services made in the developed world.[8]

As we have seen, public and private banks are crucial players in development and poverty reduction. Indeed, the most prominent among them, the World Bank Group (WB), has proudly proclaimed on its Washington-based edifice that "our dream is a world free of poverty." Notwithstanding that boast, during the Cold War, the WB provided concessional loans to countries based mainly on their strategic value to the United States and its allies, with little attention to the goals of poverty reduction. Furthermore, the response of the WB and its major collaborator, the International Monetary Fund (IMF), to the debt crisis of the 1970s and 1980s produced catastrophic results. The structural adjustment programs (SAPS) the WB/IMF imposed on developing nations for receiving bailouts during and after this crisis required the downsizing of government services, the devaluation of local currencies, the elimination of tariffs, and the opening up of local economies to foreign investment and trade. Unable to compete with large-scale, technology-driven transnational corporations, local farmers and shop owners were driven out of business; as local economies stagnated and unemployment rose, those without jobs were unable to access social services.

As noted above, trade was also touted by many economists working within development finance institutions (DFIs) as the most efficient way to develop economies. Many have argued that the free trade policies of the World Trade Organization (WTO), which were ushered in by the final Uruguay Round of GATT negotiations (1981–1994), were instrumental in promoting China's astounding development, even if they may have harmed other developing countries. However, despite the WTO's commitment to free trade, and its recent commitment in the Doha Round (2001) to furthering development, developed countries are still allowed to disproportionately "protect" their domestic industries through tariffs and subsidies at the expense of their poorer trading partners. At the end of the Uruguay Round, rich countries' average tariffs were four times higher than those of developing countries in sectors in which developing countries were best positioned to compete (in agriculture, textiles, and clothing). The United Nations Conference on Trade and Development estimated that without such tariffs poor countries could export $1 trillion a year more, gaining up to $100 billion in additional exchange instead of suffering a net loss of $600 million, after bureaucratic costs and licensing expenses due to product patents are factored in.[9]

What should we be doing?

The facts about poverty and development recounted above paint a grim picture that obscures a fundamental truth: real progress has been made in reducing poverty since the end of the Cold War. After years in which development theory was obsessed with trying to mold the developing world into its own image of what a modern, industrial society should be – using the North Atlantic states as the model – and years after forcing developing countries to swallow a market-based therapy to cure government inefficiency that even developed countries refused to impose on themselves – development theorists now have a more nuanced, holistic view about development, a greater awareness of the complex causes of underdevelopment, and a more balanced view about the role that public and private initiatives can play together in mitigating the latter while enhancing the former. The theory and practice of development has never been better.

Is that good enough? As Thomas Pogge acidly remarks, congratulating our-selves for not allowing more poor people to die from poverty than died before is incredibly self-serving when no one has to die under a feasible alternative.[10] The recent shift away from neoliberal orthodoxy toward neo-Keynesian poli-cies promoting differential fair trade responsibilities – permitting governments of developing countries to phase out tariffs while leveraging a range of public services and economic interventions – has suggested such an alternative, as have the various schemes for mutually beneficial financial and trade arrangements that have been advanced along the southern corridor by Brazil, India, China, and South Africa (BICS). But these promising initiatives are also strained by power differentials and the inefficiencies associated with government corruption. Moreover it remains to be seen whether a market economy based on capitalism, in which capital is privately owned and invested with an eye toward short-term profitability, offers a likely chance for eliminating poverty in our lifetimes while doing so sustainably.

We will examine the viability of global capitalism as a framework for sustain-able development in a later chapter, along with a host of economic and political reforms. For the time being, let's begin by asking a more basic moral question: Why should we be doing more about relieving poverty and underdevelopment than what is being done now?

One answer is that we shouldn't be doing anything more. People who incline toward this view offer different reasons for their answer. One reason – call it the *fatalism* view – agrees that things as they currently stand are bad and morally unacceptable but insists that any effort to make things better will either fail or make things worse. For instance, reasoning from the ethical standpoint of human rights, one might condemn the inhumane indignities suffered by the poor but argue that those of us living outside their range can do nothing to help them. Because *we* can't be morally obligated to do something that *we* can't in fact do ('ought implies can') we are at most obligated to urge *others* to aid the poor to the extent that *they* can. Because the poor outnumber those who are capable of aiding them, only some poor can be helped, and nothing more can be done for the rest. Alas, the poor will always be with us – not because they are intrinsically incapable of raising themselves out of poverty, but because there will never be enough provid-ers to help them.

Given the abundant resources and technical capabilities of wealthy govern-ments, this response seems rather disingenuous. USAID economist Don Sillers has assembled the following table, based on USAID Poverty Projector data, which suggests that global poverty could be greatly reduced by transferring modest amounts of income from rich to poor.[11]

Table 0.1 The cost of raising the global poor above four poverty lines: comparing targeted and universal basic income transfers

Poverty line US $/day at 2011 PPP	Projected headcount ratio 2015 (share of population below poverty line)	Average shortfall per day per poor person (PPP$)	Transfer per poor person per year (PPP$)	Number of poor (millions)	Annual transfer with perfect targeting (billion PPP$)	Annual cost with perfect targeting (billion US$ at 2011 prices)	Annual transfer with no targeting (billion PPP$)	Annual cost with no targeting (billion US$ at 2011 prices)
Targeted transfer								
1.90	11.7%	$0.578	$211.29	737.2	$155.8	$70.8		
3.20	31.3%	$1.114	$406.76	1962.4	$798.2	$332.3		
5.50	54.5%	$2.500	$913.11	3419.0	$3,121.9	$1,269.2		
10.00	75.5%	$5.745	$2,098.48	4736.5	$9,939.4	$4,125.8		
Universal transfer								
1.90		n.a	$693.98	6,275.1			$4,354.8	$1,978.4
3.20		n.a	$1,168.80	6,275.1			$7,334.3	$3,053.1
5.50		n.a	$2,008.88	6,275.1			$12,605.9	$5,125.1
10.00		n.a	$3,652.50	6,275.1			$22,919.8	$9,513.9

The table displays four poverty levels typically associated with developing societies (low income, lower-middle income, higher-middle income) and high-income developed societies: extreme (below $1.90/day per person); severe (below $3.20/day per person); moderate (below $5.50/day per person); and high (below $10.00/day per person).[12] It also displays two transfer policies, one targeting only those individuals who fall precisely under the designated poverty level as determined by proxy means tests (PMTs), and another that guarantees a universal basic income (UBI) without targeting. Because PMTs estimate family income based on household surveys regarding levels of child education, household building materials, home appliances, and other indirect measures of consumption, they are not reliable indicators of income. Therefore, to insure that no one who should be targeted is left out, it might be better to guarantee everyone a universal basic income – a policy India might soon adopt.[13]

Notice that this latter policy is more costly than the targeting policy to implement, since it would involve government administration and run the risk of over-targeting. In sum, while transferring as little as $155.8 billion could raise 11.2% of the global poor out of extreme poverty (above $1.90/day), and transferring $798 billion could raise 31.3% of the global poor out of severe poverty (above $3.20/day), this could only happen under unlikely conditions of perfect targeting and costless administration. The safer policy of providing poor people a basic income above the aforementioned cutoffs would be far costlier, amounting to as much as $4.35 trillion and $7.33 trillion, respectively (although these amounts significantly decrease to $1.98 and $3.05 trillion, respectively, using dollar market exchange calculations).[14]

As daunting as these last figures appear – they represent about 3.43% and 5.78% (1.56% and 2.41% using dollar market exchange calculations) of global domestic product for 2017 ($126.7 trillion PPP) – Pogge reminds us that as much as $300 billion could be generated in three years through a global 7 cent/gallon gas tax alone (a Tobin tax on selected international financial transactions could generate even more poverty funds). Closing tax havens and lowering licensing fees could generate another $300 billion. Furthermore, improved methods of targeting, while certainly increasing costs above the levels noted above, would make poverty remediation more affordable than implementing a UBI, however desirable the latter might be ideally.

A stronger argument against doing anything more for the poor combines a utilitarian approach with a controversial theorem. This *lifeboat* ethical view, most famously developed by Garrett Hardin, resurrects Thomas Malthus's argument, advanced during the infancy of Britain's industrial revolution over 200 years ago, that population growth outstrips food production and environmental carrying capacity.[15] Hardin accordingly concludes that saving the poor from starvation backfires by expanding their numbers beyond sustainable levels.

This argument has largely been refuted. Thanks to the Green Revolution of the 1970s, food scarcity has ceased to be a natural fact. Indeed, studies show that rising income security depresses population growth. The widely accepted *demographic transition* hypothesis postulates an initial stable population phase of high birth/high mortality (typical of Europe during the eighteenth century and pre-WWII Asia and Africa), followed by a second phase of high-birth/low-mortality population growth (typical of Europe during the Industrial Revolution and post-WWII Africa and Asia). This second phase, which prevailed in the developing world when the lifeboat argument seemed plausible, has been surpassed by a third phase of low-birth/ low-mortality population stability at about 2.5 children per family (typical of over half the developing world today). A fourth phase, of low-birth/low-mortality population *decline*, has now emerged in present-day Europe and Japan. According to demographic forecasts, world population will *level out* at about 12 billion sometime over the next 50 years.[16]

As we shall see, environmental variants of the neo-Malthusian argument that urge low (or no) economic growth appear plausible in light of what we know about climate change and human-caused environmental destruction. But these arguments at most recommend limiting the scale of carbon-intensive development in the developing world *and elsewhere*, not letting poverty go unchallenged.

Let's assume, then, that we are not doing enough to eliminate poverty and under-development. Knowing the causes of underdevelopment – who is responsible for it and who has benefited from it – might help us clarify our duties in this regard. We will address the causal question in a moment. However, Peter Singer has argued that private morality can give us some guidance about what more we could be doing at a personal level. He suggests an analogy between our duty to rescue someone in life-threatening circumstances close at hand and our duty to rescue distant others from life-threatening poverty. He explains the duty to rescue in terms of a simple principle: If we can stop something very bad from happening without having to give up anything of comparable value, we should do it. Most of us, Singer reasons, would concede that we should go to great lengths, short of putting our own lives at serious risk, to pull a drowning child out of a pond. Because we know that people are dying from poverty right now, we should likewise go to great lengths, short of placing our own life at risk, to save them by donating substantially to famine relief and other forms of assistance.

In Chapter 9 we will examine Singer's claim that our personal duty to do more for the cause of fighting poverty is perfectly analogous to our duty to rescue someone in a life-threatening emergency. It suffices to note for our present purposes that another controversial premise is at play in Singer's argument: There is no morally relevant difference between the drowning child next to me and the starving person 2,000 miles away. Distance, as such, is morally irrelevant, once it is established that donations will save lives. It is also irrelevant that other bystanders are just standing around the pond doing nothing or that government (the local fire department) is saving someone else from drowning in the pond. At bottom, not only do the lives of all count equally, but our efforts toward easing suffering and promoting well-being should not discriminate among persons, depending on how close they are to us (spatially or emotionally).

Singer here endorses a principle of rational moral impartiality that is central to the utilitarian ethical approach he favors. Without regard to who is suffering or why they are suffering, utilitarians urge us to act in such a way as to reduce suffering as much as possible – or, to state the injunction as a positive moral demand, to act so as to maximize overall well-being. Singer therefore urges that we reduce poverty and improve the lives of others as much as we can, regardless of whether others help out in this endeavor and regardless of whether our efforts ultimately succeed.

Singer's ethic of poverty relief is personally demanding. Other moral reasons for doing more to reduce poverty and promote development are not so demanding. Human rights and social contract ethics, for example, are typically understood as imposing duties on governments and, secondarily, on the citizens who hold governments accountable. Any government that is signatory to the International Covenant on Economic, Social, and Cultural Rights, for example, has committed itself to ensuring that anyone residing within its territory has access to adequate health, education, and welfare as a matter of human right. Should a government egregiously fail in this regard, it then becomes the responsibility of other governments and international relief agencies to intervene appropriately.

Not all governments recognize health, education, and welfare as goods that anyone is entitled to claim as a matter of human right. Still, many of these same governments recognize a duty to provide their subjects with these goods for what might be called social contract reasons. From this ethical perspective, government exists in order to efficiently implement duties of mutually beneficial and fair cooperation that citizens have toward each other. Citizens should not allow their consociates to fall below a threshold of well-being insofar as they rely on them for national defense and other collective goods.

Can a similar social contract argument be extended to justify the responsibilities of persons to non-citizens living outside their county? Iris Young has argued that globalization connects people internationally in a way that makes that extension plausible. Affluent people purchase clothing made in sweatshops across the globe. The apparel industry is therefore a prime example of transnational cooperation in which both sweatshop workers and affluent consumers benefit. Social contract ethicists ask whether the terms of cooperation are fair: Should the basic political and economic structure underlying apparel industry be changed so as to improve the wages and working conditions of sweatshop workers?

Social contract ethics also clarifies duties that governments have toward each other as they cooperate with one another in maintaining international peace and security. These days it is widely understood that peace and security depend on domestic stability, of which development is a part. Poverty, unemployment, and social inequality are prime causes of civil unrest that can spill over borders (recall, for example, the recent wave of refugees that have fled war-torn Syria). As John Rawls argues, all nations have a moral duty to cooperate in making the world a safe place. Notice, too, that climate change has become a factor in creating chronic droughts, famines, and rising sea levels – all of which contribute to insecurity. So, developed nations must cooperate with developing nations to ensure that their commerce is mutually beneficial and fair. This requires that developed nations negotiate trade and climate change treaties that assign different countries responsibilities proportionate to their respective capacities.

Duties of repair: the legacy of colonialism

So far we have attempted to determine what, if any, duty we might have to do more in alleviating poverty without examining the *causes* of poverty. In fact, none of the major ethical approaches we have examined so far – utilitarianism, human rights, or social contract theory – requires us to do so, *at least in theory*. In practice, of course, a utilitarian will need to know the causes of suffering in order to calculate an efficient way to eliminate them. Likewise a human rights advocate will have to locate the agents and institutions responsible for violating rights as well as recommend agents and institutions that can most effectively and appropriately intervene to stop these violations from happening. For their part, social contract ethicists will examine how existing institutions unequally affect the lives and fortunes of all who fall under them in order to determine whether everyone is mutually (and fairly) benefited by them.

The causes underlying unequal development are many. Some of them originate in recent events; others extend backward in time. Some are local; others are global. Recent local events, such as civil war or government mismanagement, are the most visible causes of underdevelopment. Events that emerge locally spread globally. As we noted above, the American economic crisis of the 1970s triggered the global debt crisis discussed above, just as the American economic crisis of 2008 triggered yet another global recession.

Knowing the cause of a specific harmful event is often useful in determining who has what duty to whom. To take the global debt crisis as an example, it might be argued that banks in the developed world indirectly contributed to the crisis. Flush with petro-dollars that they needed to invest, these banks encouraged developing countries to borrow from them at low interest rates. When the United States decided to curb its inflation by raising its prime interest rate, global banks followed suit, leaving behind heavily indebted developing countries who could no longer service their interest payments. As we know, the WB and IMF bailed these poor governments out of their crisis – but at a severe cost to their economies. Because many of the banks that encouraged (and benefited from) loans to these governments were participants in the WB group, it is fair to ask whether they had a duty to take partial responsibility for the crisis and offer less harsh terms to the countries they bailed out. In the end, the WB/IMF did forgive some of the debt that had accrued from their bailout. But many today would argue that it was "too little too late."

Special duties to aid those with whom we share special bonds of kinship – a concern among communitarian ethicists – also play a role in the ethics of development. Charity begins at home, and sometimes "home" might be other countries or persons who have, by their ideological commitments or political contributions, become a part of our community. This might explain why many people believe that the United States has a duty to aid Israel (which is a high-income country) or Ethiopia (which is a low-income country).

What about special duties of repair? In the common law of torts, when a person harms another person by acting negligently, they owe that person compensation.

The same applies to governments. If a country shares partial responsibility for foreseeably causing harm to another country, it should repair the harm it has done. Reparations may be morally justifiable apart from post-war compensation by aggressor nations, as when the government of one country adopts a policy or pursues a course of action that contributes to the impoverishment of another country. As noted above, some people have argued that trade deals between developing and developed countries have severely harmed the former. For example, critics of the North American Free Trade Agreement (NAFTA) between the United States, Canada, and Mexico, which has been in effect since 1994, claim that the treaty has not only *not* reduced poverty in Mexico but has severely harmed Mexican subsistence farmers, forcing many of them to migrate north in search of jobs. Meanwhile American businesses have benefited enormously from free trade with Mexico. Should the United States government assume partial responsibility for Mexicans losing their jobs by compensating them, perhaps by raising its quota of ordinary Mexican work visas above the current ceiling of 50,000?

This brings us to the question of the colonial legacy and the harm it caused former colonies in Asian and Africa. Some have disputed whether colonialism harmed the developing world. Indeed, many other causes have been cited to explain why developing countries find themselves so poor in comparison to developed countries. Jared Diamond (1997) argues that geography might have something to do with it. Put simply, geographical factors that enabled inter-societal transmission of high-yield seed lines, large beasts of burden, technologies, and pathogenic immunities gave Europe and Asia a head start in population growth, urbanization, and civilization. It therefore explains why North and South America, along with sub-Saharan Africa, Australia-Micronesia, and portions of Southeast Asia were vulnerable to European conquest with the aid of "guns, germs, and steel." Even today tropical zones pose developmental challenges in the form of higher rates of insect-born disease, which in turn causes a correspondingly higher rate of fertility and lower rate of productivity.

This geographical explanation does not deny the destructive impact that European colonization had on the rest of the world, but explains why Europe, in particular, came to dominance. European dominance had nothing to do with European racial and cultural superiority but with geographical factors that compelled Europeans to multiply and unite their numbers in densely populated fortified cities from whence they became proficient in waging war over scarce resources.

Other geographical factors are cited in explaining the development divide. The possession (or lack thereof) of natural resources appears to impact development in unexpected ways. It might be thought that lack of natural resources holds countries back. However, this explanation overlooks the fact that good government can counteract lack of natural resources, as happened in the case of Japan, which is among the wealthiest countries on the planet.

Instead there appears to be a more sinister connection between resources, underdevelopment, and colonialism. In a cruel twist of fate, countries with abundant natural resources have been the target of an especially destructive form of colonialism. Areas with abundant natural resources and high population density, such as the former Belgian Congo, attracted authoritarian colonizers who were bent on establishing "extractive regimes." In contrast to the settler colonies of North America that, at least in theory if not in practice, recognized the sovereignty of indigenous peoples, respected property and treaty rights, and established limited government (for settler communities), extractive regimes in Africa recognized virtually no limits on government power. The legacy of this second kind of colonialism – typically justified by a right of conquest in the name of a civilizing mission, not by a right of discovery permitting the settlement of "uncultivated and uninhabited land" – deprived many former colonies of any lawful and accountable governance with which their post-colonial subjects could identify. The long history of corrupt, authoritarian rule – first by Europeans and then by their own people – paved the way for today's murderous civil wars and pillaging of resources. In the Congo alone as many as 5 million people have died since 1994 from starvation and disease caused by endless warfare to gain control of the country's vast mineral resources; under the brutal rule of Belgian King Leopold II, as many as 10 million may have died.

To be sure, colonial regimes varied markedly in their brutality. Government by indirect rule, favored by the British in many of its colonial possessions, governed through local leaders of tribes and ethnic groups. Reliance on patronage in this system – a style of procuring political loyalty that still persists in many parts of the developing (and developed) world – fueled its own brand of corruption and intertribal conflict. Here, the arbitrary carving up of colonial territories across tribal and ethnic lines alone provided a fertile ground for this destructive legacy.

If we assume that European colonialism is the main reason why many former colonies find themselves politically and economically underdeveloped – a hypothesis that is plausible if not demonstrable – then it is reasonable to infer that European countries owed their former colonies compensation for the terrible harm they inflicted on them. That harm has continued to affect the lives of present-day Africans, just as the wealth that was stolen from them continues to benefit present-day Europeans.

We will examine what role compensatory justice might play in the ethics of development in later chapters. However, even if it is wrong to blame Europeans today for harms caused by their ancestors – and equally wrong to excuse former colonies for perpetuating the corrupt, divisive, and authoritarian patterns of governance they inherited – the issue of colonialism remains far from settled. Put simply, the status of the developing world *today* has been likened to that of an extractive regime under a more benign guise. Leaving aside corrupt dictators who plunder their own country's natural wealth for their own ends – which often involves selling this wealth to the developed world in exchange for the military hardware that keeps them in power – development theorists have questioned the unequal and exploitative commercial *dependency* between developed and developing countries that has persisted into the post-colonial era.

Over 60 years ago Raul Prebisch, along with Hans Singer, argued that the apparent "comparative advantage" developing countries possessed in their wealth of natural resources was instead a structural *disadvantage* in trading with developed countries. Relegated to the *periphery* as suppliers of primary resources to the industrial *center*, developing countries would suffer a net drain of wealth as they purchased in exchange value-added goods made by the developed world from these very same resources. Today, developing nations are locked in a pitched battle with developed nations over the escalating tariffs that the latter impose to prevent the former from selling them the value-added commodities they need to produce in order to develop their own industry.

Chapter summary

Now that we have a very rudimentary understanding of the overall state of development in the world today, what is being done to improve it, and what ethicists have argued we should be doing to improve it, we will conclude with a chapter by chapter summary of how this book proposes to elaborate these findings.

Chapter 1 addresses the most basic philosophical question motivating this book: What is development? Rather than presume a single right answer to this question, we will look at the history of development theory and question its foundational premise: that there are ascertainable standards of good (or superior) societal and individual functioning that apply to all societies at all times. Crucial to this inquiry is the complexity of human functioning itself: societies and individuals adapt to their environments by means of learning processes that reflect multiple strands of moral and technological development. It is unclear whether these different strands develop in harmony with one another or along a single path. In the final analysis, we might not be able to ascertain universally defensible endpoints of moral and technical functioning across societies, even if we can ascertain higher levels of moral and technical functioning relative to sequential problems that many complex societies face.

The second part of this chapter looks at how people today measure development. Economists long favored measuring development by a nation's gross national (or domestic) product as well as average per capita income. Because economic factors alone do not tell us anything about development outcomes or distribution, the United Nations has proposed other metrics. The Human Development Index (HDI) and the Gender Development Index (GDI) focus on average lifespan, educational attainment, and gender inequality on the assumption that fulfillment of basic needs and/or development of basic human capabilities should be the gold standard for measuring development and well-being. We conclude this chapter with some objections to the capabilities approach that question its practical usefulness as well as its universality. These objections, in turn, converge with a broader critique of development as an ideology masking Western domination.

Chapter 2 begins our in-depth survey of ethical approaches by examining the relationship between human rights and development. It is widely believed that respect for human rights is basic to the development of societies and individuals. Indeed, this belief informs a 1986 UN declaration affirming a human right to development, which states (conversely) that development is essential for the exercise of human rights. This document, like most documents, does not define what it means by a human right. In this chapter we examine a number of different (and perhaps competing) interpretations of this concept. According to a time-honored view, human rights are claims against governments to respect the dignity of individual persons. Some philosophers therefore see human rights as protecting the innate human capabilities, interests, and/or agency of individuals. Depending on which capabilities and interests they take to be essential, they then propose minimal or maximal criteria of development which existing human rights treaties more or less accurately mirror. Other philosophers, by contrast, begin with human rights treaties and interpret human rights in a less individual-centered way to accord with the legal rights these treaties confer on groups, such as indigenous peoples, or on individuals to collectively access public goods that have only an indirect relationship to protecting individuals' capabilities, interests, and agency. According to this approach, one promising candidate for a human right might be the human right to a sustainable (social and natural) environment.

There has been much debate about the ranking of human rights. Should classical (or first-generation) civil and political rights be considered the primary model of a human right or should (second-generation) welfare and developmental rights? In establishing criteria for legal enforcement, does it matter which kind of human right is being violated? Finally, if human rights are claims, it behooves us to ask to whom these claims are addressed. Are they addressed to governments only or are they addressed to non-state actors? Must we understand them exclusively as claims that arise within interactions between government functionaries and their subjects or can we understand them as claims that also arise between persons and impersonal social institutions? For example, can they be understood as claims against world society to develop more humane economic and political structures?

Chapter 3 highlights the importance of utilitarianism and social contract ethics in discussing world trade as an engine of development. The debate over free versus fair trade touches on concerns that social contract ethicists have about utilitarianism: its privileging of total or average well-being over fairness in the distribution of well-being. We will examine whether this charge is fair. For their part, social contractarians have advanced different principles of distributive (or developmental) justice. At the very least, social contractarians insist that economic cooperation should be free and agreeable to all participants. Other social contractarians go farther and insist that cooperation be fair and uncoerced. For instance, Robert Nozick (following the reasoning of seventeenth-century philosopher John Locke) insists that fair cooperation should disallow forms of acquiring and exchanging property that leave some participants without means of subsistence. John Rawls endorses an even stronger principle. He insists that the distributive outcome of cooperation is to everyone's advantage, so that inequalities are morally unacceptable unless they benefit the worst off. In addition to this prioritarian principle, Rawls proposes a principle of international trade that prohibits monopolies over patents, licenses, and technologies that condemn poor countries to a state of underdevelopment.

We conclude Chapter 3 with a discussion of the WTO and one of its most controversial provisions: Trade-Related Aspects of Intellectual Property Rights (TRIPS). On what moral grounds can patents and licenses be justified? Should developing countries be allowed to manufacture generic drugs without having to purchase a license for doing so? Are there ways to incentivize production of drugs and other use-values that will specifically target the neediest and most vulnerable of the world's population?

Chapter 4 examines the ethics of development aid as it applies between states and global financial institutions. First, we will examine whether, aside from self-interest, there are any moral reasons why wealthy states should aid poor states. Do states have a responsibility to protect against human rights deficits in other countries? Do they have a social contract duty to assist nations in developing into independent members of the international community? If so, how far should this duty extend? Is it right for governments to stipulate conditions on how their aid is used? Are certain kinds of aid morally preferable to other kinds? Is there a paradox in using aid as a vehicle for development?

Turning to international financial institutions, much criticism has been directed against the WB and IMF for how they have provided loans to countries for purposes of development. Some of the same questions raised with respect to governments aiding governments apply here as well. Should these institutions make receipt of concessionary loans conditional upon satisfying political and economic criteria? Should global banks operate under different criteria than their for-profit counterparts? Should their sole concern be improving economic performance in client states, guided by utilitarian reasoning? Or should they be concerned about how their loans will impact the broader cultural and political life of the nation they are intended to develop?

Chapter 5 moves beyond standard questions that occupy development ethicists to examine the intersection of development and the common provision of international public goods (IPGs), above all, climate change control, which profoundly impacts international security, economic stability, and biodiversity. Since 2015, this intersection has composed the centerpiece of the new Sustainable Development Goals (SDGs). Because climate change control depends on international cooperation, public duties of governance will guide our thinking in these matters. Here the question arises whether burdens and benefits of international cooperation should be distributed equally or in proportion to national capability. How does utilitarianism and social contract theory guide our thinking? How much should we maximize the well-being of future generations when considering the burdens and benefits of sustainable development?

Chapter 5 concludes by examining whether the prevailing capitalist system is compatible with sustainable development. Does this economy by its very nature generate underdevelopment and unsustainable growth? Can green capitalism avoid these outcomes? Or is socialism the answer?

Just as Chapter 5 questions the developmental sustainability of the global economic system, Chapter 6 poses this question with regard to the global political system. In what respects does the system of sovereign states promote, rather than obstruct, sustainable development? On one hand, claims to local sovereignty can be seen as advancing communitarian self-determination. Indigenous peoples have leveraged this ethical appeal in resisting domination, colonization, and exploitation by national governments, which in turn have leveraged this appeal in resisting oppressive international trade regimes. On the other hand, communitarian arguments have formed the basis of restrictive immigration policies that wealthy nations have used to limit cross-border migration of even the neediest refugees, as we shall see in Chapter 6. This constitutes a serious harm insofar as increased migration from poor to rich countries has produced a significant benefit for developing countries in the form of remittances.

The previous six chapters mainly address development-related duties of public morality that fall on states, international governing bodies, and the global economic and political order in which they operate. The remaining chapters focus on duties of private morality that concern multinationals, development workers on the ground, and private individuals (you and me).

Chapter 7 discusses duties that multinationals have toward the people in developing countries with whom they transact business. Some multinationals have included human rights guidelines in their charters and recent efforts have been made to incorporate such guidelines into the charters of all businesses. However, multinational retailers and the sweatshops with whom they contract have been the center of intense ethical debates that are best approached from the standpoint of social contract theory. These debates focus on the ethics of sweatshop exploitation. We examine what exploitation means and why it is wrong, even in contexts in which workers receive somewhat higher than average wages. We also examine whether businesses have a right (or even a duty) to outsource domestic jobs to overseas sweatshops. Does communitarian loyalty to the company's domestic workers (the stakeholder model of business ethics) trump loyalty to shareholders? Conversely, might it not be the case, using utilitarian ethics, that maximizing overall well-being requires investing in undeveloped foreign labor markets?

Chapter 8 surveys the many ethical dilemmas that aid workers on the ground confront. Many of these involve having to accommodate what aid workers regard as immoral practices – patriarchal customs that discriminate against women, corrupt government officials, and so on – in order to deliver development assistance. Other dilemmas involve the difficulty of navigating assistance in a truly collaborative manner when aid workers and their agencies possess so much power over their clients. Aid agencies, for example, have a history of absorbing much of the local talent. Given their privileged position, they may feel entitled to run a development program the way they see fit, according to the best practices of their donor country rather than the best practices of the area they are operating in. Thus, hierarchies of knowledge and power feed into inappropriate forms of technology transfer that may end up fostering dependency rather than empowerment.

We conclude this book on a personal note. As citizens we can pressure our leaders to do more for the developing world by providing higher levels of better aid and adopting trade and immigration policies that are more sympathetic to the people of that world. But what should we do as private persons? One response urges us to live our daily lives in a sustainable manner. Modeling a sustainable life for our children and consociates may seem insignificant, but multiplied across millions it can ease the burden that we in the developed world – and by extension, those in the developing world – will have to shoulder. Another response urges us to donate more of our income to development organizations. Utilitarian reasoning might require that we donate as much as we possibly can until we and the people in the developed world whose lives we are trying to better enjoy a comparable standard of living. Communitarian virtue ethicists counter this argument by reminding us of our duties to kith and kin. Improving the lives of those with whom we are bound by love and affection entitles us to divert our income to developing *them*. Social contract ethicists offer yet another way to assess our responsibilities. If we are tied to the world's poor through relations of economic and political interdependency, are we not duty-bound to help them as a matter of reciprocity?

Summary

This introduction provides facts about the current state of poverty, inequality, and environmental endangerment that are necessary in order to reason ethically about global development. Although progress has been made in raising people out of extreme poverty, levels of inequality have risen with as many as a third of the world's population living in a state of material insecurity and underdevelopment. Efforts by governments and international organizations to promote development have fallen short of expectations, and in some cases have made a bad situation worse.

The failure of government relief efforts is not a cause for despair once we realize that relatively modest sums of money well spent could reduce poverty-related deaths to almost zero. Removing the institutional causes of poverty is well within the limits of practical possibility. This becomes even more apparent when we appreciate the role of European colonialism in creating and perpetuating underdevelopment.

Governments and private persons, especially in affluent, developed countries therefore have a duty to work harder in reversing underdevelopment. The public morality of government policy and the private morality of personal action each have two prongs: promoting well-being and acting justly. While governments are mainly charged with promoting global well-being (including development), private individuals are mainly tasked with acting justly toward distant others who are harmed by their actions. Human rights and social contract ethics can guide our thinking about developmental justice. Well-being, by contrast, mainly falls within the province of utilitarian and communitarian reasoning.

Notes

1   The WB's International Poverty Line (IPL) has been criticized for being arbitrarily calculated and set artificially low. The IPL is the mean of the poverty lines of the world's 15 poorest countries as set by their governments. By comparing the purchasing power of each national currency across a broad spectrum of goods and services, a common standard of purchasing power parity (PPP), stated in what US dollars can purchase in the US, is then calculated. Leaving aside the fact that income reveals little about the satisfaction of basic needs, PPP calculations underestimate the real purchasing power of the poor, not the least because they are insensitive to variations in rates

of inflation between different goods. Poor people spend 50% of their income on food staples, whose PPP costs do not significantly vary from country to country, in contrast to the often-extreme variations in the PPP costs of luxury goods and services. So when world food staple prices doubled in 2008, the poor saw their income halved, to the point where they had nothing left over. However, because food costs compose only 5% of a nation's total consumption (the vast bulk of which is heavily tilted toward the middle and upper classes), this crisis only increased the total cost of goods and services worldwide by 5%, with national poverty lines shifting up by 5% instead of 50%.

2   Simon Kuznets hypothesized that inequality tracks phases of development: the transition to industrialization increases inequality markedly, which gradually tapers off and then decreases as levels of education rise and birth rates decline. The hypothesis appears most applicable to the industrial phase of development, but is contradicted by growing inequality in post-industrial nations like the US and G10 countries. While absolute extreme poverty has been reduced worldwide, relative poverty within developing countries has grown.

3   Kim (2013). Accounting giant PricewaterhouseCoopers estimated in a September 2014 report entitled, "Two Degrees of Separation: Ambition and Reality: The Low Carbon Economy Index", that if current trends persist, the world will use up its "carbon budget" – the amount of carbon emissions compatible with limiting overall warming to two degrees Celsius above pre-industrial levels – by 2034. To stay within this budget, by 2030 the G20 nations will need to reduce their carbon emissions by one-third, and continue doing so by one-half by 2050.

4   Goldin (2016, p. 120). Half of the world's forests have been lost, and while deforestation has abated since the 1990s – it now destroys around 5 million hectares of forest every year – 12 million hectares are lost every year to land degradation and desertification, costing $42 billion in lost incomes.

5   Ibid., p. 122. Rising sea levels, for instance, threaten to inundate coastal areas that are home to 1 billion people (25% of Bangladesh is less than a meter above sea level).

6   In 2004 the per capita carbon dioxide emission in the United States was 20.6 tons in comparison to China's 3.9 (6 as of 2014) and Bangladesh's 0.2 (the global average was 4.5). Growth in GDP is estimated to be eight times more important than population growth in explaining the rapid growth of China's carbon dioxide emissions, which now lead the world.

7   Ibid., p. 111.

8   Ibid., p. 96. The debt crisis of the 1970s highlights the compensatory duties owed by developed countries to the developing world; the crisis was triggered by the United States drastically raising its interest rates to manage its own "stagnation" crisis, with the initially low-interest loans held by developing countries to help them "take off" on a course of rapid industrialization – aggressively promoted by foreign banks flush with excess petro-dollars from skyrocketing oil prices – subsequently being readjusted upward at higher unsustainable rates. It took almost 20 years of threatened and real loan defaults by developing countries before international institutions began to respond to this financial crisis. Despite this progress, many poor countries did not qualify for debt relief or cancellation. As of 2012 the WB determined that developing countries owed $4 trillion in foreign debt, with the poorest countries having to pay $34 million *per diem* to service loan repayments.

9   Perhaps the costliest and deadliest provision of the WTO trade agreement is the 1995 Trade Related Aspects of Intellectual Property Rights Agreement (TRIPS) and related provisions that protect product patents for 20 years and beyond, thereby impeding and delaying the production of generic drugs that could save the lives of millions of people. Half of all poverty-related deaths are caused by disease, with tuberculosis and tropical diseases such as malaria accounting for 12% of the global burden of disease (GBD). A little more than 10% of global health research spending targets diseases that comprise 90% of GBD, with drug companies targeting the health needs of high-income customers. Only the latter can afford drugs whose prices, thanks to product patent monopolies, have been inflated to anywhere between 10 to 30 times the normal market price and upwards of 100 times the cost of production. A country like India that, prior to 2005, had produced generic copies of drugs for its poor population using alternative production techniques, was forced by threat of trade sanctions to sign on to TRIPS.

10 Pogge (2008, p. 11, 20–23).
11 Sillers' table is based on the World Bank's regional poverty aggregation data for 2013 (http://iresearch.worldbank.org/PovcalNet/povDuplicateWB.aspx). His 2015 projection is based on the IMF's GDP growth projections through 2023 as published in the World Economic outlook database (www.imf.org/external/pubs/ft/weo/2017/02/weodata/index.aspx). For a discussion of this table and an earlier table in Sillers (2017), which Dr. Sillers has graciously updated and revised for our textbook, see D. Sillers and S. O'Connell (2016).
12 To the right of the column listing the percentage of global population falling below each of the four poverty lines are two columns, one showing the average amount a person who falls below the designated poverty line earns, the other showing the average amount that would have to be transferred to ensure that no one fell below the line. Thus, the average person falling below the $1.90 PPP level has a daily income of $0.58 below $1.90, or $1.32. In order for that person to reach the $1.90 threshold s/he would need an additional annual income of $211.29. In order for no one to live below the threshold of $155.8 billion would need to be transferred using perfect targeting. The table also shows two ways to calculate transfers (for both perfect targeting and universal income). One uses purchasing power parity dollars (PPP$), showing how many 2011 dollars would purchase a basket of goods in the US in 2011. The other uses a market exchange formula. This is important because when 2011 dollars are exchanged for local currencies to buy a local basket of goods, their purchasing power is about double (on average $70 will buy about $140 worth of goods in developing countries).
13 In 2011–12 UNICEF funded two UBI pilots providing at the higher end Rs 150 ($2.25) per child/month and Rs 300 ($4.50) per adult/month in 12 villages in Madhya Pradesh, India. The results were positive. Recipients saved and used their income wisely to fund their children's education and increase their standard of living.
14 As Sillers notes, these figures are misleadingly high, since the costs for running UBIs would be partly defrayed by savings from the welfare programs they would replace.
15 Hardin (1974).
16 Goldin (op. cit., pp. 57–58).

Suggested reading

H. E. Baber and Denise Dimon (eds.) (2013). *Globalization and International Development: The Ethical Issues*. Peterborough, ON: Broadview Press.

This anthology contains a comprehensive selection of writings by philosophers and development experts on poverty, globalization, colonialism, neo- and post-colonialism, population and the environment, gender, cultural relativism, multiculturalism, and immigration.

Jared Diamond (1997). *Guns, Germs, and Steel*. New York: W. W. Norton & Co.

Diamond's book provides a historical analysis of how environmental circumstances led to varied development patterns across myriad world regions. It also provides evidence for the underlying environmental circumstances that may have led to western hegemonic power.

Ian Goldin (2016). *The Pursuit of Development: Economic Growth, Social Change, and Ideas*. Oxford: Oxford University Press.

This book provides a short, concise, and accessible history of development up to the present day. Written by a leading developmental economist, it does not delve into the ethics and philosophy of development.

Paul Haslam, Jennifer Schafer and Pierre Beaudet (eds.) (2012). *Introduction to International Development: Approaches, Actors, and Issues*, 2nd edition. Oxford: Oxford University Press.

This anthology of articles provides a comprehensive introductory survey of all aspects of development. Philosophical and ethical issues are discussed in passing.

José Antonio Ocampo (ed.) (2016). *Global Governance and Development*. Oxford: Oxford University Press.

This anthology contains the most up-to-date technical discussions regarding the evolving role that the UN, Development Finance Institutions, governments, development agencies, and the private sector are playing in development. Recommended for more advanced students.

Organization for Economic Cooperation and Development Data Website (2016). www.oecd.org/dataoecd/52/18/37790990.pdf. This website provides development data regarding ODA.

Jeffery D. Sachs (2015). *The Age of Sustainable Development*. New York. Columbia University Press.

Written by a leading theorist of development, this highly accessible book provides an exhaustive, panoramic survey of development opportunities, challenges, and risks, from all angles.

World Bank Website (2018). https://data.worldbank.org/. This website provides open access to global development data.

Online Sources and Visual Media

Cinema Libre Studio (Producer) and Philippe Diaz (Director) (2008). *The End of Poverty?* [Motion Picture]. United States: Cinema Libre Studio in association with the Robert Schalkenbach Foundation.

This movie provides an overview of the history of global economic inequality and the causes for its continued existence.

References

Goldin, Ian (2016). *The Pursuit of Development: Economic Growth, Social Change, and Ideas*. Oxford: Oxford University Press.

Hardin, Garrett (1974). "Living on a Lifeboat." *Bioscience* 24(10): 561–568.

Kim, Jim Yong (2013). "Ending Poverty Means Tackling Climate Change." *The World Bank*. www.worldbank.org/en/news/opinion/2013/07/10/op-ed-ending-poverty-includes-tacking-climate-change.

Pogge, Thomas (2008). *World Poverty and Human Rights*, 2nd edition. Cambridge: Polity Press.

Sillers, Don (2017). "If a Basic Income that Takes Every Human Above the Poverty Level Would Be Introduced, How Much Wealth Would Have to be Redistributed?" *Quora*, July 24, 2017. www.quora.com/If-a-basic-income-that-takes-every-human-above-poverty-level-would-be-introduced-how-much-wealth-would-have-to-be-redistributed.

Sillers, Don and S. O'Connell (2016). "Person-Equivalent Poverty: An Introduction." *USAID Economics Brief*, September 22, 2016.

1 Development

The ethics of development begins with the ethics of ranking societies and individuals. We don't need to rank societies and individuals in order to help them meet their most basic needs. Emergency food, clothing, shelter, and medical care can be provided to the desperately needy on an ad hoc basis. Nor need we rank societies and individuals who are not desperately needy as judged by their own standards. Aboriginal peoples in New Guinea were doing just fine (thank you) until they were "discovered" by outsiders. It is only when we think about how those who are *chronically* needy fare relative to everyone else, not only in terms of their low levels of consumption but also in terms of their lack of power in surviving as free and equals in a world dominated by legal and economic elites, that their vulnerability appears – to them as well as to us – as a phenomenon of "underdevelopment."

In theory, the problem of vulnerability, or domination by others, can be solved by removing oneself from those others. In practice, this is virtually impossible to do. So, the question of development, or relative power and capability, cannot not be dismissed. One might here object that the idea of development did not originally manifest itself within an ethical criticism of domination but arose instead within a colonial ideology justifying domination, specifically that of white, European-descended peoples over darker-skinned Africans and Amerindians. That this objection still finds salience among critics of development poses a challenge we shall have to address head on.

The concept of development refers to at least two distinct processes. Societies are said to develop, or evolve, by becoming structurally more complex. This kind of social development is connected to another kind: the social development of individuals. As social structures become more complex, individuals interacting within them assume new roles and develop new capabilities. The more structurally complex their interaction becomes, the more deliberate (and less habitual and routine) their way of relating to themselves and to others becomes.

This chapter begins by exploring the idea of societal development. This idea has a long pedigree dating back to the European Enlightenment, if not earlier. Before there was social science, philosophers operating out of the Enlightenment tradition speculated that the universal destiny of humanity was to become free, principally by adopting the kinds of institutions – the so-called "rights of man and citizen" – that rationally minded Europeans, shaking off the yoke of religious and monarchic authority, were adopting for themselves. The first generation of social scientists at the dawn of the twentieth century borrowed much from this philosophical legacy but wrapped it up in the mantle of respectable empirical science. These new accounts of modernization had staying power throughout and beyond the twentieth century. The critics of development as modernization, however, have raised empirical, conceptual, and ethical objections to the entire development project. Is there some way to incorporate this salubrious criticism into an account of development without abandoning the concept altogether?

After proposing one way this might be done, we turn to contemporary views about measuring development. Here our attention is also drawn to the idea of individual development. Can we elaborate a defensible theory of universal human capabilities that can serve to ground judgments about individual and societal development? Is such a theory about normal human functioning susceptible to ideological and/or ethnocentric manipulation?

What is progress? The Enlightenment debate: Locke and Rousseau

Development theory in its *economistic* form can be traced back to early modern moral philosophy. John Locke famously extolled the greater industrial and agricultural productivity as well as individual progress in material well-being that a monetized exchange economy grounded in private property and a division of labor afforded, in comparison to the impoverished lifestyle yielded by North American Indian economies based on simple hunting and gathering (Chapter V, *Second Treatise of Government* [1690]):

> [I]t cannot be supposed that God meant [the world] should always remain common and uncultivated. He gave it to the use of the industrious and rational (and *labour* was to be *his title* to it) (para. 34) . . . There cannot be a clearer demonstration of any thing, than several nations of the Americans are of this, who are rich in land and poor in all the comforts of life . . . yet for want of improving it by labour, have not one hundredth part of the conveniences we enjoy; and a king of a large and fruitful territory there feeds, lodges and is clad worse than a day labourer in England (para 41).

Locke's dismissal of the impoverished lives of native Americans compared to the lives of his English compatriots also contains a moral condemnation of sorts: those who are not rational and industrious (the Americans) disobey God's command to stake out private property claims and increase bounty for all through cultivation and hard labor. The uncultivated land they occupy is "waste" that is divinely predestined to be settled by acquisitive, hard-working Europeans. Indeed, even the lowliest of wage earners within Europe's stratified society of rich and poor lives better than a tribal chief.

One can read into Locke's moral indictment of native Americans a more contemporary allusion to what we today call "the tragedy of the commons" or "free rider" problem. This problem involves individuals taking freely from a common store of goods without individually contributing to its growth and provision. For Locke, and most economists today, the temptation to ride freely on the work of others can be solved by converting common property into private property. If individuals are responsible for their own provision, then they will have greater incentive to maintain and grow it. Hence, during the nineteenth and twentieth centuries tribal peoples in Africa, North American, and Australia were encouraged (often compelled) to convert their communal property into private holdings.

Just over half a century later Jean-Jacques Rousseau, citing Locke against himself, would impugn the moral inequality necessitated by Locke's conception of economic development:

> Even those enriched exclusively by labor could hardly base their property on better claims. They could very well say: "I am the one who built that wall; I have earned this land with my labor." In response to them it could be said: "Who gave you the boundary lines? By what right to do you claim to exact payment at our expense for labor we did not impose on you? Are you unaware that a multitude of your brothers perish or suffer from need of what you have in excess; and that you needed explicit and unanimous consent from the human race to help yourself to anything from the common subsistence that went beyond your own?"[1]

Rousseau's diatribe against progress opened up a debate that has continued to this day: an economy that encourages hard work by offering prospects for unlimited material gain also opens the door to greater social inequality and, most worrisome, greater political domination of rich over poor. In Rousseau – a lover of untrammeled nature – we see the beginnings of the Romantic reaction against industrial capitalism and the beginnings, as well, of a new tragedy of the commons, in which nature is regarded as an exploitable resource for private gain and collectively unsustainable consumption.

Aside from inspiring the French Revolution, Rousseau's intention was not to impugn the idea of progress among his contemporaries but broaden it beyond its narrow economic understanding. Enlightenment philosophies of history developed by Condorcet, Kant, and Hegel around the turn of the nineteenth century inclined to measure progress along the moral and political dimensions set out by Rousseau, specifically in terms of the universal realization of individual freedom. Civil and political rights would figure predominantly in their vision of a rational society, along with a notion of a market economy based on private property. Sharing Rousseau's fanciful depiction of "savages" as lacking in reason and ambition, many of them would endorse denying them these rights, pending their "enlightenment" under European tutelage.

The dynamic of crisis-driven development: Marx

The tension between economic and moral progress, evident in the growing impoverishment of the industrial working class, would come to a head in Marx's understanding of world history as a contradiction- and conflict-driven process tending toward the eventual elimination of domination, misery, toil, and alienation in a stateless communist utopia.

Because the Marxist vision of development provided a critique of mainstream development theory during the post-WWII era, it bears some elaborating. Inspired by the philosophy of G.W.F. Hegel, Marx believed that laboring activity was the motor force behind human development and social change:

> Hegel grasps the self-development of man as a process . . . comprehends objective man as the result of his own work. The actual, active relationship of man to himself as a species-being . . . is possible only insofar as he actually brings forth all of his species-powers – which in turn is only possible through the collective effort of Mankind, only as a result of history – and treats them as objects, something which immediately is again only possible in the form of alienation.[2]

Hegel famously argued that the entirety of world history could be read as the story of the human spirit striving to bring forth its essential species nature as free, something he believed the European society of his time was in the process of accomplishing. Powering history was humanity's own reflection on its state of un-freedom. African and Asian societies, he judged, were unfree compared to Europe insofar as they hadn't developed the capacity to dominate nature through science and hadn't liberated the individual from collective domination and despotic authority. However, in developing science and free political institutions, European society had to undergo its own crisis-laden learning process; it had to abandon natural and communal forms of life – viz., it had to "alienate" people from nature and themselves – while at the same time emancipating slaves and serfs.

Marx's conception of world history, which he dubbed *historical materialism*, jettisoned Hegel's metaphysics of a providential human spirit in favor of class conflict as the motor of human development. Marx believed that a critical level of population growth compels simple communal societies to become economic class societies. In early class society, an aristocratic ruling class of warriors and priests charged with coordinating and defending the apparatus of production lives off the labor of slaves and serfs. Inevitably, Marx reasoned, new technologies and ways of organizing production (social labor) run up against old property and political relations. In Europe, the evolution of the communal guild system of craft production into the modern industrial factory, and the parallel evolution of the communal system of cultivation based on the manorial commons into large-scale, enclosed (viz. privatized) farms, ushered in the end of feudalism and the emergence of capitalism. Capitalism creates new freedoms – economic, civil, and political – but at a severe social cost. Money, trade, and profit become the new idols, replacing religion and social stability. As Marx pointedly observed in *The Communist Manifesto* (1848): "All that is solid melts into air, all that is holy is profaned, and man is at last compelled to face, with sober senses, his real conditions of life."[3]

From Marx's time down to the present day, the preceding image of societal development as a technological, crisis-driven process of liberation – from nature, religion, and authority – has continued to captivate development theory. But Marx thought that communism (his word for a stateless utopia beyond domination) – not capitalism – was the endpoint of history. Capitalism, he argued, fails to liberate humanity from toil but instead subjects the mass of industrial workers (the proletariat) to the most alienating form of factory work: "The work of the proletarians has lost all individual character, and . . . [the worker] becomes an appendage of the machine, and it is only the most simple, most monotonous, and most easily acquired knack, that is required of him."[4] The division between physical and mental labor robs labor of its freedom, creativity, and sociality – the very qualities that enable it to develop people's powers. Marx accordingly reasoned that workers organized in factories would rebel against their dehumanization and impoverishment, this time propelled by ever-worsening crises of overproduction – a symptom of the growing concentration of wealth among the ruling capitalist-investor class. Out of the ashes of capitalism would rise a newborn humanity free to develop its powers fully:

> In a higher phase of communist society, after the enslaving subordination of the individual to the division of labour, and thereby also the antithesis between mental and physical labor, has vanished; after labor has become not only a means of life but life's prime want; after the productive forces have increased with the all-round development of the individual, and all the springs of common wealth flow more abundantly – only then can the narrow horizon of bourgeois right be crossed in its entirety and society inscribe on its banners: From each according to his abilities, to each according to his needs.[5]

This oft-quoted passage is of interest to us for two reasons: It looks ahead to the capabilities theory of development we discuss below; and it begs several questions that must be answered before the ethics of development can get off the ground. As for the first reason, Marx rejects a simple recipe for development based on increasing economic consumption and distributing wealth equally, concluding that what is most important to justice in a fully developed society is ensuring that each has the resources needed to fulfill his or her individual needs "for all around development." As for the second reason, Marx assumes that this moral aim of development depends on eliminating scarcity and creating abundance for all by developing "the forces of production" to the greatest extent possible. Eliminating scarcity is important because doing so reduces social conflict and enables us to develop our loving, sociable natures to the point where *being* a generous person is more important than *having* more possessions.

Marx conceded that the overall humanitarian goal of eliminating scarcity might require short-term suffering and reverse development. His comments on British colonial rule in India, written for the *New York Tribune* between 1853 and 1858, defend the necessity of British despotism and its destructive and deadly imposition of free trade and modern capitalism in that region, even while condemning its inhumanity. That said, it is not Marx's endorsement of tutelary colonial despotism that is important for those of us today living in the twenty-first century. It is his problematic understanding of how scarcity might be eliminated.

Wouldn't the development of industry necessary to eliminate scarcity require more – not less – alienated labor? Assuming that automation could eventually replace dehumanizing work, freeing us to develop our all-around capacities, we are then confronted with the implications of this never-ending expansion of needs and powers. Put bluntly, wouldn't the drive to develop our humanity in ever new and expanding directions make scarcity – and the potentially unsustainable development of industry necessary for trying to eliminate it – inevitable? Recall Marx's view that technologically mediated labor expands human powers and thereby creates new needs, which is to say, new scarcities. So it seems that instead of reducing the apparatus of production, humanity's Promethean appetite for a better life will necessarily condemn it to harness the power of that apparatus more intensively. Reducing the workday to a minimum – Marx's hope for a leisurely existence spent on developing our all-around powers through mental and expressive activity – seems increasingly remote. So, alienated labor, social conflict, *and* unsustainable development would seem all but insurmountable even in a communist "utopia" – unless, that is, human beings opt for different social needs whose satisfaction requires a more modest, sustainable level of development.

Post-WWII dynamics of development: modernization theory

Marx believed that all societies would have to develop into capitalist societies before developing into communist societies. This explains his ambivalence toward European colonialism, whose destruction of local economies in the name of free trade – such as the deadly decimation of the Indian textile weaving economy that followed the forced importation of machine-manufactured British textiles – belied colonialism's developmental potential. In any case, Marx's utopian vision of a stateless, democratically managed economic system, liberated from any alienating system of commodity exchange, seemed to reject two pillars of the modernization theory of development that was being elaborated by a second generation of social theorists.

In the seminal writings of Max Weber and Emile Durkheim, modernization became synonymous with science-driven secularization.[6] For them (as for Hegel) culture, not economics, was the dynamo of development. While they believed that the decline of religion and the rise of reason would promote the creation of scientifically administered, industrial capitalist societies efficiently regulated by a bureaucratic state, they observed that different religious cultures mattered in this regard. Weber himself explained the backward and undeveloped nature of non-European societies in terms of their peculiar cultural resistance to secularization. Weber believed that an active orientation to worldly change uniquely resided in the ethical heritage of Abrahamic faiths and that only Christianity – specifically Protestantism – provided the "spiritual" conditions for realizing modernity as a distinctly *rational* form of capitalist society based on individual responsibility (Weber 1958). He subsequently relegated non-Western religious worldviews (including Islam) to the status of economically and politically backward cultures. Variants of this controversial "Orientalist" thesis continue to circulate today among those who, like Samuel Huntington, posit a fundamental "clash" between the egalitarian individualism of Western civilization and the rest of the world.[7]

In the final analysis, Weber and Durkheim were as ambivalent about modern progress as Rousseau. The upside to modernization was an increase in individual freedom and material welfare; the downside was class conflict and the weakening of communal feelings of solidarity, including commitment to moral values for their own sake. In this respect, their sociology of modernization was a harbinger for the rise of fascism and communism a few decades later.

Talk of modernizing Europe's colonies was overshadowed by World War II and the Great Depression – capitalism's epic failure to solve its own endemic crises of overproduction. Post-war development efforts focused on the economic reconstruction of Europe. The WB and IMF created by the Bretton-Woods Agreement (1944) promoted a new kind of welfare state capitalism based on the economic theory of John Maynard Keynes, whose support for social safety nets and income redistribution was thought to ease inequality and class conflict while securing domestic and international peace. However, despite President Harry Truman's famous 1949 Inaugural Address proclaiming the end of the "old imperialism," his announcement that the West would raise the "primitive and stagnant" economies of Africa and Asia up from their cultural backwardness invoked a new developmental imperialism (Escobar 1995).

National liberation movements in former colonies, combined with geopolitics of the Cold War, revived interest in modernization among Western development theorists. Inspired by Walt Rostow's theory of economic stages and Talcott Parsons' theory of pattern variables, the new modernization theory posited the capitalist democracies of the West (the *First World*) – not the Communist dictatorships of China and the Soviet Bloc (the *Second World*) – as the model the undeveloped *Third World* should emulate.[8] Influenced by Weber and Durkheim, Parsons' modernization theory held that traditional social roles oriented toward maintaining collective identity were less adaptive than modern, technically specialized vocational roles whose performance could be evaluated by rational measures of achievement and rewarded in a manner conformable to individual self-interest and acquisitiveness.

From modernization to dependency

Modernization theory discounted obstacles to development caused by the terrible legacy of European colonialism. In the 1960s Marxists and "dependency theorists," such as Immanuel Wallerstein, appealed to this fact in arguing that throughout history different world economic systems have been structured around relationships of domination and dependency.[9] According to Wallerstein, global capitalism today necessarily creates both a developed *center*, occupied by the United States, Western Europe, and Japan, *and* an underdeveloped *periphery*, comprising most of the Third World. Within this world system, the periphery depends on the center to purchase its exports, which largely consist of primary goods, in exchange for center's imports, which comprise value-added secondary goods.

The neoliberal era

While Marxists conceded the possibility of development under a global form of socialism, dependency theorists believed that global core-periphery dependency was systemically entrenched in a way that would likely perpetuate uneven development under any economic system. However, both Marxists and dependency theorists endorsed state-centered economics. This understanding, which was largely embraced across ideological divides, was contradicted by the unanticipated "stagflation" that afflicted the US during the oil crisis of the 1970s and the relative impotence of government price controls and economic stimulus to combat it. The *neoliberal* economic paradigm that came to dominate development theory from the late 1970s through the late 1990s not only rejected state-centered economic development (and so diminished the role of the UN in development), it also rejected a values approach to development of the sort that had been favored by modernization theorists. For neoliberals, development, now limited to the single aim of poverty reduction through economic growth, would be driven by free trade and private investment.

The UN ascendant: the MDG and SDG programs

The failure of neoliberal orthodoxy to deliver its promises in many parts of the developing world (see the Introduction) might simply be attributed to the hypocrisy of developed nations, who continue to restrict imports from the developing world. However, it might also be that the axiom of comparative advantage that undergirds neoclassical trade theory is simply false. As dependency theorists argue (see Chapter 3), trading primary goods in exchange for secondary goods is a recipe for underdevelopment.

In any case, the failure of neoliberalism's other agenda – the downsizing and privatization of government services – seems widely accepted by most economists today. Taken together, these failures provoked a renewed values-oriented approach to development led, once again, by the UN. The mixed success of the UN's Millennium Development Goals (MDG) program included the rise of emerging economies (chiefly in China and India) and the restoration, especially in Latin America, of state-centered, neo-Keynesian economic policy. In tandem with the global economic fragility of the twenty-first century and the potentially catastrophic specter of climate change impact on food production, water access, disease control, and much else, recent development approaches, such as the UN's Sustainable Development Goals (SDG) program, have become more diverse in their aims, methods, instruments, and agents. As of this writing, development theory is in the process of reconsidering (a) the ills of "overdevelopment," such as climate change, environmental degradation, poor nutrition leading to obesity, diabetes, and coronary disease; (b) private-public partnerships; and (c) new collaborations among developing countries themselves.

Critical analysis: does development follow an internal logic or an accidental path?

Our survey of development theory reveals a significant fault line dividing those who believe that development is either mainly economic or cultural. It is fair to say that development has meant progress along both paths of rational problem solving: through technical development of efficient methods of economic production on one side, and moral development of schemes of cooperation and conflict resolution on the other.

Two questions arise regarding this dual perspective model of development. First, does enhanced learning, or rational problem solving, proceed according to a rigid logic, so that we can specify a universal pathway and endpoint of development for all societies? Second, does enhancement of one kind of learning proceed harmoniously with enhancement of other kinds?

One way development theorists have tried to answer this question is by comparing the way societies may be said to evolve in learning to adapt to internal and external challenges to the way individual persons learn to adapt to other persons and their external environments in the course of childhood maturation. If we assume that children learn to reason morally and cognitively along a single path of irreversible developmental stages, then it is plausible to imagine that societies, which might be thought to institutionalize these rational capacities in scientific, legal, economic, and political systems, follow a similar logical trajectory. If, on the other hand, children across different cultures do not follow a single development path, then it is reasonable to conclude that societies do not either.

The idea that enhanced learning proceeds according to a single logic has been proposed by psychologists explaining the development of *individuals*. Jean Piaget famously proposed that child cognitive development proceeds through four stages of *decentration*, with each stage (or general cognitive scheme [*gestalt*]) building on the preceding stage. At the first stage, which Piaget dubs *sensorimotor-symbiotic*, the infant responds unreflectively to stimuli without distinguishing whether its source is internal or external. At the second stage of *pre-operational* cognition the child has reflectively grasped the limits of its passive response to stimuli and now intentionally acts upon a world it knows to be outside itself but without distinguishing whether the things that make up the world are persons or inanimate objects. At the third level of *concrete-operational* cognition the child begins to use logic to infer the conservation of quantities, weights, and volumes across superficial variations and has learned to distinguish inanimate physical things from entities exhibiting degrees of agency. Finally, by around 10 years the child has begun to develop *formal-operational* cognition, enabling it to abstract general (formal) rules of classification and inference from more concrete, context-specific rules.

The application of this stage-sequential model of child *cognitive* development to social evolution becomes clearer when we see how the dynamic of reflection, formal abstraction, and conceptual analysis driving the process describes features of child *moral* development. Using Piaget's *genetic structuralism* as a guide, Lawrence Kohlberg elaborated a three-stage sequence of moral development that specifically highlights the last two stages of Piaget's developmental sequence involving operations that proceed from concrete to abstract (formal) reflection. According to Kohlberg's experimental findings, the *pre-conventional morality* of the very young child exhibits mainly concrete reflection: the pre-adolescent's perspective is largely egocentric, defining right and wrong in terms of behavior that elicits personal reward or punishment. *Conventional* moral cognition expands (decenters) this perspective in the direction of a standpoint that is both particular (concrete) and general (formal): the dominant legal and moral rules of one's family, religion, or nation. At the level of *post-conventional* reasoning the child learns to reflectively question these specific societal prohibitions and permissions on the basis of formal procedures of moral reasoning that abstract from concrete social rules, such as utilitarianism (maximizing well-being for humanity), social contract theory (treating each person, qua interactive partner, fairly), and human rights (respecting the equal dignity of each individual, qua human being).

Using this scheme of individual development (ontogenesis) we can now understand how the human species might be said to evolve or develop socially (phylogenesis). Drawing from Piaget and Kohlberg, the German social theorist Jürgen Habermas proposes an analogy between individual and social development.[10] According to Habermas, tribal societies that use magic to supplicate and control nature fail to logically distinguish the physical world from the social and personal worlds. Using Piaget's scheme, their level of technical cognition still displays some features that correspond to the pre-operational stage of child development. Their morality and "law" correspondingly reflect a pre-conventional view of justice in which persons exact vengeance on animals as well as other persons for perceived harms, unintended or otherwise. Pre-modern civilizations have developed formal operational reasoning in the form of mathematics and geometry but reason morally from a conventional list of concrete "dos" and "don'ts." At this middle stage, justice and right conduct are no longer understood egocentrically but have become decentered, reflecting what a given society accepts as good and right for its members. Only beginning with the ancient Greeks do we see ethicists like Socrates entertaining more abstract procedures of reasoning, with the concept of the inherent dignity of the individual as a possessor of human rights emerging only 2,000 years later.

Amalgamating Piaget and Kohlberg with Weber and Durkheim, Habermas concludes that modern societies exhibit a great deal of Piagetian decentration: such societies logically distinguish factual knowledge of a "disenchanted nature" from moral duty and aesthetic taste, which they institutionalize in science, law, and art, respectfully; and they apply this decentered cultural matrix to differentiate economy, state, and family, thereby carving separate private and public spheres and, most importantly, a sphere of individual conscience and freedom that cannot be infringed by society. Advances in communicative – not technological – rationality drive this evolution.

For Habermas, this process of decentration portends both risk and opportunity. The gradual evolution of economic and governmental systems that increasingly assume a life of their own independent of society's advanced moral self-understanding and democratic control increases the technical efficiency of cooperation at the cost of individual and collective freedom. As we shall see, it is debatable whether modern processes of social development that exhibit high levels of rational decentration and differentiation ultimately advance sustainable forms of individual development.

For now, let us leave aside the question of whether the rational differentiation of society into technical systems on one side, and ethical lifeworlds on the other, counts as freedom-enhancing for the individuals impacted by this kind of development – and ask a more basic one: Is the very idea of social evolution conceptually and empirically viable?

To answer this question, we might begin by asking whether Habermas's own logic of social development is well supported by developmental psychology. The empirical evidence supporting a universal logic of child development is ambiguous, partly because of the difficulty in testing this hypothesis across cultures possessing somewhat different skill sets that have been developed in response to different problems. Conceptually, the analogy between child development and societal development is even weaker. As Habermas notes, development of technical cognitive skills outpaces moral development, and individuals (such as Socrates) may exhibit advanced moral reasoning relative to their respective societies' institutionalized legal codes. Finally, any single measure of development risks elitism and ethnocentrism, over-generalizing or over-privileging some cognitive-moral capacities. As Durkheim noted, the kinds of hyper-reflective moral capacities favored by Piaget, Kohlberg, and Habermas as natural developmental endpoints might be unnatural endpoints for persons inhabiting simple communities based on traditional (and relatively static) forms of family-based subsistence farming and homogeneous mores (Escobar 1995). Even normal development in societies displaying complex divisions of labor and relations of contractual exchange can produce pathologies – anxiety, depression, alienation, and self-centeredness – that do not promote happiness or freedom.

Therefore, instead of conceiving social development as unfolding an innate, universal logic, one might conceive it as following *particular pathways* whose trajectories have been shaped by historical accidents. As we saw in the introduction, there were many historical accidents – geographic and demographic – that favored the early emergence of civilizations in Asia and Europe capable of developing sophisticated military technology. The rise of capitalism and an independently functioning market economy in Europe presupposed the conquest of the Americas and subsequent expropriation of the latter's gold, silver, and people. It also presupposed the existence of relatively independent city-states as centers of commerce, free labor, and technical craft production, along with nascent banks providing credit. Last but not least, it presupposed a decentralized state system, rapid population growth, and the emergence of ethical individualism as an outgrowth of reformed Christianity. The fortuitous confluence of all these accidents made Northern Europe a capitalist center that was well positioned to dominate the world system though its demographic, administrative, and technological advantages. The subsequent "accident" of European colonialism made the rest of the world become more like Europe; many of the challenges that compelled European development eventually trickled down to European colonies. (Tragically, given European elites' pervasive racism, the moral ideal of equal inclusion under the law was emphatically *not* one of the European developmental accomplishments that trickled down.)

The gradual evolution of economic and political institutions in response to what, by the twentieth century, were fast becoming common global challenges makes it difficult to clearly distinguish European from non-European paths of development. Indeed, it makes distinguishing pre-modern from modern society difficult – so much so that development must at best seen as something piecemeal, rather than holistic in the manner suggested by the "stages" of development model associated with Piaget's genetic structuralism or Marx's (and Habermas's) stages of social evolution. In fact, as we shall now see, there is nothing in this pluralistic path-dependent model of development that dictates that enhanced problem solving along a technological pathway can't be accompanied by diminution of problem solving along a moral pathway.

Critical analysis: is development harmonious?

A central question now before us is whether technical and moral pathways of development collide, converge, or intersect in some third way. Oversimplifying Marx's own thinking on the primacy of economic contradictions between productive forces and property relations in motivating historical development at all levels of society, orthodox Marxists were inclined to believe in the inevitably of a technologically driven trajectory of universal progress (technological determinism), which for them would eventually usher in the revolutionary establishment of a fully emancipated, contradiction-free communist society. For orthodox Marxists, moral ideas and political institutions more or less "mirror" and serve to legitimate technological-economic institutions, thereby ruling out any major conflict between these pathways of development.

Recently, Michel Foucault has suggested a somewhat darker version of this technological reductionism. He notes, for example, that in the late eighteenth-century England's replacement of a domestic (or cottage) textile industry based on human-powered spinning wheels and looms by more efficient steam-powered factory looms ushered in the demise of the extended family and the birth of the nuclear family that would eventually have wide-ranging implications for configuring Victorian sexual mores (with women being consigned to unpaid domestic child care and men being consigned to paid jobs outside the home). In this context, Foucault's controversial theses regarding the accidental, capillary intersection of "micro-technologies" of disciplinary power – involving the novel ordering of space and the temporal sequencing of corporeal motion in hospitals, prisons, schools, factories, and military training – is intriguing (Foucault 1979a, 1979b).[11] The creation of humans who self-identify as individual subjects, viz., humans who have been subjected to apparatuses of self-governance qua "sexualized bodies" in conformity with surveillance apparatuses of state and society geared toward engendering productive bodies (what Foucault calls biopower), illustrates the impact of technology in "developing" individual capability and "freedom." Such techno-systems preserve individual capability and freedom in effective technical designs so that, for example, the factory system's minute division of labor represents the *material sedimentation* of a certain kind of individual agency that cannot be undone.

Foucault qualifies this technological account of European "development" with an analysis of the human sciences. Besides inventing individualizing techniques of observation, examination, and classification (the archive), these sciences elaborate "moral" discourses that serve to interpret and legitimate – and thus also constitute – technological and governmental apparatuses. Yet, changes in moral reasoning regarding "scientific" standards of normalcy that accompany technological changes are sufficiently independent of the latter to evolve *counter-discourses* of technological resistance to normalization. For example, the women's movement during the late nineteenth and twentieth centuries can be understood as a protest against the dominant psychological science of the time, whose gendered morality prescribed the "domestication" of women as child bearers and caretakers.

Foucault's technological explanation for the historical, technologically conditioned constitution of self-identified gendered individuals in modern society thus moves between a convergence and a collision view of development. Philosophers working in the tradition of German idealism (especially Schiller and Hegel) as well as political economists (beginning with Adam Smith) had earlier elaborated a collision view. Even Marx was ambivalent in his assessment of the emancipatory potential of technology, which could just as easily cripple and de-skill individual capability as express and realize it.

Rejecting the Weberian view of technology as value-free neutral instrument, twentieth-century philosophers such as Martin Heidegger and Jacques Ellul condemned modern technology for what they perceived to be its inherent objectification of human existence, stratification of society into technocratic dictators and manipulated masses, and underdevelopment of human social and aesthetic capabilities.[12] Arguing in a similar vein, Theodor Adorno and Max Horkheimer maintained that the calculating form of instrumental reason that fully emerged during the European Enlightenment (but which they believed was already implicit in the mythology of antiquity) had logically developed into a totalitarian, scientifically administered society.[13] With the exception of utilitarian reasoning – which perfectly complemented the welfare state – these thinkers observed how contemporary moral understanding of social contractarian fairness and human rights dignity perversely drained these ideas of their critical individualism and refashioned them in such a way as to reinforce submission to authority. More radically – and in agreement with Foucault – they regarded the individual moral subject as a construction of social control. What remained of liberal emancipatory morality was something that could only be glimpsed in the implicit protests of modern art.

Other thinkers developed more nuanced views about technological and moral pathways of development that hypothesized the supremacy of cultural values over technology. Herbert Marcuse believed (as did Marx) that modern technology was neither essentially innocent nor essentially alienating, but reflected in its design the dominant political values of the time.[14] Marcuse's student, Andrew Feenberg, has elaborated this thought in his distinction between primary and secondary forms of instrumentalization, the former abstracting technical elements from their contexts and reducing them to quantifiable processes suitable for control, and the latter reversing this process by concretely synthesizing technical elements into value-laden designs.[15]

Like the legal system, technology functions as a mechanism for steering human behavior, while also expressing and embodying – and potentially realizing – human freedom. Feenberg criticizes capitalist production technology for incorporating designs that selectively reinforce hierarchy and de-skilling in order to efficiently manage a minute division of labor oriented exclusively toward the single value of profitability. He presents information-communication technology (ICT) as having the potential to enhance higher capabilities associated with democratic debate and action. Today, critical theorists debate the ambivalent impact of ICT on development. In its present social configuration under global capitalism, it remains an open question whether ICT institutes a digital divide that exacerbates hierarchies of knowledge and power or creates a decentralized global public space for disseminating information and arguments.

Summary: the undecided meaning of development

Technical progress and increased efficiency gained through scientific administration need not coincide with moral progress in realizing enduring values associated with freedom of choice, expanded intellectual and reflective capability, and democratic self-determination. Authoritarian regimes, like the Communist government of China, may be remarkably efficient in reducing poverty and social inequality while restraining freedom of speech and democratic dissent. We have also seen that the power conferred upon technical and managerial elites disempowers workers, consumers, and citizens. Because modern forms of institutional organization frustrate the realization of agency in important respects, it is no longer obvious that Western norms of rights, justice, and development that find effective material form in today's institutional techno-systems *are* progressive relative to the norms and techno-systems they replaced.

The ambivalent functioning of modern institutions has been appropriately highlighted by postmodernists and poststructuralists, as well as by Frankfurt School critical theorists.[16] They call into question the emancipatory claims made on behalf of reason, and note that all institutions and correlative norms of discourse and comportment are shaped by power relations. Developmental ethicists must therefore confront the uncomfortable reality that the ideas of moral and technological progress on which they themselves rely for normative guidance are inherently contestable (Allen 2016). Thus, contesting the dominant industrial model of agriculture associated with the Green Revolution, Vandana Shiva (2005) defends appropriate peasant-based agricultural technology as part of an "Earth democracy" grounded in locally centered, biodiverse, soil-sustainable, organic food production. Ecologically more radical, Arturo Escobar's call for a "decentered" notion of development beyond and against the dominant strands of Western industrial development invokes the spiritual interpretations of freedom inherent in non-Western and indigenous religions that reject hyper forms of individualism, anthrocentrism, materialism, and rationalism (Escobar 1995).

As we have seen, fractures in the Western understanding of freedom emerge within its own genealogy. Some people find freedom supremely manifested in labor-saving technologies or in technically mediated monetary transactions and legal relationships. While technologies free us from work, monetary and legal transactions free us from being morally accountable to others so that we can pursue our personal interests without needing to justify or coordinate them by engaging in risky, time-consuming conversations. Conversely, others find freedom supremely embodied in moral interactions that facilitate critical self-reflection and social detachment. Still others see freedom exemplified in social institutions that embed monetary and legal modes of strategic self-assertion in economic, political, and interpersonal relationships. Here individual freedom ceases to be defined by legally sanctioned egoism or morally sanctioned social detachment and assumes a social valence, where the achievement of one person's aim is mutually recognized to require the achievement of other persons' aims in a scheme of social cooperation.

These competing visions of freedom motivate conflicting solutions to contemporary developmental problems. Technocrats, libertarians, and social democrats frame the emancipatory yield of their respective solutions to global underdevelopment in diametrically opposed ways. Consider once again the potential of markets as engines of development. Neoliberal technocrats thinking along utilitarian lines might well endorse freeing economic markets from moral constraints they believe hamper their efficient functioning as technical systems. Lockean libertarians, by contrast, will urge freeing markets from regulatory constraints that hamper individual choice, and they will do so in the name of human rights. Finally, social democrats will appeal to social contract ethics in demanding the liberation of markets from forms of social domination that hamper fair, voluntary cooperation.

Measuring development

It is one thing to talk about what kind of freedom best comports with development, but if what we mean by development can't be measured, then it is of little practical use. As we saw in the introduction, the World Bank (WB) sets its International Poverty Line (IPL) by taking the average of the 15 lowest national poverty lines as defined by income converted to Purchasing Power Parity (PPP) dollars. A nation's poverty in relation to other nations is based on national average per capita income and, most important, the number of its inhabitants whose incomes fall below the IPL.[17] The latter can be calculated using Gross Domestic Product (GDP), a country's output, the proceeds from which may be largely owned by affluent foreigners;

or it can be calculated using Gross National Product (GNP), which measures the domestic and foreign income of citizens. The difference between using GDP and GNP is not insignificant; Angola recorded a huge increase in GDP between 2001 and 2007 even though most of its increase – in domestic oil product – went to foreigners and corrupt government elites.

Income only measures development *indirectly*; it can be spent on goods and services that do not impact development or impact development unevenly, depending on individuals' differing needs. Development theorists have therefore suggested better metrics of development. The Human Development Index (HDI) developed by Amartya Sen, Paul Streeten, Mahbub ul Haq, and others builds on the International Labour Organization's 1976 declaration that development should aim at satisfying the *basic needs* of everyone in the shortest time possible. As such, it bypasses individual household and per capita income and consumption because these don't reflect the fact that different levels of income are required for people with different needs and different endowments to achieve basic or equal development of overall *capability*.

HDI takes the average of three indices (life expectancy, education, and gross domestic product [GPD]) scaled from 0–1 within countries. The Gender Development Index (GDI) uses the same components but penalizes for gender deviations by taking the harmonic mean of male and female scores. Thus, (supposing parity among male and female populations) if both men and women have an equal educational attainment of 0.6, the GDI is just 0.6. But if men have an educational achievement of 0.9 and women have an educational achievement of 0.4, the GDI is 4/9, or 0.45.[18]

By focusing on countrywide rankings, GDI and HDI take a step backward from the WB poverty headcount measure based on the number of people living below the IPL. Their use of GDP rather than GNP also distorts real average income. Furthermore, these metrics obscure distributional inequalities within a country, so that great gains in HDI and GDI among the most affluent groups can easily make it seem that progress is being made, even though regression has occurred among the vast majority of poor, as is especially obvious in the case of income and life expectancy. Improvements in GDI can be achieved by doubling 10,000 privileged women's incomes to $200,000 each rather than doubling to $2,000 the income of 1 million female domestics (88). And because GDI, like HDI, summarizes all three indices, it obscures whether women's gains in one area offset losses in the other two.

Thomas Pogge recommends that instead of just aggregating factors and dividing by population (as WB indices for income and consumption, HDI, and GDI do) we need to begin with individuating factors of difference: age, gender, and social status. We need to know whether increases in literacy go to landlords or the landless, whether improved medical care benefits the young or the old, men or women, etc. We can then assess the relative deprivation of women, say, as the mean difference across segments of the population (divided by age, household income, situation, etc.).

The capabilities approach

The HDI and GDI have got one thing right: the most salient factor of development at the individual level appears to be successful human functioning (such as life expectancy) and primary goods essential to that functioning. The question arises whether these very general metrics leave out other, *specified* primary goods and capabilities that should be considered essential to development.

Sen and Martha Nussbaum advanced their respective capability approaches as detailed specifications of John Rawls's "primary goods" approach. According to Rawls, primary goods are goods that any rational person would want in order to obtain whatever other goods he or she wanted. These are the goods that a society can distribute in order to ensure that everyone involved in social cooperation is treated fairly. He summarizes these as basic rights, income, opportunities, and self-respect. Notice that the addition of basic rights and self-respect enriches the "all-purpose means" to development beyond simple income, education, and longevity.

Like Rawls, both Sen and Nussbaum emphasize freedom (basic rights) as perhaps the most essential capability requisite for development. Nussbaum in particular has elaborated her capabilities approach with an eye toward grounding a richer understanding of freedom and human rights (see Chapter 2). Nussbaum provisionally lists about 10 capabilities (paraphrasing, these are life, bodily health, cognition, emotion, practical reason, social affiliation, concern for other living things, play, and control over one's environment). Some of these, such as life and bodily health, appear to be more basic and therefore less controversial than others, such as concern for other living things. Nussbaum responds to the objection that her list is biased by noting that any list of basic capabilities will be subject to revision in light of critically informed public opinion and that the development and exercise of some capabilities may be more crucial to the development of freedom and the specification of human rights than others.

Capabilities are not equivalent to actual human functions but to *potentials* for functioning that can be specified, developed, and voluntarily activated. Nussbaum distinguishes *basic* innate capability from naturally developed *internal* capability and socially developed *combined* capability. Thus, language is an innate capability that develops naturally in an adult person and can be further developed by public education.

Capabilities or primary goods

Are capabilities a better developmental metric than primary goods? The argument for the capability approach can be summarized accordingly: Unlike health, intelligence, and other capabilities, primary goods, such as income, are not goals in their own right. As Marx famously argued in the *Economic-Philosophical Manuscripts of 1844*, the goal of development is *emancipation* – being able to *do* and *be* something, rather than to *have* something. And given persons' different natural capacities for converting income (resources and goods) into capabilities (opportunities for doing and being something), development science as a mechanism of distributive justice should focus on capabilities, not resources, as the primary currency to be distributed.

Rawls resists this conclusion, however, arguing that capabilities are difficult to measure and, as a function of natural endowments, fall outside the purview of social justice. In other words, he does not consider health, vigor, intelligence, and imagination as primary *social* goods that society can freely redistribute according to standards of justice. Rather they are *natural* goods that are influenced, but not directly controlled, by the basic structure of society.[19]

Nussbaum disagrees. She points out that Rawls's criticism could apply to some items on his list of primary social goods such as social respect, which is an innate natural capability that depends on appropriate social interaction for its development. She concludes that because society is responsible for providing the social bases underlying natural capabilities like social respect, it makes sense to compare different societies in their provision of equal opportunities for ensuring that each person can realize his or her natural endowments in the form of combined capabilities. Although measurable achievements in health, as with other capabilities, do not perfectly measure the degree to which a society has guaranteed them, when combined with other data regarding natural differences, such measurements can approximately do so. Furthermore, inequalities in measurable capabilities across gender, region, social class, etc., can signal inequities in the distribution of resources.

Despite the usefulness of a capability approach, the idea that capabilities could replace primary goods as the principal *lingua franca* of a theory of *distributive justice* remains problematic. As Pogge notes, in order to compensate those with fewer natural endowments for capability, there would have to be universal agreement on a list of valuable capabilities, a method for measuring their achievements, a calculus for weighing achievements of different capabilities, and a method for measuring the relative value of a person's diverse overall endowments with respect to overall capability achievement.[20] More philosophically worrisome is the presumption that persons can be *vertically* ranked according to natural capability endowments, rather than assessed along a *horizontal* axis of different capability endowments, which is more in keeping with the democratic, egalitarian tenor of modern liberal political thought.

Critique of development as capability

The conceptual problems surrounding the definition of development parallel those confronting the definitions of capability *and* disability.[21] In both instances observation (social acceptance) of what counts as human functioning, or successful adaptation, is used to derive a *norm* of agential functioning (capability). Leaving aside the conceptual difficulty – first observed by David Hume – of inferring a norm (an "ought") from a fact (an "is"), the definition of optimal human functioning must somehow specify historically based, contextually speci-fiable potentials for functioning that are not merely adaptive to oppressive and disabling social norms. In today's high-tech global economy, low levels of lit-eracy and formal education qualify as disabling in a way they might not have been 200 years ago. However, the de-skilling of labor that was once performed as craftwork and is now reconfigured to adapt to automated assembly lines – what Marx famously critiqued under the heading of alienated labor – is also disabling. Even if the division between mental and physical labor is not a structural feature of the organization of production under capitalism, a one-sided cultivation of technically demanding work skills to the detriment of other social and reflec-tive capabilities might well be. To reiterate Foucault's concern, the tendency to uncritically accept the dominant understanding of what counts as normal human functioning can lead those who embrace this understanding to overlook their own partial development while judging as pathologically abnormal those who appear to be differently abled.

Summary

This chapter has explored the meaning and measurement of development. In trac-ing the meaning of development back to the European Enlightenment we observed a fundamental tension between economic growth and moral progress. An influen-tial development economist, Simon Kuznets, optimistically hypothesized (as had Marx before him) that this tension would be lessened in later phases of develop-ment. If we follow the "Kuznets curve," social inequality rises and falls during the course of development. The transition to industrialization increases inequality markedly, which gradually tapers off and then decreases as levels of education rise and birth rates decline. The hypothesis appears most applicable to the industrial phase of development but is contradicted by growing inequality in post-industrial nations like the US and G10 countries. In the final analysis we conclude that social development does not appear to follow a pre-ordained logic analogous to individ-ual cognitive development, let alone one that is harmonious. Rather, convergence of the world toward a single developmental pathway seems to be the combined product of European history and its colonial legacy. This pathway does not show that technological development and economic growth harmoniously correlate with moral development, despite their complex intersection.

Turning to the second concern of this chapter, the measurement of develop-ment, we saw that the capability approach, which has been presented as an alterna-tive to economistic metrics favored by the WB, shares some of the problems that we noted in our discussion of Piagetian theories of children's cognitive and moral development. In particular, its specification of capabilities and, in Nussbaum's theory, specification of their higher development as foundations for human rights, runs the risk of elitism and ethnocentrism. This risk might attend any developmen-tal metric. Therefore, whatever metric guides development theory should reflect a wide range of multicultural inputs (spiritual capabilities included) expressing multiple social standpoints.

Questions for discussion

1 What is meant by *historical materialism*? Do you agree with Marx on this point? How have we seen *historical materialism* play out internationally? Are there examples that rebut this view?

2 What do you think about global technological progress? Is it inherently beneficial or damaging? Does it depend on how we implement new technology?

3 Do you agree with the *capabilities approach*? What capabilities do you think are left out, if any? Is this approach too broad? Does it include capabilities that you do not think belong? If so, why?

4 What are some of the major problems with accurately measuring levels of development? How do you think we should try and measure development?

Notes

1 Rousseau (1987, p. 69).
2 Marx (1994, p. 84).
3 Ibid., pp. 161–162.
4 Ibid., p. 164.
5 Ibid., p. 321.
6 See Max Weber (2003) and Durkheim (2014).
7 Huntington (1996). Edward Said (1978) developed the classical critique of Orientalism.
8 Parsons and Shils (2001) and Rostow (1991).
9 See Wallerstein (1974).
10 Habermas (1979).
11 Foucault (1978, 1979).
12 Heidegger (1977) and Ellul (1964).
13 Adorno and Horkheimer (1972).
14 Marcuse (1964).
15 Feenberg (2010).
16 Among the more prominent "postmodernist" and "poststructuralist" critics of modern social institutions and modern ontology are Jacques Derrida, Michel Foucault, and Jean-François Lyotard. Post-development and post-colonial theorists such as Arturo Escobar and Edward Said apply postmodernist insights to underscore how power relations impact the linguistic construction of social knowledge and social reality, resulting in what Said characterized as "Orientalism," or the social construction of "non-Western" societies as essentially different from their Western counterparts in their capability for development.
17 The headcount index for calculating poverty neglects the depth (or average shortfall) of poverty among those falling below the poverty line as well as their relative inequality. The poverty gap index reveals the average shortfall below the line as a summed percentage of individual shortfalls divided by total societal population; the squared poverty gap index reveals both the average shortfall and the severity of inequality among individual shortfalls by weighing greater shortfalls more heavily than lesser shortfalls. For an explanation of these indices, see the *World Bank Poverty Handbook, Chapter 4: Measures of Poverty*, at http://siteresources.worldbank.org/INTPA/Resources/429966-1259774805724/Poverty_Inequality_Handbook_Ch04.pdf.
18 Pogge (2010, p. 86).

19   Rawls (1971, p. 62).
20   Pogge (2002, pp. 167–228).
21   See the UN's distinction (contained in section I.c.6–7 of the World Programme of Action Concerning Disabled Persons [1983]) between *cross-cultural* standards of *impairment* (loss or restriction of normal physical and psychological *functioning*), standards of *disability* (restriction of normal *activity* resulting from impairment), and *culture-specific* standards of *handicap* (disadvantage in *adapting* to social roles and norms).

Suggested reading

Amy Allen (2016). *The End of Progress: De-Colonizing the Normative Foundations of Critical Theory*. New York: Columbia University Press.

Allen criticizes the normative theories of social evolution advanced by the Marxist Frankfurt School tradition and offers in their stead a contextual account of progress that is more sensitive to historical contingencies and the embeddedness of modern processes of societal rationalization in power relations.

David Ingram (2018). *World Crisis and Underdevelopment: A Critical Theory of Poverty, Agency, and Coercion*. Cambridge: Cambridge University Press.

Ingram critically examines the cultural and political subtext of global development theory and practice while proposing institutional reforms at the international level that address the structural sources of poverty and underdevelopment.

Martha Nussbaum (2000). *Women and Human Development: The Capabilities Approach*. Cambridge: Cambridge University Press.

Nussbaum's argument in this book, which holds human dignity at its core, outlines a number of capabilities that should be adequately supported in all democratic societies. These capabilities are also key to the prospect of development.

David Owen (2002). *Between Reason and History: Habermas and the Idea of Progress*. New York: SUNY Press.

Owen critically examines and defends a theory of social evolution based on a Piagetian account of individual cognitive development. Owen offers what is perhaps the most detailed explanation and analysis of genetic structuralism as a theory of individual and social development.

John Rawls (1971). *Theory of Justice*. Cambridge, MA: Harvard University Press.

Rawls's theory in this book, which can be broadly defined under the label "justice as fairness," attempts to overcome the problem of distributive justice. With respect to this chapter (and remaining chapters) Rawls's discussion of "primary goods" is integral in setting goals in development.

United Nations Development Programme (2016). "Human Development Report 2016: Human Development for Everyone." *United Nations*. http://hdr.undp.org/en/content/human-development-report-2016-human-development-everyone.

This UN report provides in-depth analyses of current human development data including HDI. Each year, a similar report is published and will be valuable in assessing development progress.

References

Adorno, Theodor and Max Horkheimer (1972). *The Dialectic of Enlightenment*. New York: Herder and Herder.

Allen, Amy (2016). *The End of Progress: Decolonizing the Normative Foundations of Critical Theory*. New York: Columbia University Press.

Durkheim, Emile (2014). *The Division of Labor in Society*, tr. Steven Lukes. New York: Free Press.

Ellul, Jacques (1964). *The Technological Society*. New York: Vintage Books.

Escobar, Arturo (1995). *Encountering Development: The Making and Unmaking of the Third World*. Princeton: Princeton University Press.

Feenberg, Andrew (2010). *Between Reason and Experience: Essays in Technology and Modernity*. Cambridge, MA: The MIT Press.

Foucault, Michel (1979a). *The History of Sexuality: Volume One*. New York: Pantheon Books.

Foucault, Michel (1979b). *Discipline and Punish*. New York: Vintage Books.

Habermas, Jürgen (1979). *Communication and the Evolution of Society*. Boston: Beacon Press.

Heidegger, Martin (1977). *The Question Concerning Technology*. New York: Harper Torchbooks.

Huntington, Samuel (1996). *The Clash of Civilization and the Remaking of World Order*. New York: Simon & Schuster.

Marcuse, Herbert (1964). *One Dimensional Man: Studies in the Ideology of Advanced Industrial Society*. Boston: Beacon Press.

Marx, Karl (1994). "Economic and Philosophic Manuscripts [1844]." In Lawrence Simon (ed.), *Karl Marx: Selected Writings*. Indianapolis: Hackett.

Parsons, Talcott and Edward Albert Shils (2001). *Toward a General Theory of Action*, abridged ed. New Brunswick: Transaction Publishers.

Pogge, Thomas (2002). "Can the Capability Approach Be Justified?" *Philosophical Topics* 10(2): 167–228.

Pogge, Thomas (2010). *Politics as Usual: What Lies Behind the Pro-Poor Rhetoric*. Cambridge: Polity Press.

Rawls, John (1971). *A Theory of Justice*. Cambridge, MA: Harvard University Press.

Rostow, Walt Whitman (1991). *The Stages of Economic Growth*, 3rd edition. Cambridge: Cambridge University Press.

Rousseau, Jean-Jacques (1987). *Discourse on the Origin and Foundations of Inequality Among Men*, Part Two, in *Jean Jacques Rousseau: The Basic Political Writings*, trans. Donald Cress. Indianapolis: Hackett.

Said, Edward (1978). *Orientalism*. New York: Pantheon.

Shiva, Vandana. (2005). *Earth Democracy*. Cambridge: South End Press.

Wallerstein, Immanuel (1974). *The Modern World System*. Cambridge: Academic Press Inc.

Weber, Max (1958). *The Protestant Ethic and the Spirit of Capitalism*, trans. Talcott Parsons. New York: Scribner.

2 Human rights

In 1986 the United Nations General Assembly endorsed the Declaration on the Right to Development (RTD). This right affirms that "every human person and all peoples are entitled to participate in, contribute to, and enjoy economic, social, cultural and political development, in which all human rights and fundamental freedoms can be realized" (Art 1.1). The inspiration behind the right to development was Senegalese jurist and former president of the UN Commission on Human Rights, Keba M'Baye, who in 1972 urged the establishment of a New International Economic Order that would redress global inequalities between North and South and firmly link first-generation civil and political rights to the fulfillment of second-generation economic, social, and cultural rights (1986 Annex, A. 1 and 9).

The deeper rationale behind the rights-based approach (RBA) to development was clearly laid out 11 years later by Secretary-General of the UN Kofi Annan in his Annual Report:

> The rights-based approach to development describes situations not simply in terms of human needs, or of development requirements, but in terms of society's obligation to respond to the inalienable rights of individuals. It empowers people to demand justice as a right, not as charity, and gives communities a moral basis from which to claim international assistance when needed.

Combining the Declaration on the Right to Development and Annan's Annual Report reveals an interdependence linking human rights and development:

- Development is instrumental toward achieving human rights.
- Human rights are instrumental toward achieving development.

The first point says that basic civil liberties and political freedoms cannot be exercised in a vacuum; one cannot be fully free to participate in political life or fully free to speak out and associate with others if, for example, one is starving to death, very sick, illiterate, uneducated, exhausted, insecure, and socially marginalized. The robust exercise of civil and political rights thus depends on securing economic well-being, social inclusion, acculturation, and other forms of development, which in turn require the development of economic, legal, and political institutions.

The second point says (to quote Annan): "A needs-based approach can be met out of charitable intentions, but rights are based on legal obligations (and in some cases ethical obligations that have a strong foundation in human dignity)."[1] Development is not only about helping someone out of the goodness of one's heart; it is also about basic justice, ensuring equal treatment and equal opportunities for all, commensurate with the equal human dignity of each. In short, not only does the RBA make it an ethical and legal duty on the part of government to undertake development, but individuals, by claiming an ethical and legal right to development, can hold government accountable for failing to fulfill this duty.

A follow-up 1998 UN Development Program (UNDP) Report "Integrating Human Rights and Sustainable Human Development" reaffirmed both of these points. Nonetheless, as recently as 2004 a former president of one of the leading development institutions, the World Bank, rejected the RBA, saying,

> To some of our shareholders the very mention of the words human rights is inflammatory language. It's getting into areas of politics, and into areas about which they are very concerned. We decided to just go around it and we talk the language of economics and social development.[2]

James Wolfensohn's compartmentalization of human rights and development reflects the dualism between economic and moral-legal development I noted in the previous chapter. For economists, development is a value-free economic science that focuses on delivering aid in a technically efficient manner. As such, it is indifferent to the reasons why people aid each other. Indeed, it must be indifferent in order to retain its scientific integrity as a neutral, universal project standing apart from partisan beliefs. For, according to Wolfensohn, in virtue of their being abstract and general, human rights are all but meaningless; whatever prescriptive value they possess comes at the expense of their becoming entangled in a web of subjective moral interpretation and political controversy that renders them ill-suited to advancing a common development project across different cultures and political systems.

Leaving aside Wolfensohn's questionable assumption regarding the cultural neutrality of economic science, a quick glance at Annan's defense of the RBA appears to confirm Wolfensohn's assessment. Indeed, Annan refers to different *conceptions* of human rights: (1) as legal claims that attach to both communities and individuals, and (2) as inalienable moral properties expressive of human dignity.

This chapter therefore proposes to examine the debate over the RBA by initially clarifying the moral and legal conceptions of human rights that impact the ethics of development. We then examine applications of these conceptions to a number of development problems. Given the very complex nature of both of these tasks, we will have to stick to just a few of the most important issues. We begin by discussing the difference between moral and legal conceptions of human rights. Is there a legitimate sense in which the justification for human rights resides in *two* sources: a moral interpretation of human nature and a political interpretation of social goods? Does appeal to these competing rights-based rationales for development generate controversies that fundamentally interfere with development as a universal project, as Wolfensohn fears?

We shall address two interrelated controversies that focus these questions. The first controversy concerns the alleged Western bias implicit in human rights as claims that individuals raise against their societies. Here we ask: Do human rights obstruct social development by pitting self-centered individuals against one another and their community in a way that diminishes duties to the community? The second controversy concerns the inclusion and prioritization of specific categories of rights. Here the pressing questions are: Do human rights that protect civil and political liberties have a greater claim to being human rights than economic, social, and cultural rights? Can (or should) only some human rights be legally binding and enforced? If so, can a single human right to development, or several human rights instrumental to development, be among those that are legally enforceable?

The second question we will address is how human rights might apply to a range of development issues. Governments that are signatory to human rights treaties obligating them to provide their people with the goods and services necessary for developing a dignified level of human capability exemplify one application. But we can ask whether global economic multilaterals such as the WB and WTO, as well as multinational corporations, should be bound by human rights. Furthermore, we can ask whether a right to a sustainable environment ought to be included among these rights.

Moral and legal human rights

The Preamble to the Universal Declaration of Human Rights (UDHR, 1948) describes human rights in a variety of ways that are by no means harmonious. They are described as "the highest aspiration of the common people" and "a common standard of achievement for all peoples and all nations," universal and effective recognition of which should be spread through "teaching and education." Such recognition is further tied to the "dignity and worth of the human person and in the equal rights of men and women" that have promoted "social progress and better standards of life in larger freedom." So construed, human rights are *developmental aspirations* in two senses. First, they progressively interpret freedom in terms of "better standards of life"; second, they progressively extend to all persons equally, solely in virtue of their "inherent dignity and worth." Consonant with this second aspiration, Article 2 asserts that "everyone is entitled to all the rights and freedoms set forth in this Declaration, without distinction of any kind, such as race, colour, sex, language, religion, political or other opinion, national or social origin, property, birth or other status."

Alongside this *moral interpretation* of human rights, with its emphasis on the equal dignity of the individual and social progress in living conditions, is a *legal interpretation* that describes human rights as legal *claims* that "should be protected by the rule of law." To the extent that government officials view human rights as setting forth legal limits demarcating tolerable conduct between persons and states, they acknowledge a limited responsibility to protect essential liberties from severe *criminal* predations by providing benchmarks for sanctions and military intervention.

As described above, moral and legal interpretations of human rights serve two different, and by no means harmonious, functions pertinent to development. The moral interpretation links directly to an ethics of development with its emphasis on setting forth common standards for achieving a better and freer life for everyone. But moral aspirations are open to interpretation and do not impose duties on anyone. Moreover, the idea of human dignity that underwrites the moral conception of human rights is controversial. The UDHR defines dignity in a way that upholds the *equal value* of all persons, regardless of their gender, religion, and social status. In so doing, it might be understood as endorsing the treatment of everyone the *same way*, which contravenes the religious and ethical beliefs of some cultures. The legal interpretation, by contrast, imposes very specific duties on governments that are universally accepted across cultures. However, the history of international adjudication and enforcement suggests that such duties are generally understood to be quite few in number. To the extent that they are enforced by threat of international sanction or criminal prosecution, they apply only to the worst human rights violations: genocide, war crimes, and crimes against humanity. So, as legal claims against governments, human rights at best deter governments from committing crimes against their own people and, when this fails, justify retribution against the worst human rights violators. In actual practice, they do not advance the forward-looking aims of development across a broad spectrum of goods, needs, and capabilities.

Given that moral and legal interpretations of human rights do not naturally complement each other in advancing the RBA, the question arises whether they can be made to do so. One way is to allow individual governments to voluntarily assume legal responsibility for securing a wider range of human rights beyond those protected by humanitarian law. Although neither the UDHR nor the RTD is legally binding, human rights *treaties* that require signatory governments to provide welfare, education, and other developmental goods and services to their people are. The people of these governments can lay claim to these goods and services as a matter of legal right. They can bring suit against their government in a domestic court for grossly failing to secure these goods; should this fail, they can lodge a complaint to the appropriate international committee charged with overseeing the implementation of the treaty right mandating provision of said goods.

Human rights treaties are one way that individual governments can selectively incorporate development-related human rights into their own domestic law in a manner conformable to the moral and religious beliefs of their respective peoples. Besides avoiding multicultural disagreement about how people should be treated, this approach allows each nation to harness the legal language of human rights to its own moral aspirations regarding development.

The weakness of the treaty approach to reconciling moral and legal conceptions of human rights mirrors its strength. By allowing each nation to pick and choose which development-related human rights duties it will enforce within its own borders, the idea that these rights can be claimed by any person living any-where in the world – Annan's hope for the RBA – is effectively placed on hold until all governments incorporate them into their legal systems. Whether a person can claim legal human rights beyond those protected in humanitarian law, which sanctions genocide, crimes against humanity, and war crimes, will thus depend on where that person happens to live. Women and minorities, too, may find that their "equal dignity" does not translate into "sameness of treatment" according to their society's interpretation of human rights.

The haphazard way in which governments incorporate human rights means that no government has a duty to protect against violations or shortfalls in the exercise of development-related human rights that occur in other countries. No country has an obligation to save people living in another country from mass starvation due to deliberate inaction by that people's own government. Indeed, even if a government that is allowing its people to starve has signed a human rights treaty prohibiting it from committing this kind of violation, there are no remedies they can pursue once appeals to domestic courts and international oversight commit-tees have been exhausted.

Sadly, the international community is reluctant to enforce even the most imper-ative of humanitarian laws. It wasn't until 2002, when the UN General Assembly adopted the Responsibility to Protect (R2P) doctrine, that a moral obligation to intervene in stanching the worst human rights violations was officially acknowl-edged. Significantly, an earlier R2P framework that protected persons from natu-ral and environmental threats to development was rejected for being overly broad and demanding – thus echoing the concerns that opened this chapter.

Human rights and duties to the community

One reason why human rights are contentious is that they are normally claimed *against* society. However, the RTD is formulated as a right *of* society – more pre-cisely, of the people of a nation – to develop themselves in cooperation with other peoples. RTD is therefore more readily interpreted as laying out duties of states toward one another and duties of people within a community toward that commu-nity. Here, the community is the bearer of a human right which individuals within and without the community are duty-bound to respect and protect.

The idea that communities can be the bearer of human rights reverses the stan-dard interpretation of human rights. Claimed by individuals *against* their com-munity, human rights are supposed to subordinate the social good to the good of the individual. But this is clearly problematic. For, as Article 29 of the Universal Declaration of Human Rights puts it: "Everyone has duties to the community in which alone the free and full development of his personality is possible." In subor-dinating duties to the community, the idea of human rights, according to Nigerian political scientist Claude Ake,

> presupposes a society that is atomized and individualistic, a society of
> endemic conflict . . . We [Africans] assume harmony, not divergence of

interests, competition, and conflict; we are more inclined to think of our obligations to other members of our society rather than our claims against them.[3]

The conflict between human rights as individual claims against the community and human rights as collective rights to development came to a head during the so-called "Asian values" debate that surfaced prior to the 1993 Vienna Conference on Human Rights. The Bangkok Declaration, signed by China, Taiwan, Singapore, and over 20 other nations, proclaimed that Asian cultures, especially those influenced by Confucianism, should not be expected to rigidly separate legal rights from traditional ethical duties to family, community, and state. Appealing to the right of social development, the Declaration echoed Ake's concern about the corrosive effect that a Western, individual-centered understanding of legal rights has on the social solidarity and respect for centralized, top-down authority requisite for undertaking stable, large-scale economic reform.

How compelling is this criticism of human rights? The criticism appears to be unwarranted if it asserts that human rights claimed by individuals are inherently incompatible with duties to the community. Suppose the community in question is an indigenous tribe whose way of life is being threatened by a larger community – the state. Preserving and developing such a micro-community may effectively depend on its members' capacity to claim their individual human right to practice their way of life without interference from outsiders. Effectively claiming this right will depend on the individual exercise of rights to organize, meet, debate, and protest that have been dismissed as Western rights by the very authoritarian governments that seek to impose their model of development on them.

Human rights, then, can be leveraged by individuals of a minority group to preserve and develop their community against outsiders and the state. Human rights protect individuals *and* groups from state-sanctioned predations – even those undertaken in the name of development. However, they do not unconditionally elevate human rights over duties to the state. Human rights law permits the derogation of some human rights for the sake of national security and other duties to the community in times of emergency. In keeping with Article 29 of the UDHR, human rights entitle individuals to social goods – education, health, welfare, and social security – provided that they support the state that secures them.

One Western interpretation of human rights, however, does seem problematic. The idea that human rights are unconditional entitlements that pre-exist society and state – the so-called *natural rights* interpretation popularized by Locke – has been understood to mean that individuals have relatively unlimited freedom to acquire property and amass wealth, no matter the social cost. This libertarian interpretation of human rights is not widely shared. Even Locke conceded that natural rights were prone to self-serving interpretation and could not regulate social interaction unless they were legislated, adjudicated, and enforced by government. But if exercising effective human rights depends on government, defining their proper scope depends on popular participation in governance, which in turn depends on a citizenry secure in its entitlement to a wide spectrum of social goods.

Prioritizing human rights for development: a second look at the Asian values debate

The Asian values debate highlights another problem with the libertarian conception of human rights. According to this conception, rights mainly protect individuals against hindrances to their freedom of speech, association, and movement. Government that violates these civil rights to the point of committing crimes against humanity may be subject to international sanction and their leaders indicted by international criminal courts. By contrast, governments that do nothing to secure their subjects' food security are spared human rights condemnation. As of this writing, the most powerful government on this planet that quite readily ratified the International Covenant on Civil and Political Rights (ICCPR) still refuses to ratify the International Covenant on Economic, Social, and Cultural Rights (ICESCR).

The dominance of the classical liberal interpretation of human rights not only reflects its easy susceptibility to legal application, but it also mirrors a priority in our moral economy: all things being equal, it is morally worse to make someone less well off than it is to omit making someone better off; and it is morally worse to commit a wrong intentionally than to commit a wrong accidentally (or negligently).

Of course, this priority in our moral economy is hardly impervious to doubt. Intentionally failing to help someone meet their basic needs for survival, when this can be done without significant effort or cost to oneself, seems equivalent to killing them. This explains why standing by idly while a child drowns when throwing her a lifesaver is all that it would take to save her constitutes criminal negligence in some jurisdictions. Again, violating a religious minority's civil right to proselytize seems less wrong than neglecting to protect its economic right to subsistence.

It is such doubts as these that lead Ake to question the libertarian idea of Western rights:

> The Western notion of human rights stresses rights which are not very interesting in the context of African realities. There is much concern with the right to peaceful assembly, free speech and thought, fair trial, etc. . . . They appeal to people with a full stomach who can afford to pursue the more esoteric aspects of self-fulfillment. The vast majority of our people are not in this position. They are facing the struggle for existence in its brutal immediacy . . . There is no freedom for hungry people or those eternally oppressed by disease. It is no wonder that the idea of human rights has tended to sound hollow in the African context.

In the passage quoted above, Ake clearly presupposes the classical interpretation of human rights. However, the signatories to the Bangkok Declaration do not. They appeal to a human right to development and interpret that right through the human rights incorporated into the ICESCR. In short, they reverse the standard priority of civil and political rights over economic, social, and cultural rights – and in so doing justify their own authoritarian model of economic and social development.

However, if moral development of civil and political freedom depends on economic development (as Ake and the Bangkok Declaration insist it must), economic development of social capability surely depends on the moral development of civil and political freedom. Before seeing why this is so, it bears noting that the Vienna Conference affirmed this view in its own declaration, asserting that efforts to prioritize some human rights categories over others were misguided, since all the disputed categories complement each other:

> All human rights are universal, indivisible and interdependent and interrelated. The international community must treat human rights globally in a fair and equal manner, on the same footing, and with the same emphasis.

The argument that all human rights are "indivisible, interdependent, and interrelated" finds ample support in the capability theory of agential development discussed in the previous chapter. As Ake notes, "freedom to choose" is meaningless if one is starving, sick, uneducated, or subject to violence and coercion. Conversely, subsistence is insecure in the absence of civil and political freedom to choose. The complementarity of human rights also finds support in modernization theory. Societies that evolve efficient economic markets must secure individuals' economic freedom through property and contractual rights; but this freedom can scarcely be *secured* without civil rights to associate and speak out and, ultimately, to petition government in its management of the economy. Making government accountable extends the logic of human rights further, toward the development of democratic political rights and social and cultural rights that enable everyone to exercise *those* rights with equal capacity.

In sum, prioritizing some *categories* of human rights over others in terms of their greater importance or urgency – especially as this relates to the broader human right of communities and individuals to develop themselves – appears futile. This becomes more apparent when we realize that some human rights – such as the right of workers to organize themselves into unions in order to protect their wages, benefits, and jobs – straddle economic, political, civil, and social rights. Still, following Henry Shue (1996), we may conclude that some rights within a given category are more *basic* than others. All things being equal, the economic right to subsistence is more basic than the economic right to acquire property. Thus, the coercive dispersal of large landholdings may sometimes be necessary to procure peasant farmers their subsistence.

Difficulty in prioritizing human rights categories should not prevent us from prioritizing human rights *protection*, especially when that protection takes a coercive, legal form. From a legal perspective it may appear that civil and political rights should be privileged over social, economic, and cultural rights. Constitutions have tended to exclusively select the former category of rights for special protection; in any case, it is widely believed that they are more essential to social cooperation than the latter category of rights. Furthermore, classical liberal rights such as these appear to be better defined and more universally accepted than economic, social, and cultural rights; and their exercise appears to be costless, requiring no expenditure of effort beyond everyone staying within their own self-regarding sphere of non-interference.

These reasons for privileging classical liberal rights are not compelling. To begin with, some countries constitutionally embed economic, social, and cultural rights alongside civil and political rights. Furthermore, classical liberal rights to free speech, free association, and freedom of religion do not come with ready-made instructions on their scope of application; they too must be concretely codified in legal statutes and court decisions, just like economic, social, and cultural rights. Likewise, their legislation and enforcement require considerable public expenditure. In the final analysis, our moral repugnance in the face of starvation would be every bit as strong as our condemnation of genocide if the starvation in question were caused by deliberate government inaction. If we still insist on limiting international interventions to the worst humanitarian crimes, it is because interventions involving sanctions and military force often inflict more suffering than they prevent.

How justifying human rights impacts development ethics

The Asian values debate and its "resolution" suggests a partial rejoinder to Wolfensohn's objection that human rights are too subjective and politically contentious to serve as a common framework for development. This rejoinder consists in assembling a long list of human rights that do not privilege (a) individualist interpretations that conflict with rights of (and duties to) communities and (b) specific categories of rights. The authors of the UDHR sagely sidestepped politics by following this pragmatic strategy: assembling a long list of legally non-binding aspirational rights would appeal to everyone without offending anyone.

It didn't take long for philosophers to question the inclusion of some items on this list, especially once nations began incorporating human rights into their laws. To take one often cited item on this list: Article 24 declares a "right to rest and leisure, including reasonable limitation of working hours and periodic holidays with pay." Formulated as an aspiration, this right might not ring any alarms and, in fact, few would dispute that rest and leisure from toil are essential to human development; but formulated as a legally binding claim on all nations this right seems unnecessary and unenforceable.

The desirability of justifying a universal list of legally binding human rights clearly animates Annan's insistence that human rights and development need to complement each other. But it is not likely that he had Article 24 of the UDHR in mind when he gave voice to this sentiment. This thought in turn motivates the following question: What philosophical understanding of human rights should have been guiding Annan's thinking about rights and development?

Philosophers have advanced two major approaches to human rights in answering this question. The first approach, call it the social contract approach, is expressly designed to circumvent Wolfensohn's concern about cultural disagreement by pruning the list of actionable human rights to those that all reasonably decent nations would accept as conforming to their own ethical beliefs about the essentials of human and societal cooperation, however much these beliefs may differ from nation to nation. The second approach, call it the human dignity approach, aims to circumvent Wolfensohn's concern by proposing a single, rationally demonstrable theory of the capabilities that any individual must develop in order to meet a basic threshold of human agency.

The social contract approach

The social contract approach departs from the idea that rights function as ground rules for social cooperation. John Rawls uses this approach to justify a modest list of human rights which function as necessary side constraints on international cooperation between minimally decent nations (or peoples), the principal agents who enact and enforce human rights treaties. Rawls maintains that all decent nations would agree to enforce a special class of urgent rights, "such as freedom from slavery and serfdom, liberty (but not equal liberty) of conscience, and security of ethnic groups from mass murder and genocide" (1999, p. 79). Especially important from the perspective of development and the Asian values debate, Rawls includes a human right to subsistence among these urgent rights. But most striking in this formulation is his additional qualification that the human rights listed above need not be exercised by all persons in the same way. Nations' differing cultural beliefs – recall the Asian values debate – will lead them to interpret and apply these commonly accepted rights in different ways. People who live in nations that are strongly influenced by Confucian or Muslim ethical traditions might prefer the way their society tailors the exercise of human rights to accord with the specific cultural roles assigned to gendered and minority sub-groups within society. Rawls explains that in order to meet a minimum level of moral decency, such societies must permit individual members of such groups to be represented by one of their own in a consultation body to which government leaders are to be held accountable. However, individuals in these societies would not be required to have an equal vote to express their personal preferences *qua individuals* in electing representatives. To require them to do so – which would effectively remake these societies in the image of Western liberal democracy – would violate social contract principles of toleration and reciprocity essential to promoting global cooperation in securing peace, stanching humanitarian crimes, and eliminating poverty.

Thus, while Rawls accepts Articles 3 through 18 of the UDHR – which he says characterizes human rights proper – as well as their secondary implications, such as the human rights covered in special conventions on genocide (1948) and apartheid (1973), he expressly rejects as a parochial Western interpretation Article 1's assertion that "All human beings are born free and equal in dignity and rights" and that they "are endowed with reason and conscience and should act towards one another in a spirit of brotherhood" (1999, p. 80 n23). He accordingly excludes Article 21 of the UDHR, which asserts that "everyone has the right to take part in the government of his country . . . through freely chosen representatives" and that these representatives will be chosen through "periodic and genuine elections" based on "universal and equal suffrage." He rejects other rights stated in the UDHR, such as Article 22's right to social security and Article 23's right to equal pay for equal work, not because they reflect a Western liberal bias, but because they presuppose specific types of economic and legal institutions that are best characterized as one among many possible means for securing a basic right to subsistence.

A social contract approach to global cooperation might yield a different list of human rights than the rather meager selection proposed by Rawls. Even Rawls concedes that "the case for liberal democracy" as a human right is made "[s]hould the facts of history, supported by the reasoning of political and social thought, show that hierarchical regimes are always, or nearly always, oppressive and deny human rights."[4] Indeed, the historical case for liberal democracy now appears to be irrefutable. Others have argued against Rawls's assertion that states, rather than individuals, are the proper and primary agencies of global social cooperation. They maintain that in today's globalized world, states have ceased being self-governing over all that affects them, and that people everywhere are now increasingly subject to supra-national regimes of governance, such as the WTO, the WB, and the UN. Given the supra-national nature of global cooperation, it makes more sense to insist that "cosmopolitan citizens" are the proper and primary agents that a global social contract theory should attend to. Regarded simply as individual human beings, such citizens merit equal treatment – and equal rights – simply in virtue of their innate dignity.

The human dignity approach

As noted above, social contract approaches to theorizing about the proper scope of human rights need not be as restrictive as Rawls's. Whether universal suffrage is a right basic to political cooperation and the exercise of other basic rights depends on the historical track record of nations that have granted their subjects less freedom. It also depends on who is selected to be the primary parties to the social contract: culturally identified nations or more abstractly considered cosmopolitan citizens.

Selecting cosmopolitan citizens rather than culturally identified nations as the primary parties to a global social contract leads to the adoption of a human dignity approach to human rights. This approach can also justify pruning back or expanding the rights listed in international treaties based on a consideration of capabilities and moral powers that are deemed essential to leading a life of human dignity.

The human dignity approach asserts that a right is a human right if and only if its purpose is to protect human capabilities. The notion that the human species possesses a dignified status above all other beings is quite ancient. The idea that each individual human possesses dignity equal to any other, however, first emerged during the European Enlightenment. Philosophers writing during this period disagreed about what human attributes bestowed equal dignity on persons. Immanuel Kant famously asserted that it was the capacity to set ends for oneself *rationally* – what he called self-determination, or autonomy – and, more importantly, to take responsibility for those ends by ensuring that they were compatible with respecting this same faculty in other human beings. This moral interpretation of human dignity entails *duties* to respect others' autonomy; after this moral idea was coupled with the modern understanding of an individual legal claim against the state, it entailed the idea of human *rights*.

Following Kant's understanding of human dignity as a basis for human rights, we end up with the formula that a right is a human right if and only if it protects the rational moral agency of individuals. This is a restrictive interpretation, because some philosophers do not regard young children and mentally handicapped adults as rational moral agents (indeed, Kant himself, like most of his male contemporaries, did not regard women, black Africans, or indigenous people as such, a disturbing fact that diminishes his later condemnation of colonialism and slavery). So, despite conventions protecting the human rights of children and mentally disabled persons, a strict Kantian would deny that children and mentally disabled people should have human rights, even though she might happily insist that they have other moral and legal rights based on their other important needs and interests.

Of course, a revisionary Kantian might also conclude that children and mentally handicapped persons properly have human rights in virtue of their *potential* to develop the faculty of rational moral choice or, more expansively, in virtue of their being members of an animal *species* that normally develops this faculty in most of its members. But holding this more inclusive understanding of how the rational moral agency qualification should be applied opens up a number of challenges. For example, it might be wondered why very intelligent non-human animals that display altruistic behavior should be denied human rights when these are granted to profoundly mentally disabled persons who will never become agents. Falling back on species membership as a basis for according profoundly mentally disabled persons privileged consideration as human rights holders seems just as question-begging as appealing to race as a basis for according Europeans special rights denied to Africans.

Other interpretations of human dignity need not have the restrictive implications that a Kantian interpretation appears to have. The challenge then becomes selecting out the capabilities and powers that human rights should protect once they are no longer exclusively linked to rational moral agency. For instance, all humans and even some non-humans could claim basic rights to subsistence and bodily integrity, but whether they could claim basic rights to education, political participation, and other aspirations linked to higher-order functioning would be debatable.

One approach to interpreting human dignity, the capability approach, seems to recognize that human rights protect both an innate status possessed by infants and cognitively disabled persons (and perhaps some non-humans) *and* potentials for developed functioning possessed only by rational adults. Recall that Martha Nussbaum and Amartya Sen originally introduced this approach in order to show that distributing primary goods was not the primary aim of developmental justice but the fair provision of capability. In *Women and Human Development* (2000) Nussbaum extends the thinking behind this approach to derive categories of human rights. According to her, human rights are both legal claims that aim to protect capabilities and moral aspirations that aim to develop them. So understood, human rights can be grounded in:

> *innate* capability potentials possessed by infants and children (basic capabilities); *naturally developed* capabilities of mature persons (internal capabilities); and *external* capabilities whose development and exercise is advanced or hindered by institutional circumstances (combined capabilities).

While basic capabilities ground the "worth and dignity of basic human powers" sufficient to justify equal human rights to life and bodily integrity to infants and mentally disabled persons, internal and combined capabilities ground higher levels of human functioning whose neglected development suffices to establish a state-condoned human rights deficit (Nussbaum 2000, pp. 78–86).

The capability approach succeeds in capturing the equal human dignity of infants and mentally disabled persons as a function of innate capability potentials – thereby securing them the bare status of human rights holders – while at the same time explaining why additional human rights accrue to normally functioning adults as they develop these potentials into higher-level capability. Thus, while it would be violating the human right of an infant (or profoundly mentally disabled person) to arbitrarily terminate its life and not provide for its basic needs, it would not be violating its human right to religious freedom or political participation by denying it access to religious community or the ballot, as it would in the case of a normally functioning adult.

Whether appeal to capabilities alone is sufficient to establish the content and extent of all our human rights is debatable. Take one item from Nussbaum's list of capabilities: bodily health. This is a scalar idea whose meaning has evolved historically along with the evolution of healthcare. A hundred and fifty years ago high infant and maternal mortality would not have been considered an affront to human dignity. Today, this dynamic understanding of healthcare as a basic right is captured by the ICESCR when it asserts a human right to the "maximal attainable health" possible. "Possible" here can mean "attainable for average persons of a certain age living in particular society given that society's resources" or it can mean "attainable for everyone of any age and society given planetary resources." While the former interpretation can be accused of setting our human rights aspirations too low, the latter formulation can be accused of setting it too high. A human right to healthcare must imply development beyond an impoverished society's average standard of health, but it cannot imply that everyone on the planet enjoy the maximal attainable health possible in some abstract sense, given institutional and other practicalities.

Institutional practicalities: a critique of the human dignity approach to human rights

Neither the social contract approach nor the human dignity approach fully explains institutional human rights practices. For example, at the outset we observed that groups (or communities) as well as individuals have been recognized as legal human rights claimants. Indeed, the human right to development is essentially formulated as a right of communities; the same applies to the human rights covenants protecting indigenous peoples and minorities. Neither state-centric nor cosmopolitan applications of the social contract approach seem capable of recognizing these groups as human rights claimants. The human dignity approach fares just as badly in this regard. It is hard to think of many of the communities protected by the right to development, not to mention the rights of indigenous peoples and minorities, as possessing the "dignity" we normally accord to individuals based on their rational moral agency, basic needs, and interests, or capabilities.

An advocate of the human dignity approach might try to square her theory with these group-specific human rights by suggesting that the human rights of groups can be reduced to the human rights of their individual members. The human right of community C to X would then be equivalent to the human right of individual P in C to X.

Is this right? Suppose, hypothetically, that the human right of an indigenous community to development is interpreted through the lens of the human right of indigenous peoples to maintain and preserve their culture. Suppose further that the culture of the community in question prescribes practices or social roles that a person within the community rejects as incompatible with her human dignity and individual development. The community's human right to development would not be reducible to the individual member's right to development. The majority within the community might view the individual member's decision to develop herself as she wants as an *external threat* to the internal solidarity and identity of the group. Here, the human right of the community to regulate its own association democratically conflicts with the human right of an individual member of that community to live her own life of dignity. So, regardless of whatever accommodation is worked out between the community and that individual in resolving this contradiction, it is clear that a community's right to development need not directly mirror an individual's right to development.

In a more mundane sense, the human right to national membership (citizenship) implies secondary rights to a vast assortment of social goods, such as national defense, that are irreducible to any good that an individual alone might claim to be essential to her human dignity. Indeed, national defense, like many other social goods, imposes reciprocal duties and costs on individuals that cannot be understood to advance their individual needs, interests, or capabilities taken singly. National defense may be instrumental toward securing each individual's human right to security, but the service demanded of those who participate in national defense often puts their lives and rights at risk. In fact, many civil and political rights that promote human dignity in one or more of its meaningful senses might have to be temporarily suspended for the sake of exercising the right to nationality.

Other human rights that are currently acknowledged in legal practice, such as the right to healthcare and the right to participate in democratic elections, do not obviously promote individual human dignity in any straightforward sense. Preventing pandemics may require quarantines and mandatory vaccinations that might harm some individuals in the pursuit of their health; the same can be said of democratic elections: the outcomes might or might not advance a public good such as collective self-determination, but even when they do, they need not directly advance each and every individual's basic human needs, interests, or capabilities.

Even the much criticized human right to leisure and periodic holidays with pay makes sense as part of a broader human right to institutionally guaranteed welfare and communal development, even if its exercise is not essential to an individual's leading a life of dignity. In short, as Allen Buchanan reminds us, it is wrong to think that legal human rights procuring provision of public goods must "mirror" moral human rights assigned to individuals to protect their individual humanity.[5]

Applying human rights to development: Is there a human right to a sustainable global environment?

In the remainder of this chapter I will briefly examine how the institutional practice of human rights might bear on development. First, we will examine how that practice might impact the development of a sustainable global environment, which, as we saw in the introduction, has become crucial to the recently adopted Sustainable Development Goals (2015).

Despite the fact that a human rights framework was not incorporated into the 1992 United Nations Framework Convention on Climate Change (UNFCCC) or the Kyoto Protocol (1997), the Chair of the Inuit Circumpolar Conference submitted a petition in 2005 to the Inter-American Commission on Human Rights on behalf of the Inuit of the Arctic regions of the United States and Canada arguing that the impact of global climate change caused by the "acts and omissions" of the United States violated the fundamental human rights of the Inuit peoples. Subsequent petitions by the Maldives and Small Island Developing States sought to incorporate a human rights framework in the negotiating process of UNFCCC. A report entitled "Climate Change and Human Rights" (2008) that was developed by the International Council on Human Rights (ICHR) notes the advantage of shifting from aggregate cost-benefit analysis (emissions rights) to analysis of climate impact on individual human lives (human rights) in setting minimally acceptable outcomes and procedures for legal implementation.

What advantages did the ICHR have in mind when it proposed shifting the discussion of global climate change from an ethics of balancing costs and benefits – the standard utilitarian approach – to an ethics of human rights? To begin with, treating harms caused by global climate change as problems that can be resolved through simple negotiation ignores the fact that the Inuit and other small islands peoples have virtually no bargaining power of their own to leverage against the powerful, populous industrial nations that equate their interests with the maintenance of levels of domestic consumption and production so damaging to our global climate. Furthermore, treating these harms as matters that can be justly resolved through negotiation presumes that a state's or industry's right to deplete or pollute is equal in moral weight to the right of individuals to an integral environment, so that balancing costs to both parties is morally acceptable. Things look very different, however, if the right to an integral environment is a human right that carries much greater weight than the right to do business; for a human right is not the kind of right that can be bargained away or even compromised for the sake of respecting some lesser right.

To be sure, no treaty currently exists that stipulates a human right to a sustainable climate. However, that doesn't mean that such a right doesn't exist. Should petitions such as those presented by the Inuit and other small island nations reach international courts, a difficult decision will have to be made whether a right to a healthy environment merits a level of protection comparable to that assigned to other actionable human rights. The Statute of the International Court of Justice (ICJ), which issues advisory opinions that sometimes address human rights violations, states that, besides treaties and customary international law, its decisions will be based on such "subsidiary means" as general principles of law recognized by all nations, past judicial decisions, and most importantly, the teaching of highly qualified publicists (i.e., experts) (Article 38.1). The use of such subsidiary means seems to require, as some legal scholars note, further appeal to legitimate interests, *jus cogens* (peremptory and compulsory) norms, and most importantly the normative idea of humanity and the dignity of the human person as discussed in both binding and non-binding conventions.

Human rights and business as usual: Should non-state actors be held liable for obstructing human rights?

You will recall that the libertarian model of human rights favors a very restrictive interpretation of human rights. The human rights that are targeted for high-level coercive enforcement are those whose violations amount to crimes against humanity, war crimes, and genocide. This model presupposes an interactional view of human rights, where the perpetrators and victims are both persons. Although stanching such violations remains a prerequisite for development, it does not directly advance development. Sanctioning human rights violations and punishing perpetrators of humanitarian crimes is "backward-looking," whereas developing institutions is forward-looking.

Thomas Pogge (2008) therefore recommends supplementing an interactional understanding of human rights with an institutional account. Supplementation is necessary because internationally recognized legal conventions, such as resource extraction and lending privileges, rules of trade and product licensing, and many other international institutions – including structures of investment and labor exploitation intrinsic to a global market economy – harm people in their exercise of human rights. As Iris Young notes, the backward-looking interactional model of human rights, which mirrors the liability model familiar to criminal and tort law, can't apply in registering institutional harm, because the institutions in question are the outcome of many different decisions over time – some of them quite innocent – and because, too, virtually all of us contribute in some way to their maintenance.[6] In lieu of assigning causal responsibility for human rights–related harms – or deficits, because the failure to allow persons secure access to the goods vouchsafed to them by human rights is a matter of degree in both intent and effect – Young recommends assigning differential responsibility for changing the institutions that cause them (see Chapter 9). According to her model of responsibility, even those whose human rights are disrespected by existing institutions may share some responsibility (however small) in maintaining them (for example, by not organizing resistance to them, whenever it is safe to do so) and because they have the most to gain from changing them, they may share some responsibility in this regard as well.

Case study: Bolivian water rights v. human rights

Do global institutions, transnationals, and governments violate human rights "legally"?

Succumbing to pressure from the World Bank to refinance old debt on a new $600 million loan, Bolivia sold Aguas del Tunari (a local subsidiary of transnational Bechtel) the rights to Cochabamba's water supply and distribution for 40 years and passed laws that even required the purchasing of licenses in order to collect rainwater. Bechtel then proceeded to increase water prices by an average of 200% ($15/month for an average family earning $60/month). This action sparked five months of rioting that led to the cancellation of the contract barely six months after it had been ratified in 1999. A new law (Ley #2878) passed in 2004 recognized traditional water rights, guaranteeing water rights for irrigation and indigenous farming communities. But in that very same year, a second "water war" erupted in El Alto, which had had its water rights sold to the French multinational Suez in 1997. Pegging rates to the dollar, water prices rose 35%. Aguas del Illimani, the private consortium owned by Suez, charged households $445 for installing water service and ended up leaving 200,000 people without service. Water service is crucial, however, since lack of clean water is the chief cause of child morbidity and mortality in Bolivia. In 2002 the UN Commission on Economic, Social, and Cultural Rights declared that "The human right to water is indispensable for leading a life of human dignity. Water and water facilities must be affordable to all."

In many cases, however, responsibility for changing institutions falls on governments, global economic multilaterals, and businesses. Because governments are the enactors and enforcers of human rights treaties, they are designated the addressees of human rights obligations. In the case discussed in the inset above, the government of Bolivia was sued in court for violating a treaty to which it was signatory, even though its harmful action was "coerced" by the WB in what was considered a fully legal action on its part.

The above case raises a question that profoundly impacts the future of development: Should global economic multilaterals (GEMs) like the WB also be the addressees of human rights law? In fact, complaint mechanisms have been adopted by states to protest rights-infringing policies of GEMs. After the UN committee exercising oversight of the ICESCR issued a statement in December 2001 asserting that global agreements on trade and property rights (such as TRIPS) could not conflict with states' human rights obligations – including the duty not to adopt "retrogressive measures" – the WTO ratified a declaration, *put forth by 20 developing nations*, that affirmed "the WTO members' right to protect public health and, in particular, to promote access to medicines for all" (WTO, Doha Declaration on the TRIPS Agreement and Public Health).

To be sure, neither the WTO nor the IMF/WB has entrenched international human rights law in their operational mechanisms. In light of the enormous impact their decisions have on the right to human development, perhaps they should. But why not extend the same responsibility to respect human rights to transnational corporations (TNCs), like Bechtel and Suez?

The Special Rapporteurs commissioned by the United Nations Human Rights Council (UNHRC) and the Office of the High Commissioner for Human Rights (OHCHR) have proposed operational human rights standards that could be applicable to both GEMs and TNCs in line with John Ruggie's 2009 Report to the UNHRC. This report enjoins TNCs to exercise "human rights due diligence" by (a) adopting a human rights policy, (b) undertaking and acting upon a human rights impact assessment, (c) integrating human rights policy throughout all company divisions and functions, and (d) tracking human rights performance to ensure continuous improvement.[7]

Conflicting rights: transnational corporations (TNCs) versus individuals

Currently, TNCs can only be held accountable for human rights violations that count as international crimes as defined by the Rome Statute of the ICC. TNCs domiciled in Europe can be sued for civil human rights violations only in European courts. The latter case is problematic because the European Court of Justice (ECJ) also recognizes corporations as human rights claimants. This raises a question familiar to us from our discussion of the tension between the human rights of communities and the human rights of individuals. Should the human rights of individuals carry greater weight over the human rights of businesses?

Regardless of whether the human rights of individuals should carry greater weight than the human rights of communities, it seems plain that the rights of communities should carry greater weight than the human rights of TNCs. Assuming that TNCs should be accorded some legally actionable human rights – it is questionable whether they should – the communities in which TNCs operate merit legal priority simply in virtue of their special role in protecting and developing the capabilities of their members. If human dignity also carves out a special duty to respect the interests, needs, and capabilities of individual persons apart from their communal membership, this too can be leveraged as a moral hedge against the untrammeled freedom of TNCs to do business with the blessing of government elites.

Summary

We began this chapter by examining whether human rights were too subjective and political to motivate and guide an ethics of development. Reasons for thinking that they might be revolve around the different – and by no means compatible – moral and legal senses attached to them. The human right to development is formulated as a right that attaches to communities in ways that might sometimes conflict with the human rights of individuals. Furthermore, there exists considerable political and theoretical disagreement about the proper content and ranking of human rights. Despite these tensions, we saw that there are nonetheless good reasons for holding that different categories of human rights are complementary, so that narrowly focusing on the enforcement of civil and political rights involving humanitarian crimes, while necessary for securing the conditions of development, does not advance the economic, social, and cultural rights essential for sustainable development. Here the proper focus should be on reforming the legal conventions that currently obstruct the ability of vulnerable persons to securely access the goods necessary for developing their (and their community's) capabilities. Such a reform might also mean incorporating a right to a sustainable global environment as a human right and designating GEMs and TNCs as well as state governments as those responsible for upholding human rights, generally. More radically, drawing from lessons taught by indigenous cultures, such an environmental human right might itself be facilitated non-anthropocentrically, by assigning rights to nature, as the Bolivian and Ecuadorian constitutions did in 2008.

Questions for discussion

1   What are the major differences between (a) civil and political rights and (b) economic, social, and cultural rights? Are (a) and (b) independent and distinct, or are they mutually compatible? Explain your reasoning.

2   What are the pros and cons of both the social contract and human dignity approaches to human rights? Which of the two do you find most important for human rights development? How are these two approaches compatible and/or incompatible with one another?

3   How do community rights relate to human rights? What problems may arise by thinking that all human rights are grounded in the moral dignity of the individual? Can you think of some examples where individual rights may supersede community rights? How can communities and/or groups be protected using these conceptions of human rights?

4   Do you believe that non-state actors ought to be held accountable for obstructing human rights?

Notes

1   Bristol (2012, p. 661).
2   Wolfensohn (2005, p. 21).
3   Ake (1987, p. 5).
4   Rawls (1999, p. 79).
5   Buchanan (2013, p. 18).
6   Young (2007, pp. 159–186).

7   See "Report to the Human Rights Council of the Special Representative of the Secretary General
On the Issue of Human Rights and Transnational Corporations and Other Business Enterprises"
adopted by the HRC on July 2011 and the more recent "United Nations Guiding Principles on
Business and Human Rights" (2013).

Suggested reading

Thomas Pogge (2008). *World Poverty and Human Rights*, 2nd edition. London: Polity
Press.

Pogge's book attempts to show the disconnect between affluent nations and poverty
around the world, suggesting that a minimal amount of economic support could radically diminish poverty. This work presents a type of cosmopolitan view to the problem
of global distributive justice and human rights.

Amartya Sen (2005). "Human Rights and Capabilities." *Journal of Human Development*
6(2): 151–166.

Sen's paper offers a valuable distinction between human rights and capabilities. He
ultimately argues that the two cannot be subsumed under one another and that the development of both must come from the result of public reasoning.

United Nations General Assembly (1948). *Universal Declaration of Human Rights*. www.
un.org/en/universal-declaration-human-rights/index.html.

This UN declaration is the fundamental document concerning common standards of
human rights.

References

Ake, Claude (1987). "The African Context in Human Rights." *Africa Today* 34(1/2): 5–12,
Human Rights: The African Context (1st Qtr.–2nd Qtr., 1987).
Bristol, Graeme (2012). "Architecture and Human Rights." In Thomas Cushman (ed.),
Handbook of Human Rights. London: Routledge.
Buchanan, Allen (2013). *The Heart of Human Rights*. Oxford: Oxford University Press.
Nussbaum, Martha (2000). *Women and Human Development*. Cambridge: Cambridge Uni-
versity Press.
Pogge, Thomas (2008). *World Poverty and Human Rights*, 2nd edition. Cambridge: Polity
Press.
Rawls, John (1999). *The Law of Peoples*. Cambridge, MA: Harvard University Press.
Shue, Henry (1996). *Basic Rights: Subsistence, Affluence, and U.S. Foreign Policy*, 2nd
edition. Princeton: Princeton University Press.
Wolfensohn, James (2005). "Some Reflections on Human Rights and Development." In
Philip Alston and Mary Robinson (eds.), *Human Rights and Development: Towards
Mutual Reinforcement*. Oxford: Oxford University Press.
Young, Iris Marion (2007). *Global Challenges: War, Self-Determination, and Responsibil-
ity for Justice*. London: Polity Press.

3 Development through trade

Utilitarian, social contractarian, and communitarian considerations

The World Trade Organization (WTO) proudly announces that "the WTO agreements recognize the link between trade and development and contain special provisions for developing countries." It continues by noting that the launching of the Doha Ministerial Conference in 2001 has led the WTO to place "development issues and the interests of developing countries at the heart of the WTO's work."

Those who have participated in the countless demonstrations protesting what they believe to be the harmful impact of WTO policies on the poor would disagree. Although the WTO has recently adopted provisions allowing for the differential treatment of least developed countries (LDCs) – specifically by allowing them to gradually phase out import quotas and tariffs that protect their fragile economies from foreign competition – it has generally insisted that free trade, or trade that is unregulated by quotas, tariffs, artificial price supports, and subsidies is the ideal to be striven for. In practice, developing countries that have sought to benefit from privileged membership in the WTO have had to eliminate or greatly reduce domestic measures that have been designed to protect workers in their domestic industries. Meanwhile, the most powerful nations have retained so-called "escalating tariffs," which protect their production of refined goods from foreign competition, and many other tariffs, quotas, and subsidies, which protect domestic industries in agriculture and textiles.

This raises several important ethical questions: Leaving aside the fairness and sustainability of capitalism as such (see Chapter 5), does justice in the area of trade require treating all nations the same way, regardless of their level of development? If differential treatment is fair, then how can this be justified? Assuming that adoption of a universal policy of free trade equally applicable to all nations is fair, is it also conducive to development? In general, must trade benefit all parties equally in order to be fair, and is fairness more important developmentally than security, freedom, cultural integrity, or overall well-being? Does global free trade undermine democracy and human rights (Rodrik 2011)?

We begin this chapter by considering the peculiar advantages that utilitarian ethics and social contract ethics have in answering these questions. Although the human rights approach establishes benchmarks for the development of individuals and community that trade policies must respect, it does not expressly address the justice and proper aim of trade policies. Once we have examined the contribution that social contractarian and utilitarian reasoning can make to understanding the ethics of trade as it relates to development, we turn to the argument that is most often advanced on behalf of free trade – that trade is mutually beneficial for all nations, no matter their relative or absolute disadvantages in productive efficiency. This discussion leads us to examine whether such a benefit, even if true, would lock developing nations into a spiral of dependency. Finally, we examine whether other factors of transnational commerce besides trade, such as flows in capital and labor, should be governed by standards of justice and development. This focus permits us to consider communitarian ethics, which purports to explain why it is proper for communities to restrict flows in goods, capital, and labor for the sake of preserving a less tangible form of local well-being: cultural identity, social solidarity, and political democracy. We conclude by asking whether, from a communitarian or cosmopolitan ethical perspective, there should be limits to property and extraction rights.

Beyond human rights: utilitarian ethics and social contract theory

We ended the last chapter by noting how human rights might place limits on trade agreements and commercial transactions that impact development. Selling public water rights to a privately owned transnational corporation in a way that endangers a community's access to a life-sustaining resource threatens violation of a human right to life. Other commercial transactions that violate human rights include the illicit trade in human beings – human trafficking – which can sometimes involve kidnapping, slavery, and coercive labor exploitation. Smuggling of arms, drugs, cultural artifacts, protected animal and plant species, and ivory also impact indirectly the development and the enjoyment of human rights. But to recall the above example, "legal" forms of trade entitle governments to traffic in dangerous weapons, pesticides, and waste products – not to mention sell off vital resources – in ways that have the same effect. So, only in theory do human rights prohibit trade agreements that prevent persons from accessing the security, health, and subsistence they need in order to achieve a minimally decent *threshold* of development. Because governments are charged with protecting these rights, they and the people they "democratically represent" must oppose unregulated free trade (Rodrik 2011).

One might wonder: Aside from guaranteeing everyone a minimum threshold of development, should considerations of fairness and improvement in overall well-being also be factored into how we assess the ethical impact that trade policies have on development? Human rights link welfare to equal treatment. They require that each person and community be guaranteed a minimum of welfare essential to developing an equal capability for living a life of dignity. However, human rights allow welfare to be decoupled from equal treatment once this minimum is achieved. Indeed, welfare and equality (justice) compete as important development-related values. Improving most people's lives substantially by implementing policies that increase inequality and social domination modestly can be right by utilitarian standards. Conversely, foregoing modest or relatively insignificant improvements in economic well-being for the sake of increasing equality can be right by social contractarian standards.

Ideal and non-ideal ethical theory

One way to understand how well-being and equality can collide – and one way to begin sorting out the different applications of utilitarianism and social contract theory to trade policy – is to note an important distinction that ethicists make between ideal theory and non-ideal theory. Ideal theory aims to lay out a blueprint of the best or most just society that is practically attainable under ideal circumstances, limited only by the necessary moral and material constraints imposed by the human condition. Non-ideal theory, by contrast, lays out a blueprint for achieving a second-best society under less-than-ideal circumstances, one whose imperfect justice, being transitional toward achieving ideal justice, takes into account the changeable realities of the world as it currently exists. These realities include such things as the current state of moral psychology, in which some people are tempted to not comply with what they know to be right conduct, as well as unfavorable circumstances such as extreme material scarcity and inequality.

A simple thought experiment clarifies the ideal/non-ideal theory distinction. In an ideal world – providing ample if not abundant resources for all to achieve a modicum of well-being and inhabited by people who consistently hewed to minimal standards of morality, including respecting human rights and caring for others – people would be generally satisfied with their lives. Under these conditions the coercive power of the state needed to maintain domestic and international security could be relaxed. With the elimination of violent conflict and poverty, the uprooting and unsettling of communities through migration would significantly decline. Not only would cultural and moral differences not lead to violent conflict, but different communities, arrayed along a spectrum ranging from affluent to non-affluent, large to small, powerful to weak, would cooperate with one another on the basis of mutual respect and caring. Under these conditions, nations would assume global responsibilities proportional to their respective size and capability. Trade between countries would not be compelled by need and competitive growth imperatives; it might well be freer, too, once the need to protect fragile domestic businesses from foreign competition wanes. In any case, international trade and investment flows between "equal" partners would be much less exploitative and intense than is currently the case.

The vision of a "realistic utopia" sketched above is one that Rawls himself proposes in *The Law of Peoples* (1999) as an ideal instantiation of a just social contract to be striven for among all nations (or peoples). It is realistic insofar as it keeps within the bounds of human psychology and culture as we know it, in which we feel stronger loyalties to kith and kin than to foreigners, and prefer bounded forms of political association to unbounded ones of the sort exemplified by a single global state. Although this utopia does not envision perfect equality between nations or between persons (taken as citizens of a particular nation or of the world as a whole), it does envision much less inequality than what currently exists. Furthermore, the utopian provision of adequate material resources to each and every one that is sufficient to enable equal opportunities for development also maximizes global well-being according to utilitarian principles. For, according to the principle of marginal utility, additional increments of consumption beyond a modest threshold yield decreasing increments of satisfaction and well-being. In short, a more equal world without starving masses and multibillionaires – and living within more sustainable limits of economic growth and consumption, generally – would be on balance better (healthier and happier) than the current one.

However, until that ideal world is achieved, we might have to live according to different principles that are better suited to our current circumstances in which utilitarian and social contractarian approaches, and their respective aims (well-being and equality) might not harmoniously converge. For instance, under non-ideal circumstances, the peoples of the world will need to divert considerable resources away from development toward the maintenance of national and domestic security. "Outlaw" nations must be sanctioned when they threaten international aggression or commit humanitarian crimes against their own or other nations' peoples. Borders must be safeguarded in dealing with destabilizing waves of migration and "burdened societies" that fall below a threshold of political stability, and the economic viability of developing nations must be assisted by developed countries to the point where they can manage their own affairs and occupy a place of equal standing on the stage of international relations. To achieve this goal, rules of fair trade might have to stray from the social contractarian ideal of equal treatment and accord poor nations certain rights to protect their industries from competition not afforded to wealthy nations. The existence of geopolitical threats will pressure nations to grow their economies and defense capabilities, so poorer countries, too, will have to sacrifice a higher level of consumption and perhaps much else for the sake of saving to build up their economies.

I have suggested that social contractarian ethics dictates different norms and policies depending on whether it is asked to guide our thinking about non-ideal or ideal circumstances. Under non-ideal circumstances, its egalitarian principles might have to be compromised by more utilitarian considerations aimed at bringing about overall well-being. But as I intimated above, utilitarian ethics has its own versions of ideal and non-ideal theorizing. For instance, an ideal world in which everyone sought to maximize the greatest amount of planetary well-being might provide a near-equal distribution of resources and opportunities among all the world's inhabitants (again, this would seem to follow from the principle of marginal utility, which asserts that additional levels of consumption beyond the satisfaction of basic needs yields increasingly less happiness). If recent demographic trends are a reliable indicator of what might be expected as a result of increasing economic security for those at the bottom, global population growth would level out and possibly decline as women and their families assumed roles commensurate with an educated middle-class lifestyle. Whether (following the utilitarian philosophy of John Stuart Mill) such a world would also protect the greatest amount of individual liberty compatible with overall respect for persons' rights and duties – including the perfect freedom to purchase goods, labor, and services across borders – is less clear. Be that as it may, in our non-ideal world, utilitarianism counsels that sacrifice in short-term happiness – and perhaps sacrifice in freedom and equality – should be undertaken for the sake of maximizing long-term happiness (whether or not this state also maximizes freedom or equality).

Utilitarian ethics and development

In this book we will mainly focus on applications of utilitarian and social contract ethics to our current world, which by almost all moral standards is far from ideal. Utilitarianism seems especially pertinent to the economics of poverty and under-development. According to one strand of classical economic theory, it might be necessary to increase overall development of society before attending to human rights deficits and other forms of social injustice. A Marxist, for example, might argue that developing a relatively affluent society is necessary before social domination can be eliminated and equal human rights realized. More recently, Simon Kuznets argued (along similar lines) that economic development within a society generally requires initially increasing production and consumption unequally before distributing production and consumption equally. Today, many defenders of free trade echo Kuznets's thinking: long-term economic growth that is prerequisite to advancing human rights and justice is best facilitated by a relatively unregulated market whose short-term consequences might include greater inequality and less welfare for some.

In sum, an unjust institution might be morally tolerable if it is the most expedient among several realistic alternatives to achieving substantial economic development. However, higher levels of consumption yield marginally lower increments of material satisfaction, so that eventually, even by utilitarian reasoning, once a modest level of average material affluence has been achieved along with development of higher capabilities, freedom and social justice become more valued as components of well-being. At this level of development, social contract ethics becomes especially applicable.

Social contract ethics and development

We know from reading Rousseau and Marx that social inequality can hinder development. A community's human right to development can be threatened if it finds itself at a disadvantage in negotiating trade agreements and other commercial transactions. The same can be said of individual persons. They may have sufficient access to the goods guaranteed to them by human rights and still be incapable of exercising sufficient control over factors that impact their lives. Domination by others can render them incapable of advancing conditions that might further develop their capabilities; they can be subjected to coercive threats and exploitation.

Social contract theory applies here because it aims to lay out moral principles that specify fair terms of social cooperation between communities and between persons. Because this theory is particularly pertinent to the question of trade as an exemplary form of mutually beneficial cooperation, this chapter will explore the many varieties of this theory in greater detail. All defenders of the social contract approach to social ethics emphasize the importance of voluntary consent in legitimating forms of cooperation that are accepted by all parties as mutually beneficial. At the same time they disagree how far social inequalities should be permitted to threaten the freedom of the poorest and weakest parties to the social contract. They therefore disagree how far this last group should benefit from cooperation in comparison to their more powerful and wealthy co-partners. Finally, as a matter of related concern, they disagree about which classes of persons ought to be included in the social contract. The terms of social cooperation that have historically emerged have excluded racial, ethnic, and religious minorities; women; indigenous peoples; and colonized subjects. In the words of Charles Mills and Carol Pateman, although the *ideal* norms espoused by social contractarians might have condemned slavery and patriarchy, the *historical* norms they endorsed did not; in reality the social contracts that have bound societies up to the present have been "racial," "sexual," and "settler" contracts.

Prudential social contract ethics

The least ethically demanding – but arguably most realistic – social contractarian approach descends from the arguments pioneered in Thomas Hobbes's *Leviathan* (1651). This approach assumes that morality springs from self-interest and a form of prudential (or strategic) reasoning that favors caution and pre-emptively reducing risks posed by others, who, competing for the same scarce resources as ourselves, must be regarded mainly as threats to our freedom and well-being. Although our natural reaction is to dominate threatening others if we can, our reasoning calculates that a less risky option is to join with them in agreeing to a social contract which, by imposing the threat of greater sanctions, limits everyone's power to dominate anyone else. Minimally, this social contract requires creating a legal system that compels parties to the contract to respect the basic freedom of others to procure their livelihoods without infringing on the freedom of others to do the same. Those who make and enforce the laws, in turn, will have their interest in domination curbed by the thought that yielding to this temptation is not in their long-term self-interest, as it might incite the rebellion of their subjects.

The Hobbesian version of social contract ethics requires the establishment of law and order conducive to maintaining the compliance and loyalty of most people in society (lawbreakers having effectively opted out of the contract). It is therefore imperative that such an order protect the freedom necessary for people to acquire and exchange property pursuant to securing their own short- and long-term preservation. So long as the resulting distribution of property is not perceived as threatening the lives of most citizens or as rendering them worse off than the distribution that would obtain without the system, order will be maintained. For Hobbes, mere consent to legal order – even if it is constrained by fear of a worse alternative – is all that is necessary to declare the order just. Democracy, which some philosophers (such as Rousseau) interpret as the most important (political) vehicle for *collectively* expressing free consent, is *not* considered by Hobbes as prerequisite for just legal order. Because fear of violence (legally or illegally sanctioned) is the main motive underlying all consent to legal domination, individual self-interest, rather than the common good as expressed by a democratic vote, is and ought to be the only rational moral concern of the individual legal subject (skepticism regarding whether any democratic system can rationally yield an outcome that is good for everyone is another reason to not insist on it as a necessary feature of just legal order).

The so-called realist school of international relations, which departs from Hobbes's model of the social contract, interprets the duties of the developed world to the developing world mainly through the lens of *national* self-interest. If we extend the strategic reasoning that leads to the establishment of a social contract, then establishing a lawful international order that secures world peace is a duty that all self-interested peoples should readily endorse. Although the establishment of a sovereign world government possessing effective, centralized power might be the ideal order for maintaining global peace, the weakness of the UN and other international legal institutions in compelling outlaw nations to obey laws forbidding aggression under current non-ideal circumstances recommends a more realistic alternative: retention of a decentralized state system in which it is the supreme interest of powerful nations to increase or maintain their power in order to hold each other and weaker nations in check with the threat of sanctions.

Because people expect their own government to promote their own interests ahead of the interests of foreigners, they will feel duty-bound to respect and protect the human rights of foreigners only when it secures them some benefit. For example, it might sometimes be in the interest of a people to encourage their government to permit the entry of refugees and other migrants, respect and protect human rights of foreigners, and even assist burdened countries in order to maintain peace and security. However, cooperating with other foreign governments in achieving these mutually beneficial security aims (including controlling the effects of global warming) will always be dependent on a shifting strategic calculus of self-interest. If circumstances change and that calculus shifts, peoples may justly close their borders to human and commercial traffic, refrain from respecting and protecting the human rights of foreigners, and refuse to help burdened societies. In the final analysis, because trade agreements will be negotiated from a standpoint of strategic self-interest in which the most powerful will leverage their superior threat potential in exacting the most favorable terms for themselves, there is no expectation that trade agreements voluntarily contracted between rich and poor countries would (or should) benefit the poor as much as the rich.

Libertarian social contract ethics

A more ethically demanding version of the social contract that descends from John Locke's *A Second Treatise of Government* (1690) departs from a more robust understanding of voluntary cooperation based on a more complex understanding of human motivation. According to this version, purely self-interested persons would not calculate that it was in their rational self-interest to trust others to abide by the terms of any agreement. In order for stable (long-term) forms of social cooperation to arise whose participants feel bound by something more than threat of sanction, we must assume that persons are motivated to put aside their self-interest in respecting the basic freedom of others for its own sake. According to this view, respecting the freedom of others to procure their self-preservation would entail a duty on the part of the community to ensure that each and every participant to the contract be guaranteed an equal opportunity to acquire and exchange property sufficient to living modestly well.

Unlike Hobbes's version of the social contract, which allows that persons can and would (indeed should) surrender their basic freedoms and rights to a law-and-order government for the sake of protecting themselves against the greater threat of anarchy, Locke's version allows that persons cannot nor should not surrender these freedoms and rights. To do so, according to Locke, would entail abdicating their very humanity as responsible members of society. Our natural right (and natural duty) to freely pursue our self-preservation in a manner that respects and protects the similar right and duty of others accordingly limits the rightful power of government over us. Locke's contemporary expositor, Robert Nozick, concludes in *Anarchy, State, and Utopia* (1974) that the only legitimate government is one that limits its coercive power to protecting our individual freedom to acquire and exchange property. According to him, taxing the wealthy to increase social equality (as distinct from providing a basic safety net for the indigent and unemployable) is unjustly coercive (not unlike stealing), having been done without the consent of the wealthy.

Applied to the international arena, Lockean social contract theory endows all inhabitants of the world with basic property rights (including a right to subsistence for the unemployable), which governments are duty-bound to respect and protect. Furthermore, because this version of the social contract stakes rightful ownership to just historical entitlement based on voluntary acquisition and exchange, it condemns current patterns of ownership and wealth distribution rooted in slavery, colonial expropriation, and imperial domination. These unjust violations of the natural rights and duties framing the social contract call for some form of restitution, or duty on the part of countries that benefited from past crimes to provide some compensation to the countries now disadvantaged as a result of them. Finally, because our natural rights to own and exchange property take precedence over whatever political rights and duties our government imposes on us, government cannot limit these rights except in order to protect them. In an ideally free world, these rights would be unlimited; cross-border transactions and migrations would be unrestricted, and tariffs and other "artificial" (or unnatural) barriers to free trade would be eliminated. In our current non-ideal world of security threats and illicit trafficking, the right of individuals to freely move themselves and their goods must be restricted, but the state would have to show why doing so was necessary in order to protect the freedom, lives, and property of its own citizens. Importantly, ensuring the equity, or equal benefit, of trade and other contractual agreements remains but a subordinate concern of Lockean social contract theory.

Welfare-enhancing social contract ethics

The third and most demanding version of the social contract theory is exemplified by John Rawls's *A Theory of Justice* (1971). Rawls criticizes Locke's understanding of natural rights and historical entitlement because it still permits class structures and forms of domination that appear to be morally unjustifiable. Rawls insists, more than Hobbes and Locke, that voluntary consent to any cooperative scheme be tied to contractual terms that are fair to everyone, including those who are born into unfavorable circumstances (for example, those who have inherited disability or poverty). Talents that persons inherit as a result of being born into favorable circumstances that advantage them in the acquisition of property are purely accidental (a function of luck) and are therefore undeserved. It follows – contra Locke – that a historical account of entitlement (desert) favors the lucky, and as such does not comport with the most basic idea of morality: fairness (or impartiality).

Furthermore, because each contributes something necessary to everyone else's cultivation of their talents – the lowly harvester feeds the educated doctor – it is impossible to sort out who has contributed how much to the social good. Therefore, from a purely moral point of view, everyone should be entitled to an equal share of social goods. However, Rawls allows that a cooperative scheme that distributed unequal shares might be agreed to by all, but only if this scheme benefited the people who are left worse off. Thus, there is nothing morally objectionable about paying a doctor substantially more for the use of her talents than a farmworker, as determined by a market principle of supply and demand, so long as the farmworker can receive affordable medical care from the doctor, funded perhaps by an insurance scheme supplemented from public tax revenue.

To be clear, Rawls does not endorse the idea that great inequalities are justified so long as any benefit – however small – trickles down to the poor. As Rousseau had argued earlier in *On the Social Contract* (1762), Rawls endorses a democratic understanding of the social contract that demands that those on the bottom benefit the most, so that all end up with roughly equal opportunities to participate in the political process, in which the legal terms of the social contract are interpreted and applied. In order for everyone to participate as equals in the political process, each must have not only equal civil and political rights but also equal educational opportunities to fully inform themselves, develop leadership skills, and have a fair start in life. Inequalities of wealth should not influence the formation of public opinion, legislative agenda setting, and voting, otherwise democracy devolves into oligarchy, or domination of the wealthy over everyone else.

To justify the ideal of a liberal democratic society that disperses wealth and limits social inequality while providing equal opportunity for all, Rawls deploys a thought experiment in which we imagine ourselves, along with our fellow citizens, as choosing principles for the design of just society. To ensure that our reasoning is impartial, we impose a *veil of ignorance* on ourselves that denies us any knowledge about our personal circumstances and permits only general knowledge of psychology, economics, political science, and the like. Psychology tells us that naturally self-interested persons will not be envious of others' wealth and power (contra Hobbes) so long as they believe it to be acquired fairly, a principle that every reasonable and rational person can be motivated to act upon. Faced with having to distribute their society's primary goods – or goods that any rational person wants such as liberties, income, self-respect, and opportunities for acquiring positions of employment and running for political office – participants reasoning under a veil of ignorance will imagine themselves as potentially occupying the least favorable and most vulnerable positions in their society. Given the uncertainties surrounding their own actual position, they will adopt a risk-aversive strategy for choosing principles whose application would maximize the condition of the least favorably positioned. They would not choose principles that maximize human excellence (an aristocracy of the talented few) nor would they choose utilitarian principles that maximize the greatest happiness for the greatest number (for all they know, they might be one of the minority that lives in slavish misery). Instead, they would choose (two) principles that enshrine (respectively) basic economic, civil, and political liberties compatible with a like freedom for all and a distribution of scarce offices based on merit, coupled with a sub-principle of distributive justice that regulates inequalities in income to the advantage of the worst off (what Rawls calls the *difference principle*).

Under non-ideal conditions, these principles would have to be qualified. For example, in a society that has a long history of race-based slavery and discrimination, it might be proper to institute transitional remedies, such as affirmative action programs, that relax ideal principles promoting color-blind, merit-based distribution of scarce positions in professional schools and employment. So, like Nozick's application of the social contract under non-ideal conditions, wherein the current distribution of unequal opportunities stems in part from past injustice, Rawls's application of the same entails an auxiliary principle of compensatory justice.

As I noted above, Rawls extends his social contract argument to the international arena. In doing so he makes two notable changes. First, he redefines the aim of agreement: a law of peoples governing fair cooperation between nations instead of a principle of justice specifying fair cooperation between individuals. This change reflects Rawls's conviction that people inhabiting different kinds of society might reasonably disagree about whether liberal democratic institutions that privilege individual freedom are uniquely and universally the most just in comparison to other institutional arrangements. Second, he qualifies his application of the veil of ignorance thought experiment to account for this disagreement. The experiment is now divided into two parts: First, it shows that impartial representatives of liberal democratic societies that prioritize individual freedom over a thick (e.g., religious) conception of the common good would agree to an international law (a "law of peoples") stipulating (among other government duties) protection of basic human rights (including a right to subsistence) and assistance in the development of burdened societies. Second, it shows that impartial representatives of decent (less free and undemocratic but politically accountable) societies that prioritize a thick conception of the common good over individual freedom would also agree to such a law. Agreement on a law of peoples between the representatives of these two different kinds of societies – one individualist, the other associationist – requires that the duties specified in the law not be interpreted in a narrow, liberal democratic manner. To recall my discussion of Rawls in Chapter 2, an associationist society, for example, could reasonably understand the human right to religious freedom in a way that favored a dominant religion or disfavored a minority religion, so long as it tolerated freedom of religious conscience.

It is important to note that many critics of Rawls question how he applies his social contract reasoning to global society. They favor applying the reasoning Rawls used earlier in justifying liberal democratic principles of justice. For them, an ideal global society would consist of only liberal democracies (perhaps regulated by a supreme cosmopolitan liberal democracy) in which inequalities between nations and between the world's inhabitants would be adjusted in accordance with the difference principle. Such an ideal world society, in their opinion, would equalize conditions of development to a far greater degree than Rawls's own law of peoples envisages.

As for realizing that ideal in non-ideal circumstances, these critics are more emphatic than Rawls in pointing out that the causes of global poverty extend beyond the political corruption, human rights abuses, and patriarchal oppression of women that Rawls rightly attributes to many burdened societies. These global causes include an unfair distribution of resources and unfair rules of global trade. As Pogge notes, developed countries all too willingly purchase the resources that authoritarian regimes in burdened societies steal from their own people. He also condemns unfair trade agreements that allow developed countries to protect their domestic industries while freely competing in the markets of developing countries (thus denying developing countries more than $300 billion in exchange). The overall impact of such uneven terms of trade can be catastrophic to developing nations whose labor-intensive industries compete at a disadvantage against larger-scale, high-tech transnational corporations. Again, developed countries take advantage of developing countries' undeveloped markets by dumping their own highly subsidized and artificially discounted commodities in these markets with disastrous effects on local business. Finally, the provision of the WTO agreement governing licenses, copyrights, and patents, Trade Related Aspects of Intellectual Property Rights (TRIPS), costs developing countries billions of dollars in licensing fees while driving up the costs of pharmaceuticals (and prohibiting the production of low-cost generics). Here, as noted in Chapter 2, TRIPS provisions contradict states' human rights duties to their own citizens.

Pogge accordingly proposes social contractarian principles for changing rules of trade and compensating for the past and present harms they have inflicted on the world's poor. Pogge, for instance, recommends trade sanctions on corrupt authoritarian regimes as well as a Global Resource Dividend (GRD) tax. This tax would ultimately be paid by affluent consumers of non-essential, environmentally hazardous resources, such as petroleum, the proceeds from which would be used to compensate the poor for being unjustly denied access to their fair share of the world's resources. As for TRIPS, Pogge criticizes its protection of products (as distinct from processes) and proposes an alternative, non-market-based set of incentives (the Health Impact Fund) for funneling tax revenue toward the development of drugs and other health-related technologies that would have the greatest impact on reducing worldwide morbidity and mortality.

Summarizing the developmental value of utilitarian and social contract ethics

In sum, utilitarianism and social contract theory supplement the human right to development in at least several ways. First, they provide additional methods for resolving tensions between the various human rights whose exercise promotes development. For example, during times of civil strife, or whenever the human right to security conflicts with the human right to free movement, utilitarianism and social contract theory might endorse the protective detention of refugees in camps, either to reduce the possibility of greater harm or to restore frameworks for social cooperation. Likewise, these theories can be called upon to temper harsh trade sanctions that are intended to compel governments to cease violating human rights, once it is determined that the sanctions themselves harm or destabilize the population they are supposed to be helping.

Second, they supplement our thinking about the ethics of development in both ideal and non-ideal circumstances. Once human rights are satisfied, it might be asked: What development duties remain, beyond simply increasing overall well-being and social justice, understood as a factor of well-being? However, until that ideal is achieved – and before it is achievable – utilitarianism and social contract ethics can clarify our intuitions about balancing economic development and moral development. As we shall see in Chapter 5, they can also clarify our intuitions about *intergenerational* justice: whether it is just for present generations to benefit from policies that harm future generations, or (conversely) whether it is just for younger generations to benefit from policies that harm older generations.

China as test case

China's remarkable development illustrates how a shift from utilitarian to social contractarian considerations can clarify these questions. Throughout its reign, China's Communist government has devoted itself single-mindedly to pursuing economic growth for the Chinese people. Its experimental policies, ranging from agricultural collectivization in the early years, through the Cultural Revolution and beyond, including its current market-based socialism, have not always met with success (indeed, some of have been disastrous). But today there is no disputing the impressive strides China has made in eliminating and reducing poverty. For most of its history, China's Communist Party has enjoyed wide support from the Chinese people, despite imposing sacrifices on them, including restrictions on civil and political rights. However, beginning with the Tiananmen Square Protests of 1989, a younger generation of educated and affluent Chinese began demanding more freedom. Today, inequality between urban and rural regions, coupled with the growth of an educated and cosmopolitan middle class, is generating pressure to open up the political system, eliminate restrictions on civil liberties, and redistribute economic gains to those at the bottom.

Trade has been an important part of China's story. Exports produced in its manufacturing centers have driven its economic growth. From a utilitarian perspective, China's manufacturing and trade policy might seem relatively unproblematic, if one assumes that among all realistic alternatives it was most likely to raise a substantial portion of its population out of poverty quickly.

From a social contractarian perspective, this policy appears more problematic. What enabled China's exports to compete so successfully on the world market was a combination of questionable domestic and foreign trade policies. China's foreign trade policies may have exploited moral loopholes regarding fair dealing with other countries; the Chinese government may have deliberately under-enforced licensing and copyright agreements to which it was party; it may have extracted technology transfer agreements from foreign companies as conditions for doing business; it may have devalued its own currency so as to gain a competitive advantage on world markets for its underpriced exports; and it may have protected its domestic industries through hidden quotas on imports. Of course, China's exploitation of these loopholes appears less morally problematic if the trade agreements it signed with developed countries were not fair to begin with – a possibility we have already broached – or if violating them promoted a higher good, such as the reduction of global poverty and inequality.

The same probably cannot be said of China's domestic trade-related policies. China's domestic policy of focusing economic development in urban manufacturing and industrial centers may have required practices of labor exploitation, environmental degradation, price controls on domestic agricultural goods, and restrictions on labor mobility. Leaving aside allegations that China has used prison labor and that as many as 30 million workers may have been subject to forms of slavery and other coercive labor practices – allegations that the Chinese government disputes – there is no denying that China's manufactured goods cost less to produce than similar goods manufactured elsewhere because Chinese workers have been paid substantially less and labored in less safe, and less healthy, working conditions. It may be, too, that the food consumed by a poorly paid urban Chinese working class was made affordable by government price controls that harmed rural Chinese farmers.

Our aim in this chapter is not to scrutinize the morality of China's domestic labor and trade policies as such but to underscore the link between China's domestic economy and its connection to a model of development based on achieving both growth and domestic justice through trade. But why did China's leadership think that trade was the most expedient path toward achieving these goals?

The ethics of trade

Economists dating back to Adam Smith have touted trade as the great engine of economic growth. Their ethical reasoning has been predominantly, but not exclusively, utilitarian. Working through the law of supply and demand, markets in general, they argue, are the best mechanisms for determining the true social values and costs of commodities; by signaling over- and under-supply of commodities relative to demand through price fluctuations, they help guide investors and consumers in efficiently distributing their combined assets. However, because no one can predict market fluctuations from one moment to the next, individual fortunes can be made or lost in an instant. There is nothing intrinsically fair about market outcomes; hard-working people can wake up one morning without a job, due to their company closing shop or outsourcing its personnel to persons living abroad who are willing to do their job for much less.

That said, market outcomes can be said to be ethical in a utilitarian sense. The efficient distribution of resources according to supply and demand produces the greatest overall utility as measured by standards of subjective and (less obviously) objective standards of well-being. From the standpoint of global development, this claim becomes more plausible if we adopt marginalist thinking. To recall what we discussed earlier, according to the principle of marginal utility, additional increments of some good beyond a point of maximum impact yield diminishing returns of utility. For example, at least one loaf of bread is needed to save a starving person, with additional loaves yielding diminishing benefits for that person. To take the above example, the outsourcing of jobs located in developed countries to people living in developing countries yields high returns in utility, *if* we assume that jobs are needed most where unemployment and poverty are high. Conversely, the harm outsourcing does to workers who lose jobs is comparatively worth it, given that developed countries have less unemployment overall and can provide unemployed workers with welfare benefits that still afford a high standard of living.

However utility-promoting market transactions might be, they need not produce a universal benefit for all affected. A person living in a developed country who loses her job to foreign outsourcing often loses substantial income (not to mention benefits, both physical and psychological) that are not compensated by unemployment insurance and lower prices of consumer goods produced by cheaper foreign labor. Economists, however, argue that universal benefit ought to be the expected outcome, at least for those who are directly involved in transacting the exchange of goods and services. After all, people would not trade goods and services if they thought it would not benefit them.

This argument assumes that persons normally act rationally, so that their choices in bartering goods and services are calculated to most efficiently bring about their desired aims. It follows that exchanges between rational persons will normally be mutually beneficial – no one will be made worse off and at least one person will be made better off. It also follows that if person A desires X and person B desires Y; and A produces Y more efficiently than B and B produces X more efficiently than Y; A will give B surplus Y in exchange for B giving A surplus X at a rate that is favorable to both of them.

These assumptions do not hold absolutely. Persons are not always rational and will sometimes act on desires they know are harmful to themselves. Also, what a person correctly calculates is in her best interest now may not be best for her in the long run. And, actions that are optimal from the perspective of each actor taken in isolation can be suboptimal from the perspective of their unintended cumulative side effects. In particular, utilitarian calculations become increasingly less certain to the degree that they presuppose knowledge of an indefinite chain of causes and effects that only an all-knowing God would be privy to.

The unreliability of utilitarian calculation poses a severe limit on utilitarianism as an ethical decision procedure. This limit is especially apparent when considering the impact of trade policy on development. Market transactions produce extra costs and benefits (called externalities) that are not reflected in the prices of traded goods. An example of an unintended benefit might be peaceful co-existence between trading parties that are loath to give up the economic benefits of trade. An example of an unintended cost might be loss of control over one's production and consumption to outsiders, which very often comes with additional costs.

All of these negative outcomes produce "buyers' remorse," which can lead persons and nations to renegotiate the terms of trade, if not withdraw from it. Resistance to the free flow of labor, capital, and commodities – expressed in forms of local, national, and regional trade "protectionism" – find their basis in this insight: that the benefits of free trade predicted by economic experts are either too distant or too uncertain.

Should all nations engage in trade?

For the sake of argument, let us assume that market transactions – we'll call them trades, for short – are beneficial to the transacting parties. When considering development, the question naturally arises whether it is always in the best interest of a nation to engage in trade with other nations. An affirmative answer presupposes that every nation produces something that other nations are willing to trade for because they want it and cannot produce it themselves or cannot produce it as cheaply. In today's high-tech world any nation could in principle produce anything it wanted, but it wouldn't be able to produce it as cheaply as some other nation. So if it is always in the best interest of a nation to engage in trade with another nation, it will most likely be because each nation possesses an *absolute* advantage in producing more cheaply something that the other nation wants.

As a matter of fact, however, a nation A will trade with another nation B for some commodity that A could produce more cheaply than B. This is puzzling: Why is it sometimes beneficial for a nation to trade for something that it could produce more cheaply itself?

As British economist David Ricardo argued 200 years ago, mutually beneficial trade presupposes only that each nation possess a *comparative* advantage in producing some good. Portugal may produce both cloth and wine more cheaply than England. However, Portugal might profitably trade wine for English cloth in a way that is mutually beneficial for both countries if Portugal has a great advantage in cheaply producing wine in comparison to cloth and England has a great advantage in cheaply producing cloth in comparison to wine. If England diverted all its wine-making resources toward cloth-making and Portugal diverted all its cloth-making resources to wine making – each maximizing its respective productive efficiencies – then each could trade with the other for what it no longer produces and both end up with greater aggregate wealth (greater surplus in what each produces most efficiently) than if they had not traded at all.

This explains why a developing country with a large semi-literate rural population and abundant fertile land can export its agricultural commodities to a developed country where those same commodities could be produced more cheaply using high-tech farming. The developed country can more efficiently divert its highly literate labor force to industries that are more profitable than agriculture, such as pharmaceuticals. It can then sell these pharmaceuticals to the developing country, in which the production of pharmaceuticals is costly in comparison to the production of agriculture.

In sum, the argument that trade is both possible and economically beneficial for developing nations, even when they are at an absolute disadvantage in almost any given economic sector, now seems understandable. In short, reluctance to pass up better opportunities for profit will sometimes constrain developed nations to forgo developing sectors of their economy in which they possess global advantages, thus compelling them to purchase goods produced in these sectors from developing countries.

There might be no better illustration of the principle of comparative advantage than China. Today, China's people are among the best educated in the world despite enjoying only a modest standard of living in comparison to higher-income countries. In this respect, it could be argued that China has an absolute advantage over more developed countries, such as the United States, in producing almost anything. China has a strong incentive to sell its goods to the United States, but what incentive does it have to purchase goods from the United States that are produced using higher-paid workers laboring under more costly working conditions?

Leaving aside China's well-known purchasing of US government debt and real estate, it would seem that China has no incentive to purchase American-made goods. True, China's absolute advantage in cheap, educated labor power is shrinking as Chinese wages have steadily risen. However, it might also be true that China's heavy industries suffer a disadvantage in comparison to its manufacturing base. Hence, it is economically rational for China to purchase industrial machinery from the United States, even though, in principle, it could produce that machinery more cost-efficiently if it were willing to divert its labor and resources in that direction. The cost of doing so, however, would temporarily weaken China's manufacturing base, thereby weakening its hold on global markets – the very condition that has driven its economic development.

Trade dependency and underdevelopment

We discussed earlier the unintended side effects of trade. The interlocking of China's and America's economies through trade and much else – American industry has deep investments in China's factories – compels these countries to seek peaceful resolution to the geopolitical conflicts that divide them. This means, too, that the governments of China and the United States have ceded partial control over their economies to each other.

It is unlikely that this interdependency – the effect of globalization – will adversely impact China's continuing development, even if the trade imbalance between China and the US eventually shifts back to the US as production costs in China rise or terms of trade are renegotiated. This cannot be said of interdependency linking most developing countries and the developed world.

You will recall that the logic underlying the principle that every nation can only benefit from trade – the idea that there are comparative advantages (and disadvantages) in any domestic economy – dictates that poor, developing countries, most of which are at an absolute disadvantage in almost any area of production, develop their economies through the specialized production of just those exports wherein they have a comparative advantage. Developing one's economy through exports deprives developing countries of domestic control over their own economic development to the extent that developed countries that originate the greatest demand for exports can increase or lower demand through the removal or imposition of protective tariffs and consumer product codes.

Product codes lower demand for exports by prohibiting products that violate safety standards and environmental regulations – the EU ban on the use of GMOs in agriculture being a familiar case in point. However, product codes adopted by an entire industry can have the opposite effect by forcing developing countries to gear their exports toward the widest mass market possible. The mass marketing of agricultural produce, for example, involves producing uniform, standardized products using high-yield seeds, fertilizers, and in many instances, labor-saving machinery. In this scenario, developing countries become locked into a global "monoculture" in which they abandon indigenous ways of farming geared to subsistence and domestic markets; they become dependent on transnational companies, such as Cargill, Monsanto, and Dow Chemical, which monopolize the production and distribution of standardized seeds, fertilizers, and pesticides.

In sum, small developing countries that cannot compete – as China did (by mainly diversifying its export economy through competitive labor practices) – find themselves at the mercy of a global market economy dominated by developed countries and transnational companies based in those countries. From the standpoint of social contract ethics, it might be wondered whether developing countries benefit equally (if they benefit at all) from this arrangement. There are several reasons for thinking that many do not.

First, economies that mainly depend on exports for development might be required to shift their productive capacity away from satisfying the subsistence needs of their own people (Fader 2013). Instead of growing food for local consumption they grow exotic crops (such as flowers) for global markets. Many developing economies that formerly attained a level of self-sufficiency in food production now find themselves importing food from abroad. They subsequently become vulnerable to global food shortages and price hikes caused by fluctuations in the global market, which are again heavily influenced by patterns of production and consumption in the developed world. This situation will get worse with climate change.[1]

Second, some of the most important export industries – agriculture and manufacturing – have become increasingly high-tech in order to lower labor costs and maximally exploit advantages associated with larger, more efficient economies of scale. The introduction of high-tech agribusiness in the developing world, which often displaces small subsistence farming, has yielded a net loss of jobs in rural areas. Many rural workers migrate to cities where they seek out scarce manufacturing jobs. These jobs, too, are disappearing as automation takes hold. So, export production does not always create jobs, but often exacerbates an already serious unemployment problem.

Third, the internal migration of labor from rural to urban centers does nothing to improve abandoned towns and adds new stresses associated with overpopulated, under-resourced urban slums. The free trade zones (FTZs), where some of these migrants find work, are mainly geared toward export processing (also called export processing zones [EPZs]). Because FTZ/EPZs often pay wages that are higher than what the local economy affords, it might seem that export-oriented development is, after all, a net gain for developing countries. However, higher wages must be balanced against the higher cost of urban living; in any case, sweatshops owned or sub-contracted by foreign transnationals are vulnerable to market vicissitudes; they will transplant themselves to any region offering the prospect of lower wages. From a utilitarian perspective, this "rush to the bottom" might benefit the poorest regions of the world, but it does not benefit those who have lost their jobs or those who must make wage and benefit concessions in order to keep their jobs.

Fourth, sweatshops located in FTZ/EPZs are typically exempt from having to pay taxes and abide by national labor regulations. Such incentives might be necessary to lure foreign transnational companies to set up sweatshops in FTZ/EPZs, but the price for doing business with them is often high, after job-related injury and sickness, environmental damage, and loss of tax revenue are factored in. Environmental costs count as one of the negative externalities accompanying market economies; clean air and water and uncontaminated land do not come with price tags. They count as public goods that are freely exploited without being adequately maintained and replenished. Although unregulated market economies discount environmental costs, export-oriented economies based on EPZs are legally permitted and encouraged to do so, exemplifying the worst abuses associated with a "tragedy of the commons."

Fifth, export-oriented development has not always led to a net gain in exchange. Arguing against the neoclassical view of comparative advantage, Raul Prebisch and Hans Singer maintained over 70 years ago that developing countries were at a *structural disadvantage* in trading with developed countries. Because developing countries are relegated to the *periphery* as suppliers of *primary* resources to the industrial centers of developed countries, they spend more money on purchasing the value-added goods processed from these resources than they receive from the sale of these same resources. Trade thus makes the rich richer and the poor poorer.

Sixth, the corollary to this structural disadvantage is a disadvantage in human resource development. In comparison to the developed world, the extraction of resources in the developing world is far more dependent on cheap manual labor. Developing economies geared toward exporting their cheap primary resources to the developed world therefore have no incentive and little opportunity – given the escalating tariffs imposed by developing countries on imports from developing countries – to diversify their economies. Discouraged from developing industries that technologically process primary resources, developing countries find it difficult to develop the technical capacities of their domestic workforce, which would enable them to compete for better-paying employment in the global market.

Combatting dependency and creating trade equity

Over the years, many economists have proposed policies for combatting trade dependency. Prebisch – who was appointed as Secretary-General of the newly created United Nations Conference on Trade and Development – recommended a developmental policy of import substitution. This policy promotes a policy of self-sufficiency, in which developing countries encourage the consumption of domestic commodities in place of imports, which in turn stimulates the growth of domestic production. This policy has shown some success in post-World War II Latin America, but it seems to work best with large, populous countries, like Brazil. It would not be feasible for a small island country such as Haiti that lacks sufficient arable land to feed its population. In any case, implementing a policy of import substitution involves protecting local businesses from foreign competition by imposing tariffs on imports. Practically speaking, a global policy of protectionism implemented by all countries would cause a global economic depression (such a global policy arguably exacerbated the Great Depression of the 1930s). So this policy would have to be implemented cautiously and selectively by developing countries, which must still import some necessities from the developed world in order to increase the technological capacity of their own industries, if for no other reason. Furthermore, the policy presupposes that developed as well as developing countries have adopted a welfare-enhancing – rather than prudential or libertarian – social contract ethics in negotiating fair trade agreements. The Doha Development Round of WTO negotiations that has been under way for almost 20 years has operated with this social contract model; the consensus is that developing countries should be allowed to protect some of their industries from destructive foreign competition, at least for a temporary period of time that would permit these industries to modernize and become competitive, while developed countries should eliminate protections that prevent developing countries from selling their goods in developed markets. Trade between developing and developing nations should not be based on the principle of prudential advantage (greatest benefit) for those with the greatest bargaining leverage; nor should it be based on the libertarian principle of free trade that insulates the acquisition and exchange of property from regulations designed to compensate for consequences that harm, or do not primarily aim to benefit, the most disadvantaged partners in trade.

Case study: Brazil vs. US in cotton dispute

Equitable trade for whom? Do bilateral trade agreements weaken WTO protections for poor countries?

In 2002, cotton farmers in Brazil requested that their government challenge US subsidies to its own cotton farmers. In a case brought before the World Trade Organization (WTO), the complaint maintained that subsidies approved in the US Farm Bill by Congress, amounting in $12.9 billion paid to farmers from 1999 and mandated through 2007, violated rules established by the WTO. Brazil argued that the payment of such subsidies led to higher production in the US and, consequently, larger exports and a substantial decrease of cotton prices on the world market that not only affected Brazil but cotton farmers in developing countries around the world. By dumping cheap cotton on the global market, Brazil argued that the US had caused "serious prejudice" to the country according to Article 5(c) as stated in the Subsidies and Countervailing Measures Agreement that one member of the WTO should not "cause adverse effects to the interests of other Members."[2] A WTO panel ruled in favor of Brazil, and the US appealed to the WTO's Appellate Body AB in 2004, but the ruling was upheld in March of 2005 by deciding that US subsidies are not exempt from Brazil's challenge under the Agreement on Agriculture's "peace clause." The case, won by Brazil, was celebrated by the "Cotton-4," the African countries of Benin, Burkina Faso, Chad, and Mali, which produced approximately 10% of all cotton on the global market, and had thrown their support behind Brazil. Brazil became the champion of protecting poor cotton farmers around the world and their right not to have their livelihood threatened by cotton subsidies paid in the US.

Expectations ran high in the developing countries who interpreted the landmark case as a first step in supporting their own farmers by challenging rich countries and their subsidies in other agricultural production. Yet the US was not willing to change its agricultural policies simply due to a ruling of the WTO. In 2014, after minor tweaks to the US subsidy policy and threats of trade retaliation by Brazil, the US and Brazil reached a bilateral agreement for the US to provide a one-time payment of $300 million to the Brazilian Cotton Institute for the adverse effects experienced by cotton farmers in Brazil. The hope that the case would bring change in subsidy policies and trade rules, and more equity between rich countries and developing countries, including the protection of the livelihood of poor farmers, seemed to vanish. However, the millions of African cotton farmers, who were not involved in the US-Brazil agreement, began to receive development assistance that was designed to enhance their ability to compete globally. Although helpful, cotton farmers in Africa remain vulnerable to the volatility of and low prices in the worldwide cotton market.

Communitarian ethics and development

Utilitarian and social contract ethics do not exhaust the approaches to moral reasoning about trade. Another approach that has gained wide currency is communitarian ethics. Unlike utilitarianism and social contract theory, communitarian ethics does not begin with the individual as the primary reference point for calculating aggregate benefits (utilitarianism) or distributing benefits of cooperation (social contract theory). According to communitarian ethics, the primary reference point for ethical reasoning should be the particular values and cultural identities that unite members of the community in relationships of solidarity.

We noted in Chapter 2 that one reason for preferring the community over the individual as a starting point for ethical reasoning is the historical priority of the community as a basis for individual development. Simply stated, the basic interests, values, and moral psychologies of individual persons are largely, if not entirely, shaped by the cultural mores of the communities with which they identify. From the moment we are born, our sense of self, including our self-confidence to act independently in the world, is forged by caring relationships of trust that extend from family to friends, neighbors, and members of our extended community. The intimate associations that make up our extended communities are ultimately bounded by the nation in which we claim citizenship. Nationality is a significant source of linguistic and cultural identity, perhaps more so in the case of smaller nations that possess a distinctive religious or "ethnic" identity. However, even vast multicultural nations, such as the United States, are perceived by its members as designating a protected sphere of national caring, so much so that feelings of patriotic loyalty can inspire them to undergo great sacrifices to secure their mutual defense. Beyond the bounds of national unity, our solidarity with strangers wanes.

Several important consequences follow from this fact about communitarian solidarity. First, as Michael Walzer notes in *Spheres of Justice* (1983), solidarity presupposes a sense of intimacy or closeness, which cannot obtain so long as non-members are treated the same as members. As he notes, a world in which there was no distinction between insiders ("us") and outsiders ("them") would be a world of strangers unbound by any caring attachments. Of course, there are relatively unbounded communities, such as neighborhoods, into and out of which residents and passersby can enter and exit at will. But within the neighborhood there will still be closed communities (families, clubs, and religious associations). More importantly, the territorial integrity of an open community such as a neighborhood or municipality will depend on its insertion within a larger community, such as a nation, that cannot be entirely open to migrations of strangers without ceasing to function as a community of mutual care. Persons will not sacrifice resources necessary to discharge basic social (welfare) functions for strangers who have no connection to them.

Communitarianism thus opposes the free movement of people *and* goods across borders to the extent that it threatens the ethical values solidifying the community. Because the values of a community are rooted in its traditions and collective democratic choices, the precise extent to which they harmonize with specific immigration and trade policies will vary from country to country. A nation whose basic values are liberal democratic – privileging individual freedom of choice over a specific, comprehensive conception of the individual's and community's good – will incline toward policies favoring freer trade and more open immigration. By contrast, a nation whose values are more collectivist – privileging, for example, a religious vision of the individual's and community's good – will incline toward policies favoring more restrictive trade and immigration.

For that reason there is no hard and fast communitarian rule prescribing what a community's trade and immigration policies ought to be. A theocratic monarchy such as Saudi Arabia will predictably prohibit entry to persons who are perceived as hostile to its aristocracy and fundamentalist religion, and it will tightly control the freedom of the few non-Muslims it admits as guest workers. Secular democracies won't be nearly as closed as Saudi Arabia's monarchy. However, they might deny entry to adherents of certain ideological or religious sects if the majority perceives them as subverting liberal democratic values. They might even refuse to trade with countries that oppose these values. And liberal democracies will protect their domestic industries through subsidies and restrictive tariffs on imports for the sake of preserving time-honored ways of life (such as family farms and artisanal crafts). Indeed, as we observed earlier, it is not unreasonable to expect that under a global free trade regime developing nations might also restrict global commerce. For example, they might resist a global "monoculture" such as "McDonaldization" if it threatens to supplant more sustainable local ways of life.

But seen from another perspective, the corrosive impact of global trade and Western mass consumerism on the developing world might be assessed more positively. Many traditional cultures in developing countries impose patriarchal norms that stifle women's development. These norms sometimes require women to live a life of domestic seclusion without education, outside employment, or inclusion in public, political life. Global trade can create a dynamic of upward mobility, an aspiration for achieving a "middle-class" life of increased income, consumption, employment, and overall opportunity that encourages families to employ and educate their female members outside the home. Microfinancing institutions (MFIs) such as Mohammed Yunus's Grameen Bank that almost exclusively target women for small business loans might not empower women politically or increase levels of consumption dramatically; the positive benefits they sometimes yield by enabling the purchasing of durable goods that can increase production must be weighed against their negatives – meager returns on investment, high interest rates, and indebtedness (Karim 2011). Needed still are better-paying jobs for women outside the local economy that connect them to the global economy. With better-paying jobs requiring higher levels of education, women in the developing world will make even greater strides toward becoming full-fledged citizens of their communities.[3]

Summary

In this chapter we have discussed how different ethical approaches – human rights, utilitarianism, social contract theory, and communitarianism – assess global trade from a developmental perspective. Human rights advocates ask whether all persons who are impacted by trade policies can achieve a minimum threshold of well-being conducive to living a life of dignity. Trade policies – and *all* unregulated forms of free trade – that harm the economies of local communities by destroying jobs, denying people opportunities to earn a livable income, or denying them access to basic essentials such as food and water, violate the human rights of both individuals and communities. However, even trade policies that respect human rights can still be unfair if they obstruct development or disrespect a community's core values and identity.

Other ethical approaches to trade and development address these last concerns. Utilitarianism attaches supreme ethical value to trade policies that promote the greatest well-being for the greatest number. Well-being, of course, can mean many things, such as freedom or stability, which do not enter into economic measurements of consumption. This explains why utilitarianism presents such an elusive approach to ethical reasoning. That said, the kinds of trade policies utilitarian ethics would promote under ideal circumstances might well favor a free flow of labor, goods, and services. Conversely, utilitarianism might favor restrictive trade policies geared toward limiting the negative externalities produced by unregulated market economies.

Utilitarianism is just as ambivalent in guiding our ethical reasoning about trade policy under non-ideal conditions. Calculations that take into account the principle of marginal utility might favor trade policies that disperse global wealth more evenly, by protecting the fragile and often less efficient economies of developing nations. People in affluent nations stand to benefit from trading with people in less affluent nations to the extent that the latter increase their power to purchase the goods produced by the former. On the other hand, trade policies that shield developing domestic markets from foreign competition might weaken the economies of more developed countries, thereby triggering global recessions that lower global consumption and production across the board.

Utilitarian ethics might not always favor trade policies that benefit the worst off. It might endorse trade policies that harm a minority of some (national or global) population for the sake of maximizing greater benefits to the majority. Under conditions of extreme scarcity, utilitarianism might even support a "lifeboat ethic," or triage principle, that permits (and possibly requires) diverting resources from the few who are the neediest to the many who are less needy (and less costly to maintain). So-called "rule utilitarians" like J. S. Mill, however, will consider the unreliability of calculating the effects of specific acts and will recommend policies based on general rules that have proven their utility over time, such as the social contractarian principle touting the benefits of free and equitable cooperation.

Social contract ethics assesses the rightness of trade policies based on their acceptability to those who are directly or indirectly impacted by them. Prudential forms of this theory assume that consent is always constrained by strategic bargaining threats. These forms therefore do not condemn trade agreements that disproportionately benefit the richest and most powerful parties.

Libertarian contractarians, by contrast, will regard the poor's consent to such trade agreements as having been coerced, unless the poor are guaranteed an inviolable right to subsistence. For instance, they will condemn as exploitative agreements that provide subsistence wages to starving workers in exchange for slave labor under a different name. They will favor trade agreements that level the playing field, so that all parties have the same freedom to buy and sell without restriction. No nation, no matter how powerful, should claim preferential treatment. Finally, libertarian contractarians will endorse compensating nations that were wrongfully exploited in the past. Pursuant to the demands of compensatory justice, former colonial governments in Europe and elsewhere are here advised to grant their former colonies a favored trade status enabling the latter to sell goods to the former at above-market prices.

Welfare contractarians go further than their libertarian counterparts. They endorse trade agreements that favor the least well-off party regardless of past historical injustice. Like Rawls, they might do so as part of a temporary policy of assisting burdened societies to the point where they can join the global society of "well-ordered" peoples as equal and independent partners. Self-interest – the mutual desire of all nations to achieve international peace and security – might be the main (prudential) reason motivating this duty in the beginning. However, welfare contractarians hope that more dignified motives, such as caring and friendship, will replace self-interest as a reason for helping nations.

Other welfare contractarians[4] demand more. They endorse international trade policies that favor the least well-off party as a matter of (distributive) justice. This comports with their view that the global order, encompassing both nations and individuals, is similar to a global government, with global economic multilaterals such as the WTO structuring opportunities for development. Accordingly, they see no reason not to apply Rawls's difference principle globally, which mandates terms of trade only if they substantially benefit the worst-off nations. Therefore they endorse trade policies that protect the fragile industries of developing nations from destructive forms of foreign competition; and they endorse rules guaranteeing that workers employed by foreign businesses receive living wages, benefits, and workplace protections conducive to development. Trade agreements that perpetuate dependency and underdevelopment clearly violate this policy of distributive justice. Less clear, however, is whether welfare contractarians would also endorse policies that impose burdens (and even sacrifices) on wealthy nations (and wealthy individuals) for the sake of improving the lot of the poor.

Finally, communitarian ethicists raise concerns about the impact of trade policies on communal values, identities, democratic choice, and ways of life that they deem to be vital to caring relationships. They criticize unregulated trade policies that allow the global spread of a mass consumer monoculture; for such a culture elevates self-centered narcissism and hedonism over preservation of tradition and community. They therefore endorse the right of communities to limit imports that corrode their cultural values, which today almost always includes respecting human rights. As for this last value, they should endorse global trade to the extent that it promotes the empowerment of women.

Although the five major ethical approaches I have discussed propose different standards for evaluating trade policies, it is likely that on many points they converge. For instance, trade policies that promote development arguably promote global security and social stability, which in turn promotes communal solidarity. Of course, these values sometimes clash in our assessment of the developmental gains afforded by any give trade policy. Weighing their impact will require finer-grained judgments that transcend theoretical speculation. For this reason, human rights, with all of their internal complexity and ambiguity, should remain the touchstone for assessing the morality of international commercial transactions.

Questions for discussion

1   What are some of the main arguments for the positive consequences of global free trade? What are some of the main arguments for the negative consequences of global free trade?
2   Should we look to develop trade policies that favor those nations that have been victims of historical injustice? Why or why not? If we should, to what extent should developed nations be responsible for compensating these injustices? How could this be done?
3   Of the five main ethical approaches discussed in this chapter, which do you find most valuable in assessing trade policies with respect to development? Why? Which is the least convincing? Why?

Notes

1   A recent report from the Potsdam Institute for Climate Impact Research suggests that roughly 16% of the world's population rely on international trade to cover their agricultural needs, with "North African, Arabic and Andean countries display[ing] the highest shares (>50%) of dependent population" (3): 66 countries, mainly situated in Africa, were found to be "unable to produce all the crop products they currently consume due to water and land constraints, even if their potentials for cropland expansion were taken advantage of. Future population growth will exacerbate this situation leading to up to 5.2 billion people dependent on external water and land resources, and thus, on international trade. Finally, up to 1.3 billion people may be exposed to longer-term food insecurity by 2050 in low-income economies (mainly in Africa), if their economic development will not allow them to afford productivity improvements, cropland expansion and/or imports from other countries" (7). http://iopscience.iop.org/article/10.1088/1748-9326/8/1/014046/pdf
2   T.B. (2005); the first section of this case study is taken from this brief.
3   The limits of microlending as a means for economic development and female empowerment are discussed by Ingram (2018).
4   Miller (2010).

Suggested reading

Naomi Klein (2008). *The Shock Doctrine: The Rise of Disaster Capitalism.* London: Picador Press.

In her book, Klein analyzes the neoliberal policies flowing from Milton Friedman and the Chicago School economists that, through free trade policies, have negatively affected the world's poor.

Charles Mills and Carole Pateman (2007). *Contract and Domination*. Cambridge: Polity Press.

Mills (author of *The Racial Contract* [1997]) and Pateman (author of *The Sexual Contract* [1988]) collaborate in this penetrating critique of classical social contract theory, which has traditionally been invoked in ways that have excluded the voices and interests of women and racial minorities.

Jeremy Rifkin (2013). *The Third Industrial Revolution: How Lateral Power Is Transforming Energy, the Economy, and the World*. New York: St. Martin's Press.

With respect to international trade, Rifkin suggests in this book the need for utilizing information technology to build lateral, rather than traditionally hierarchical, trade networks that can directly benefit both the developed and developing worlds. With respect to the effects of globalization, Rifkin provides a look at both positive and negative features of our current, highly globalized world.

Peter Singer (2004). *One World: The Ethics of Globalization*, 2nd edition. New Haven: Yale University Press.

Singer's book presents several key arguments for a development ethic largely based on the utilitarian approach to solving issues of global development, and it demonstrates many of the key problems and benefits of globalization.

Online Sources and Visual Media

Center for Global Development Website (2018). www.cgdev.org/.

This website provides numerous policy reports and resources concerning global trade data.

Tom Heinemann (Director) (2010). *The Micro-Debt* [Documentary].

This controversial documentary questions the alleged successes of micro-finance. It examines the performance of Yunus's Grameen Bank in its home country of Bangladesh and the allegation (dismissed by Norwegian government) that Yunus illegally diverted $100 million in Norwegian donations in 1996 into Grameen Kalyan, a sister company of the bank (Yunus was later fired as the bank's chief managing officer for what some believe to be political reasons).

International Monetary Fund Website (2018). www.imf.org/external/research/index.aspx.

The IMF's website contains continually updated economic reports concerning global trade and development.

Helena Norberg-Hodge (Producer) and Steven Gorelick, Helena Norberg-Hodge and John Page (Directors) (2011). *The Economics of Happiness* [Motion Picture]. Australia: Local Futures.

This documentary depicts many consequences of an increasingly globalized world and individual communities' efforts to maintain local sustainability.

References

Fader, Mariancla et al. (2013). "Spatial Decoupling of Agricultural Production and Consumption: Quantifying Dependences of Countries on Food Imports Due to Domestic Land and Water Constraints." *Environmental Research Letters* 8. http://iopscience.iop.org/article/10.1088/1748-9326/8/1/014046/pdf.

Ingram, David (2018). *World Crisis and Underdevelopment: A Critical Theory of Poverty, Agency, and Coercion*. Cambridge: Cambridge University Press.

Karim, Lamia (2011). *Microfinance and Its Discontents: Women in Debt in Bangladesh*. Minneapolis: University of Minnesota Press.

Miller, Richard (2010). *Globalizing Justice*. Oxford: Oxford University Press.

Rodrik, Dani (2011). *The Globalization Paradox: Why Global Markets, States, and Democracy Can't Coexist*. Cambridge, MA: Harvard University Press.

T. B., Simi (2005). "Brazil-US Upland Cotton Dispute." *Trade Law Brief, Centre for International Trade, Economics & Environment (CUTS)*, at www.cuts-citee.org/pdf/TLB05-02.pdf

4 Development and aid

Global financial institutions and private donors

In Europe, WWII ended with the unconditional surrender of Germany to the Allies on April 14, 1945; on the deck of the battleship *Missouri*, a representative from the Japanese government signed a document of unconditional surrender on August 4, 1945. The most destructive and devastating war in human history had ended – Germany, Austria, and Poland lay in ruins, Russia had suffered the loss of over 20 million people, England was exhausted, and the economies of other European nations were in tatters. On the other side of the globe, Japan's occupation of China, Korea, Burma, and other Asian countries and islands in the Pacific had resulted in widespread loss of life and economic disaster. Of the five great Allied powers (England, France, China, Russia, and the United States) only the US survived the war without being invaded, bombed, or occupied by one of the Axis nations. At the peak of its power, the United States used its hegemonic influence to establish both international economic and political institutions that were designed to avoid the policies that led to WWII.

Near the end of WWII, the United States, along with England and 44 other Allied nations, met to discuss a new global political and economic system that would avoid what were considered as causes of the Second World War. Called the Bretton Woods Conference, its purpose was to plan an international framework that defined the economic relations among nations throughout the world. We will cover this in greater detail later in this chapter, but for now it is important to mention that the formation of bilateral aid and multilateral aid started at this conference. As a reminder, bilateral aid is government-to-government financial aid. In most cases, governments in developed countries provide this aid in loans to developing countries. It is also often the case that a portion of this aid is funneled through international multilateral organizations such the World Bank, IMF, and the United Nations, dispersed under the auspices of United Nations International Children's Relief Fund (UNICEF) or United Nations Development Programme (UNDP), which is described as multilateral aid.

Bilateral aid and multilateral aid are part of official development assistance (ODA) already explained in the introduction. In order to track the amounts of aid provided to developing countries, wealthy countries that provide ODA are members of a group called the Development Assistance Committee (DAC), which is part of the Organization for Economic Cooperation and Development (OECD), founded in 1961 with its headquarters in Paris, France.[1] For example, total volume of ODA to economically improving nations such as Brazil and China decreased during the period 1960–73, while total aid provided remained the same in real terms. From 1974 until 1989 and the end of the Cold War, in real terms ODA increased. During the 1990s, when the proxy conflicts between communism and the West disappeared and donor fatigue set in due to the perception that aid to sub-Saharan Africa did not provide the expected results, aid to developing countries fell. It rose again after the Millennium Development Goals were agreed upon and has continued to increase, with a brief dip in 2015, until the present.

Since 2000, the allocation to certain sectors is revealing: aid to the health sector has increased due to the DAC members' commitment to the Millennium Development Goals and its focus on reducing preventable diseases such as malaria, and in response to the AIDS pandemic; aid to the education sector, however, has fallen since many developing countries have used their own resources to improve their educational systems; aid in the sectors of governance and institution-building has increased dramatically for those countries that are experiencing post-conflict challenges; aid to economic infrastructure has decreased, due to major donors of the DAC (perhaps subscribing to neoliberal policy) who support market financing for large economic projects; multisector aid is growing due to the acknowledgement by DAC members that governments in developing countries should have more input on the allocation of ODA; and non-sector aid varies significantly from year to year based on humanitarian and disaster relief, as well as debt relief.

The list of developing nations that are eligible to qualify for and receive ODA is constantly monitored and changing because of their development status. Aid can, of course, go to countries not on the ODA recipient list, but it is important to note that aid allocated to wealthy countries not on the list does not formally qualify as ODA. Countries in the Middle East, the Caribbean, and Southeast Asia are part of the growing list of countries that have been taken off the ODA recipient list because they meet the measurement indicators for social progress and increasing income levels. In light of the fact that approximately 50% of the population lives below the poverty line throughout sub-Saharan Africa, aid has continued to increase significantly to those recipient nations. Since 1970, because of the political strife and economic instability resulting at the end of the Cold War, those countries added to the list include 10 countries located in the former Soviet Union.

In 2016, the 23 members of the DAC provided a total of US$142.6 billion in net official development assistance,[2] an increase of 8.9% over the previous year. Of this amount, the US was the largest donor by volume in providing US$33.6 billion, an increase of 7% from 2015. Following the US during the same year were Germany ($24.67 billion), the United Kingdom ($18.01 billion), Japan ($10.37 billion), and France ($9.50 billion), respectively. The European Union donor countries in the DAC has grown from 15 in 2011 to 30 as of 2018, and this group provided $81.3 billion of the total volume of ODA in 2016; from the 1970s onward, this group has contributed more than half of the total ODA during the last 25 years. Yet the US ranks 22nd and contributes much less as a percentage of its gross national income (GNI). Since the United Nations established a benchmark of 0.7% of GNI that wealthy countries should give for ODA, the US has been invariably below the 0.3% average for the DAC. Only Denmark, Luxembourg, Norway, Sweden, and the United Kingdom have reached or surpassed the United Nations goal set for ODA, with Germany meeting this goal in 2016; as a percentage of GNI, Norway contributed 1.11% while the US contributed 0.18% in 2016.

In terms of gross ODA, the 10 countries receiving the largest flows of aid in 2016 include in descending order: Afghanistan, India, Vietnam, Syrian Arab Republic, Ethiopia, Indonesia, Pakistan, Jordan, Kenya, and Iraq. By region, of the gross ODA contributed, sub-Saharan Africa receives 22.8%, Southern and Central Asia 11.8%, Other Asia and Oceana 9.6%, Middle East and North Africa 9.4%, and Latin America and the Caribbean 7.3%. Some rather interesting examples of individual DAC country contributions include: Spain, whose ODA increased by 192% in 2016 for debt relief to Cuba; Turkey, whose aid increased by 63.8% for humanitarian relief; Malta, whose ODA increased by 24.6% for its general aid program; and the US, who lists its top ODA recipient countries as: Afghanistan, Israel, Egypt, Iraq, Jordan, Pakistan (of which the majority amount of ODA is for security assistance), and Kenya, Nigeria, Tanzania, and Ethiopia (which almost exclusively is in the form of economic and development assistance).

Why aid?

Aid as Self-Interest:[3] One of the main justifications for providing bilateral aid is, of course, national self-interest. According to this view, aid is employed by a country to advance its own economic and foreign policy interests. Aid is used as a reward, for example, for voting to support a US-led initiative or policy in the United Nations, or in granting the US favored-nation trade status. Almost all of the industrialized or Western nations engage in this type of aid, namely, to disperse aid selectively to those developing nations that return geopolitical advantages or economic benefits.

Aid as Prudential: Another major justification for aid to developing countries is that poor, vulnerable people who cannot help themselves and whose governments are without adequate resources need help – that bilateral aid provided from wealthier nations can indeed make a difference in the lives of people who need basic services such as healthcare, access to safe water, education, and shelter. When certain members of Congress joined with advocates on behalf of the United States Agency for International Development (USAID) to successfully resist its incorporation under the US Department of State, it was seen as a victory for those who believed aid to developing countries was not exclusively a matter of national self-interest.

Aid as Obligation: The UN Declaration of Human Rights (1976) and the International Covenant on Economic, Social and Cultural Rights (1966) maintain the perspective that aid should be considered an obligation that wealthier nations have in relation to people living in developing countries who have a right to food security, a basic primary education, and healthcare. If these fundamental needs are positive rights (as discussed in other chapters of this book), then the developed countries have the obligation to meet these needs in the form of providing bilateral aid to nations that do not themselves have adequate resources to ensure these basic needs.

Aid as Compensation for Colonial Exploitation: Another perspective on bilateral aid has an historical framework. In 1884–85 the Berlin Conference was convened and brought together all of the European nations interested in partitioning the continent of Africa as colonial possessions. Germany, France, Portugal, England, and Belgium formalized each other's colonial boundaries in west and central Africa, and after the conference in east Africa as well. Western missionaries imposed Western religion and culture, while colonial administrators imposed an economic system that denied millions of people of their human rights, land, identity, freedom, and independence. For some European leaders, as well as global social activists, economists, philosophers, and Africans themselves, the legacy of colonialism has left the African continent poorer and more vulnerable to control by global financial institutions and the larger global economic system. Compensation in the form of aid for continuing inequitable economic policies that still favor former colonial powers is therefore the only means by which developing countries in Africa can hope to improve the livelihoods of their people.[4]

Aid regimes and the dominance of the US

Historians agree that one of the most important causes of WWII was the worldwide depression that started in the 1920s and grew worse during the early 1930s. One way of dealing with the economic challenges faced by nation states at this time was to devaluate currency as a means of increasing exports. The reaction by other countries was to establish higher tariffs in order to protect their own vulnerable economy. The result was a downward spiral of global protectionism that entrenched and worsened the worldwide depression. The two political changes that followed and changed the course of history were the election of Franklin Delano Roosevelt as president of the United States in 1932, and the rise of Adolf Hitler and the Nazi Party in 1933. Hitler invaded Poland in September of 1939, and from that time until August 1945 the world was plunged into terror and destruction.

To avoid the economic instability and chaos that characterized the pre-war years and ultimately led to WWII, the United States, along with its allies, organized the Bretton Woods Conference. One of the driving motivations for the American contingent behind the conference was to begin thinking in internationalist terms, and to design through international institutions an economic order that promulgated equity, social progress, and security not only for the United States but for nations and people around the world. What Roosevelt had achieved domestically by adapting Keynesian policy, the Bretton Woods Conference would achieve internationally. And since the United States was the preeminent power in the world at the time, unrivaled in economic, military, or political power, the American representatives were convinced they had the prerogative and moral authority to not only establish the conference agenda, but to propose an international economic framework that enhanced its own prosperity as well as that of the world. This led to the establishment of three institutions that would form a new economic order: The International Monetary Fund (IMF), created to provide loans to ensure stable exchange rates when a country's currency was in danger of devaluation; the International Bank for Reconstruction and Development (IBRD), otherwise known as the World Bank, established to provide loans for the specific purpose of major European post-war reconstruction and development projects; and the General Agreement on Tariffs and Trade (GATT), which became the World Trade Organization (WTO) and was mandated to address issues related to trade. In 1945, the United Nations was also established as an international organization with the purpose of addressing challenges to peace and security.[5]

Almost immediately, the function of both the World Bank and IMF changed. The Marshall Plan, a unilateral aid and reconstruction package designed exclusively for European countries in 1947, undercut the purpose for which the World Bank was established. It was the collapse of colonialism and the rise of national independence movements around the world during the decades of the 1950s and 1960s that redirected the World Bank's focus toward economic development instead of reconstruction and rebuilding. The IMF, which was initially focused on stabilizing national currencies that, in turn, enhanced global trade, turned to providing loans to former colonial possessions that it perceived were in dire need of development assistance.

Under the leadership and with the financial support of the United States, three of the world's most historically influential institutions had been established to provide a new economic and political world order. Yet the price of leadership is criticism, and the United States's influence over both the World Bank and IMF has been an example in the wielding of unabashed power. The United States gave itself sole authority to appoint the president of the World Bank; accordingly, all 12 presidents since its inception have been American. (The European Union has sole authority to appoint the president of the IMF.) Voting rights are based on contribution quotas; thus the wealthy, industrialized countries have retained control over the decisions made by both institutions; the US wields virtual veto power over all World Bank and IMF decisions. It is not an overstatement, therefore, to say that the decisions made by both the World Bank and IMF align with, and are favorably disposed to, the geopolitical and economic interests of the US.

The decisions made by the World Bank during the Cold War years became a focus of increasing dissatisfaction not only from developing countries, but also from European and other allies. As the United States engaged in proxy wars around the globe with its military and ideological nemesis, the Soviet Union, for political and economic dominance, under the influence of the US the World Bank and IMF made decisions that led to the protection of Western economic assets in the likely prospect of nationalization and to the overthrow of Mossadegh of Iran in 1953, Arbenz of Guatemala in 1954, Lumumba of Congo in 1960, and Allende in Chile in 1973, as well as the financing of dictators and regimes that violated human rights, of which Pinochet in Chile is one of the most odious examples. During these years, the World Bank and IMF primarily functioned as a financial middleman between the US and its democratic allies and non-communist nations in the developing world to shape economic interests to those of the US. From the decade of the 1960s through the 1980s, because of the fact that the IMF and World Bank were reliant upon the US for a large portion of their funding, the US Treasury was given extensive oversight and monitoring privileges. During this time, the Treasury department rejected loan requests (over the objection of other WB members) to Sandinista Nicaragua, Communist Vietnam, and Allende's Chile, while approving requests from the dictators in the Philippines and Zaire.

The watershed moment: the oil crisis, OPEC, and the rise of neoliberalism

From the time of its inception to 1968,[6] the World Bank crafted a public image that it was a successful organization in development finance: its ideology and social mission consisted in lending for large public-sector economic programs that improved the world; it was committed to prudent fiscal decision-making; and all of its discrete projects involved a comprehensive technical analysis and solution. In 1956, however, at the insistence of the US, members at the bank voted to create the International Finance Corporation (IFC) with the mandate to encourage private enterprise overseas, and in 1960 the International Development Association (IDA), which arranged financial terms for those poor nations that were unable to pay their loans under the bank's regular terms of repayment. The IDA was established as an alternative to the UN's Special United Nations Fund for Economic Development, which did not come under US control. In the mid-1960s, the bank started to finance projects in agriculture and education in Africa.

When Robert McNamara became the fifth president of the World Bank in 1968, after his tenure as CEO and reorganizer of Ford Motor Company, and after his effort as Secretary of Defense to restructure the Pentagon as well as America's defense industry, his vision for the bank's role in the worldwide economic system changed it dramatically and forever. Immediately after assuming the presidency of the bank, he presented his plan to the board of governors that included: (1) that the bank would lend as much in the next five years as it had in its entire history; (2) that lending would refocus on poor countries in Latin America and Africa who lacked resources; (3) that priority financing would be given to education, agriculture, and population control. Borrowing activity skyrocketed from $735 million in 1968 to $1.3 billion in 1971; by the time McNamara stepped down from his position at the bank in 1981, borrowing had increased to over $5 billion and the institution's projects had expanded to over 2,600 worldwide. Most telling, however, was that even though he had given a speech to the Bond Club in New York in 1969 in which he emphasized that the World Bank was a "development investment institution" and not a "social welfare agency," by 1973 he had successfully reoriented the bank's focus from discrete infrastructure projects in developing nations to the "elimination of absolute poverty" in those poorest of nations whose populations lived in "utter degradation." Within the first three years of McNamara's presidency, staff grew by 75% and, in an unprecedented cultural change that would later drive the worldwide expansion of US-influenced financing and unacceptable and morally compromising conditionalities for structural adjustments programs, remuneration incentives at the bank were tied to the number of loans handled.

The debt crisis

A number of unpredictable crises led to a destabilization of the global economy during the 1970s. The collapse of the Bretton Woods system in 1971 was the first of these crises. Currencies throughout the world had been linked to the US dollar, which, in turn, was linked to the gold standard. Too rigid a system to continue with the growing complexity of the global economy, the fixed currency exchange rate system collapsed when the US decided to break the link between the dollar and gold.

Yet it was the aftermath of the 1973 oil crisis that led to a watershed moment for the World Bank, the IMF, and the policies that they represented on behalf of the Western nations.[7] Assuming that the cost of a barrel of oil would not be increased by the Organization of Petroleum Exporting Countries (OPEC), Western nations expected a continuation of the status quo. Developing nations, however, saw an opportunity to publicize the economic inequality between them and the industrialized countries.[8] The Group of 77,[9] a collection of developing countries formed out of the United Nations Conference on Trade and Development (UNCTAD), convinced OPEC to use the oil crisis as a bargaining tool to advocate for major changes in the worldwide economic system. When OPEC decided to triple the price to purchase a barrel of crude oil, the Western nations were shocked and forced to listen. Then again, in 1974, OPEC doubled prices for its crude oil. Almost simultaneously, food prices doubled due to production issues in numerous countries around the globe. Consequently, inflation doubled in all developed countries; inflation in the US rose from 3.3% in 1971 to 11.1% in 1973. Compounded by a stock market crash in 1973–74, the US and other developed nations faced declined growth. Combined with increasing inflation and a growing unemployment rate, the result was "stagflation." When another oil price increase hit in 1979, there was a consensus in the wealthier nations that a more conservative approach was necessary to stabilize the worldwide economy.

Soon afterwards, in order to reduce inflation the developed nations implemented restrictive monetary policies, which increased interest rates. Under Paul Volcker, the US Federal Reserve Board raised interest rates sharply in October 1979. This became known as the "Volcker Shock," and it had a direct bearing on a large number of developing countries' ability to continue their debt servicing or payments to the World Bank and IMF. Due to slow worldwide growth, increasing interest rates, and unfavorable trade conditions, developing countries were having more and more difficulty meeting their balance-of-payment obligations. In 1982, Mexico was the first country to announce that it could not meet its as-scheduled debt service without rescheduling or the infusion of more loans. The announcement was followed by wave after wave of African and Latin American countries issuing the same assertion – which lasted for the entire decade of the 1980s.

The weak response from the financial institutions within the affected international community led to what is one of the most traumatizing and harmful decades in the history of Latin America and sub-Saharan Africa. For Latin America, the poverty rate increased to 48.3% in 1990 from a rate of 40.5% in 1980; this poverty rate would return to its 1980 level 25 years later in 2005. For sub-Saharan Africa, the poverty rate also did not return to its 1981 level until the year 2005, 25 years later, and its gross domestic product (GDP) also took 25 years to return to its level in 1981. Moreover, during the decade of the 1980s, many developing countries became financial resources exporters, so to speak. Due to the debt crisis, capital inflows decreased dramatically while debt servicing rose steeply. This reverse flow of financial resources hurt South America the most when capital inflows amounted to $13 billion from 1980–81, but reverse flows of financial resources to World Bank and IMF and wealthy countries amounted to an astounding average of approximately $25 billion annually for the years 1983–89. The fact that developing countries relied heavily on short-term debt contributed to and worsened their situation, but it is undeniable that the debt crisis was not all of their own making. Most distressing, due primarily to the debt crisis, was that commitments to alleviating poverty by governments in Latin America and sub-Saharan Africa were hindered for a quarter of a century.

Exacerbating the debt crisis were the pronouncements and policies of what came to be known as the "Washington Consensus." Late in McNamara's presidency at the World Bank, he and his staff became convinced that "structural adjustment" lending was a way to help developing countries meet their debt service. Similarly, in order to address the economic challenges due to the debt crisis confronting developing countries, the IMF established a policy that was called "IMF conditionality." This measure included the approval of new loans based on structural conditionalities or structural adjustments and required governments in developing countries to engage in economic deregulation, privatization of state-owned companies, capital liberalization, open markets, and the expansion of trade. Under the influence of Ronald Reagan and his conservative policy advisors (economic and political), the US Department of the Treasury joined with the World Bank and IMF to promulgate these policies; since all of these institutions were based in Washington, DC, the policies were dubbed the "Washington Consensus." In the beginning, the Washington Consensus was concerned with reforms that focused on liberalizing, privatizing, and stabilizing national economies. Under the influence of Reagan and his advisors (the policy known as "Reaganomics"), the Washington Consensus began to absorb and incorporate into their policy reforms a neoliberal ideology or market fundamentalism that broadened their vision and approach to dealing with the economic problems of developing countries. Uncompromising in their approach, the advocates of neoliberalism maintained that economic development requires unregulated free trade and free markets, unrestricted flows of capital across borders, reduced or minimal taxation for both the corporate sector and individuals, and a minimal or scaled-back role for government that translates into minimal involvement and minimal intervention in a national economy.

As structural adjustment policies were implemented in many developing countries, there was a growing concern among international aid agencies, NGOs, and the United Nations that retrenchment of government, the reduction in social expenditures, wage decreases, and the general Washington Consensus assumption that market fundamentalism led to sustained economic growth and development, was misguided and even counterproductive. The UN's World Economic Survey reported that the average annual growth (GDP) in developing countries was 3% during the 1980s and per capita growth 1%. For the poorest and most vulnerable people, economic and social infrastructure support had been compromised. In addition, real wages had fallen by approximately 20% in many developing countries. Although it was true that structural adjustment programs provided evidence of eliminating hyperinflation, reducing developing country budget deficits, and helping to maintain debt payment schedules, there was also growing evidence made public by UNICEF that there was declining income and reduction in social services, especially healthcare services for children, throughout developing countries. And contrary to the assumptions of the Washington Consensus, structural adjustment programs and the underlying neoliberal policies – that unfettered free markets will lead to development – did not address the structural problems that gave rise to the searing poverty that a large portion of the earth's population suffered.

Case study: Zambia, the copper mining industry, and structural adjustment

Can reliance on global finance save poor countries from the collapse of global commodities markets?

In 1960 when Zambia gained its independence,[10] its first president embarked upon a nationalization policy for the country's most important industries that was intended to redress the extraction of resources under the colonial regime. This included the copper industry, which provided approximately 80% of the country's foreign exchange and a similar percentage of formal sector employment. However, due to a worldwide recession and a precipitous decline in the price of copper, the state-run copper industry experienced a drop in production and exploration for new sources of copper halted. From 1969 to the early 1990s, copper production fell by almost 60% and Zambia Consolidated Copper Mines found itself $800 million in external loan debt. Having regularly produced 90% of Zambia's export earnings, by the early 1990s this figure had dropped to 50%. A new president elected in 1993 welcomed the loan money that accompanied the World Bank's structural adjustment program for Zambia. The government agreed to privatize 280 public companies, lift all restrictions on imports and exports, eliminate custom tariffs, and eliminate price controls for all agricultural produce. The government's agreement to also reduce expenditures in order to meet debt relief payments led to a new user fee for Zambians to access healthcare services, freezes in wages for all government employees, and immediate layoffs and resulting loss of wages for between 60,000 and 72,000 workers as a result of privatization. Another burden of the debt repayment was the effect on education: in 1991, the government had apportioned $60 for the education of a child in primary school – by 1999, that figure had been reduced to $15 per child. Since the cost of the structural adjustment program was felt most by the poorest segment of Zambia's society, children were forced to quit school in order to work for their household's survival. By the late 1990s, primary school attendance rates had dropped 20% since the beginning of the decade. In 1998, Zambia's external debt was 181% of its gross national product.

From 2004, however, worldwide copper prices improved dramatically and, due to foreign investment, Zambia was able to weather the 2008 economic slowdown.[11] From the year 2005 to 2014, copper prices increased from $2,000/mt to $5,500/mt in 2014. Yet the poorest demographic groups in Zambia didn't benefit; in the copperbelt mining towns, there had been 47 hospitals before privatization, and after privatization there were only 25 still in operation. Those people living below the poverty line of $1.25 per day was reduced from 69% in 1996 to 61% in 2010, statistically minimal to the poverty reduction program that had built upon the structural adjustment strategy conditions required of Zambia by the World Bank.

Aftermath of the debt crisis

In light of the growing publicity surrounding international debt from not only civil society but an array of social activists and high-profile individuals from the worldwide entertainment industry, and with no impact evaluations to produce evidence that structural adjustments programs led to both economic development *and* poverty alleviation, the World Bank and IMF embarked on two major initiatives.[12] First, in 1996, in order to reduce external debt burdens to sustainable levels for developing countries, the institutions created the Heavily Indebted Poor Countries Initiative (HIPC); in 2005, as an enhancement to the HIPC, they formed the Multilateral Development Relief Initiative (MDRI) to assist in reaching the Millennium Development goals. Secondly, the IMF retooled and renamed its structural adjustment program as Poverty Reduction Strategy Papers (PRSPs), which required poor country loan recipients to design a strategy that identifies the economic policies needed for poverty reduction. In order to qualify for debt relief or cancellation for loans from the World Bank, IMF, and African Development Bank, for example, a country had to: (1) submit a realistic PRSP; (2) manage its economy well; (3) curtail excessive borrowing; and (4) use money allocated for debt servicing to fund social programs. According to the IMF, there are 36 countries around the world who qualified for debt relief or cancellation, of which 30 are in Africa. The turnaround from spending more on debt servicing to social programs in health and education seems to have been dramatic; the average spending on social programs in these countries is five times more than on debt repayment. According to the World Bank and IMF, overall debt in Africa has been reduced by $76 billion; debt relief to Chad alone amounted to $1.1 billion in 2015.

The IMF has also provided new lending instruments which included flexible terms on new loans, zero interest rates on concessional loans to 2011, increased financial resources, doubling of borrowing limits, and the accommodation of increased fiscal deficits. Properly crafted and implemented, these new policies for loan conditions could have provided a more ethical and equitable response to poverty alleviate. Still, the legacy of earlier structural adjustment programs and neoliberal policies that accrue to the geopolitical and economic interests of the US remains intact, with continuing emphasis on privatization of state-owned enterprises, elimination of subsidies, reduction of budget expenditures, and liberalization of the economy in general. Jamaica is a good example of this legacy.[13] Faced with growing debt much like other developing nations in the 1980s, the government accepted the IMF and World Bank's structural adjustment program. Wages were reduced and the number of nurses in the country fell by 60%, the currency devaluated, and food subsidies abolished. By 2013, Jamaica had repaid $19.8 billion; it had been given a loan totaling $18.5 billion and due to the remaining accrued interest, the country still owed $7.8 billion. Jamaica does not qualify for debt relief because the IMF and World Bank have classified it as a middle-income country.

New aid schemes

Since the beginning of the twenty-first century, the changing landscape in aid for international development has been unprecedented.[14] These new donors, or "partners" in development as they prefer to be called, are all non-DAC members and are comprised of the following three groups: southern aid providers such as China, India, Indonesia, Thailand, and Brazil; Arab aid providers such as Saudi Arabia, Kuwait, and United Arab Emirates (UAB); and private and philanthropic aid providers such as the Bill & Melinda Gates Foundation, Rockefeller Foundation, and others.

These non-DAC donors share certain policies (with the exception of the private/philanthropic providers), one of which is an explicit approach that international aid is part of a larger, comprehensive foreign policy strategy encompassing geopolitical issues and challenges, common political and economic interests, and specific recipient requests (rather than the DAC donor focus on sector-based initiatives focusing on poverty, education, health, or need). These foreign policy aid instruments include a wide range of concessional loans, trade preferences, capital investments, lines of credit, traditional grants, technical training and cooperation, and technological transfers. Most importantly, this new approach to aid also reflects a more communitarian ethic in honoring and respecting the recipient country's sovereignty, that conditionalities on aid are minimal – or in certain circumstances absent – and that the term "partner" is preferred to "donor" in order to diminish the traditional aid assumptions in the terminology of "donor/recipient."

Southern Aid Providers: During the 1980s and early 1990s, approximately 80% of those living in extreme poverty were in China. East Asia received the largest amount of foreign aid; however, dramatic economic development, the "East Asian Miracle," enabled China to lift 500 million of its population out of this poverty. Eschewing the neoliberal policies that dominated international aid in the 1980s and exacerbated the debt crisis, East Asia relied on protected trade and government involvement to spur its economic development. Currently, both China and India have emerged as two of the global economy's most influential players. Between 2000 and 2014, China has given aid to 140 countries amounting to an estimated $354.3 billion; in comparison, US official development assistance during the same period amounted to $394.6 billion. Primarily focusing on infrastructure development, in 2017 China's largest recipients of its official aid include: Cuba, Cote d'Ivoire, Ethiopia, Zimbabwe, Cameroon, Nigeria, Tanzania, Cambodia, Sri Lanka, and Ghana. China has no equivalent to USAID, CIDA, or anything similar to Western nations' aid agencies; rather foreign aid is administered through a complex and fragmented system of 23 government ministries and commissions as well as state-owned enterprises and banks. All of this, of course, adds to the charge of lack of transparency from the West.

Arab Providers: Saudi Arabia, Kuwait, UAB, and Qatar have become major international aid donors. From 1973 to 2008, Arab nations have contributed an average of 13% of DAC official development aid during the same period. Preferring bilateral rather than multilateral modes of support, these countries focus on both the Middle East and sub-Saharan Africa. With few conditionalities, Arab providers fund mostly infrastructure projects in transportation and energy, but also funnel growing amounts of aid to humanitarian and refugee initiatives. In 2014, Saudi Arabia contributed 70% of all funding, or $500 million, to the UN's continuing refugee and displacement program in Iraq. In 2014, Kuwait contributed $326 million and promised another $211 million for Syrian refugee relief.[15] Keen to prove their commitment to humanitarian causes and avoid the perception of funding terrorist groups, the Arab providers have been transparent and share their official aid assistance statistics and reports with the DAC.

Private and Philanthropic Providers: Private aid from organizations such as the Bill & Melinda Gates Foundation, the Rockefeller Foundation, the Aga Khan Foundation, and others is growing at an increasingly rapid rate. Estimates are that private flows of international aid are between $56 and $75 billion annually, approximately one-third of ODA. The actors in this part of the changing international aid landscape are becoming more and more important in certain sectors, especially health and education, and have flexibility and potentially more impact with less aid. Private/public financing is an increasingly popular approach for providing financial support for health, water, agricultural, and other key sectors in developing countries.[16] The Bill & Melinda Gates Foundation, a global private foundation, focuses on funding for the global health sector. The Gates Foundation along with the Rockefeller Foundation have been at the forefront of creating private-public partnerships (PPPs) that are beginning to change the architecture of international aid. Working within an ethical framework of communalism and of human rights, and not driven by geopolitical or economic interests, these foundations maintain that national governments in developing countries do not have the required resources to deliver universal healthcare to their growing citizenry, and it is only public/private sector partnerships that will generate enough investment/ funding to provide healthcare for the globe's poorest and most vulnerable people. PPPs have been formed with multinational pharmaceutical firms such as Bayer, Bristol-Meyers Squibb, Merck, and Sanofi to develop products that address HIV/ AIDS, malaria, and tuberculosis in developing countries. A key component to these PPPs are the reduced risk for the public and private partners. For example, GAVI, the Vaccine Alliance is part of a PPP arranged by the Gates Foundation that provides funding for vaccinations and child health in low-income countries around the world. The scaling-up of PPPs is beginning to make a profound difference in pooling financial resources to address what has been considered seemingly intractable health issues in the developing world.

Conclusion

If we look at aid policy and development from the above historical approaches, the core policies and principles of the Bretton Woods Conference still have relevance for our analysis of the ethics of bilateral and multilateral aid. Assuming that both developed nations and developing nations shared a mutual interest and perceived benefits of international peace and security, the economic policies of growth through industrialization and international free trade that was to benefit all nations regardless of their size, wealth, and political importance in the new world order after WWII, ultimately led to the solidification of an unequal relation between the industrialized and wealthy nations of the West and the agriculturally based, poor nations of the developing world. These worldwide economic structural inequalities, which benefited the industrialized nations of the West to the detriment of the developing nations, naturally led to the extraction of favorable terms – economically and geopolitically – from poor nations. Threats of withholding aid, based on a wealthy nation's prudential self-interest, became commonplace strategic thought at the height of the Cold War. The admirable goals of fulfilling basic needs through economic policies that encouraged industrialization and free trade, and the human right to such things as housing, medical infrastructure, and widespread primary education in developing countries, fell victim to short-sighted strategic self-interest related to geopolitical advantages. Lacking economic and political power, and forced to act deferentially, the developing countries were relegated to playing pawns in a global chess game. The result was humanitarian and ethical consequences of historic impact – the poorest nations in the developing world began to experience more poverty.

From the early policies of the Bretton Woods Conference that promoted financial investment and industrialization in developing countries and began to define the structural inequalities between rich and poor nations, to free market liberalization and economic policy reform promulgated by the Washington Consensus, to achieving the Millennium Development Goals through Poverty Reduction Strategy Papers, the influence and continuing effects of the neoliberal framework remains intact to this day. The policies of "one size fits all" structural adjustment programs and conditionalities flies in the face of a fair and equitable way to treat all nations by ignoring context and specific issues related to national development. Creating a "spiral of dependency" as described in Chapter 3 of this book, the violation of the free trade principles that underlie the international trade system by the developed countries for their own benefit is just one example of the hypocrisy inherent in the ethics of aid within the Washington Consensus. Rather than enhancing the human right to a minimum threshold of well-being for the citizens of a developing country, the bilateral and multilateral aid negotiations of the World Bank and IMF with poor-nation governments led to dominating "conditionalities" where governments were forced into signing agreements that resulted in the privatization of state-operated enterprises, a reduction of government intervention and lessening of regulations, an unrestricted flow of capital investment, opening of local markets to foreign imports, a reduction of all trade barriers, and a balanced budget (ironically rejected in the US as the "Balanced Budget Amendment" by the US Congress during the Clinton administration) that forbade budget deficits by reducing funding for essential basic social services such as primary healthcare as well as salaries and resources for primary and secondary education. Rather than corruption and government mismanagement that were the cause of weak economies in developing nations the World Bank and IMF so readily like to blame, it was instead the structural injustices within the aid agreements of those institutions that resulted in the expansion of the spiral of dependency that led to and exacerbated even more poverty in developing nations. Defying human rights advocates and social contract theorists that development aid should be tempered by considerations of equality, justice, *and* effectiveness, bilateral and multilateral aid agreements between the World Bank, IMF, and the governments of developing countries led to what might be thought of as contributing to the undermining of social contract theory as an ethical framework between wealthy and poor nations,[17] since it increased pressure to comply with neoliberal economic policy and allowed developed nations to take advantage of what has become known as "emerging markets" throughout the developing world.[18]

The new aid schemes are beginning to ethically counterbalance this market-oriented approach, with their emphasis on dispersals of aid within national contexts: Bolivia is different from Cote d'Ivoire politically, economically, and culturally, just as Botswana is different from Indonesia and Mexico is different from Egypt. This communitarian approach has a number of caveats and nuances, however. For the Asian providers and Middle East providers, aid is inexorably linked to political influence and favored trade status, for example. And although Asian and Middle East providers of aid focus on the issues of public morality related to aid and development, such as the principled adherence to a minimum threshold of well-being that focuses on access to the basic needs of food security, healthcare, safe water, and shelter, they are less concerned with the unjust violation of individual cases related to freedom of the press. Thus the convergence of concern for universal human rights and access to basic essentials and a communitarian respect for the independence and welfare of communities within developing countries, for Asian and Arabic providers of aid, and an evaluation of their impact on development, depends on the context of their application.

We find a similar, though not identical, complexity in our moral assessment when we turn to the growing amount and influence of aid from private and philanthropic providers. Functioning as funders of aid for a universal standard of human rights and respect for communitarian core values, these providers are reaching millions and millions of the poorest and most disadvantaged people in developing countries with each passing year. Yet a core criticism has been leveled at them.[19] If organizations like the Gates Foundation, the Grameen Bank (whose microfinance initiatives were discussed in Chapter 3), and other large NGOs acknowledge the *possibility* that their aid has unwittingly been part of a "band-aid" approach, which has kept the poor placated with the "crumbs of development" while discouraging calls for radically changing WB/IMF structural economic policies, they themselves can become advocates for change. Their development aid would then no longer merely meet basic needs that satisfy the threshold of living a life of dignity, but would promote equality, empowerment, and development toward creating sustainable and democratically accountable institutions across the board. Any moral assessment of the response of foundations and international NGOs to this criticism will require fine-tuned judgments and evaluations. As we have seen above, the road to development has many paths, not the least of which includes respect for national sovereignty, the welfare of a nation's citizenry, and justice for the poor.

Questions for discussion

1   What key policies came out of the Bretton Woods Conference, and what have been the effects of these policies internationally?
2   What is the "Washington Consensus" and how did it affect international aid? Were the overall effects largely positive or negative, and why?
3   What are the main differences between older forms of aid and so-called "new aid schemes"? What are the benefits of these "new aid" models, and what potential concerns should we be on the lookout for?
4   Is there a positive role for debt on the international scale? What are the benefits and risks of international debt schemes? How might we think about restructuring certain international institutions (like the World Bank, IMF, etc.) so as to make this process more equitable for less wealthy countries?

Notes

1   OECD (2011).
2   As defined by the OECD, net is "the gross amount less any repayments of loan principals or recovery of grants received during the same period."
3   Haslam et al. (2012, see Chapter 8).
4   Kelleher and Klein (2011).
5   Haslam et al. (op. cit.).

6   Milobsky and Galambos (1995).
7   Kelleher and Klein (op. cit.).
8   See World Economic and Social Survey (2017).
9   Formalized by the Group of 77 in the Declaration for the Establishment of a New International Economic Order (NIEO), the document was considered and approved in 1974 by the United Nations General Assembly. Within the Declaration, developing countries were asking for renegotiated trade agreements providing greater access to markets in wealthier nations, debt rescheduling on more favorable terms, the transfer of technology, larger amounts of aid for resource poor and least developed nations, legal regulation of multinational corporations and their operations according to national standards, and monitoring of capital flows in and out of their country. Within a few years there was a glut of oil on the international market, OPEC was forced to reduce its price for a barrel of crude oil and, as result of the disappearing economic leverage related to the control of oil supply and pricing, the industrialized nations rejected the proposal of the NIEO. There were some weak attempts to placate some of the developing nations with preferential trade agreements, but in general the rejection communicated the message that the economic issues confronting developing nations was not a shared or common interest, and that their participation in the decision-making process and deliberations within such institutions as the World Bank and IMF regarding the global economic system was neither welcome or needed. World Economic and Social Survey (op. cit.).
10   This summary is taken from DeStage et al. (2002, pp. 330–333).
11   See 2016 UNDP Human Development Report.
12   www.imf.org
13   Dearden (2013).
14   Mulakala and Schuler (2014); the following is a summary of this report.
15   IRIN News (2014).
16   Winters (2017).
17   Beyond the International Court of Justice (ICJ), the purpose of which is to settle disputes in accordance with international law that are submitted to it by nation states belonging to the United Nations, and the WTO, which was established to adjudicate disputes related to global trade issues, there is currently no such similarly functioning institution as a world court of economic justice to settle controversial issues in regard to debt forgiveness or colonial exploitation and reparations.
18   Kelleher and Klein (op. cit.).
19   Wallace (2004).

Suggested reading

Life and Debt (Documentary).

This 2003 film from director Stephanie Black and screenwriter/narrator Jamaica Kincaid exposes the catastrophic impact of IMF and WB structural adjustment policies on Jamaica from the 1970s through the 1990s.

Richard Peet (2007). *The Geography of Power: Making Global Economic Policy*. London: Zed Books.
Joseph Stiglitz (2002). *Globalization and Its Discontent*. New York: W.W. Norton.
Susanne Soederberg (2004). *The Politics of the New International Financial Architecture: Reimposing Neoliberal Domination in the Global South*. London: Zed Books.
World Economic Survey (Various years). www.un.org

Internet sources

The Asia Foundation: www.asiafoundation.org
The Bill & Melinda Gates Foundation: www.gatesfoundation.org

International Monetary Fund: www.imf.org
Third World Network: www.twnside.org.sg
U.S. Agency for International Development: www.usaid.gov
World Bank: www.worldbank.org

References

Dearden, Nick (2013). "Jamaica's Decades of Debt Are Damaging Its Future." *The Guardian*, April 16, 2013. www.theguardian.com/global-development/poverty-matters/2013/apr/16/jamaica-decades-debt-damaging-future.

DeStage, Rick, Ailsa Holloway, Dan Mullins, Leah Nchabeleng and Penny Ward (2002). "Learning About Livelihoods: Insights From Southern Africa." *Oxfam*. www.imf.org.

Haslam, Peter, Schafter, Jessica and Pierre Beaudet (2012). *Introduction to International Development*, 2nd edition. Oxford: Oxford University Press.

IRIN News (2014). "Gulf Countries: Growing Aid Powers." *IRIN News*, September 17, 2014. www.irinnews.org/news/2014/09/17/gulf-countries-growing-aid-powers.

Kelleher, Ann and Laura Klein (2011). *Global Perspectives*, 4th edition. London: Pearson.

Milobsky, David and Louis Galambos (1995). "The McNamara Bank and Its Legacy, 1968–1987." *Business and Economic History* 24(2): 167–195.

Mulakala, Anthea and Nina Schuler (2014). "Non-DAC Providers." *The Asia Foundation*. https://asiafoundation.org/publication/the-changing-aid-landscape-in-east-asia-the-rise-of-non-dac-providers/.

OECD (2011). "Measuring Aid: 50 Years of DAC Statistics – 1961–2011." *OECD*. www.oecd.org/dac/financing-sustainable-development/development-finance-standards/MeasuringAid50yearsDACStats.pdf.

Wallace, Tina (2004). "NGO Dilemmas: Trojan Horses for Global Development." *Socialist Register*. www.socialistregister.com/index.php/srv/article/viewFile/5818/2714.

Winters, Janelle (2017). "The Surge of Public-Private Partnerships for Health Since the Millennium." *Global Health Governance Program*. http://globalhealthgovernance.org/blog/2017/7/21/the-surge-of-public-private-partnerships-for-health-since-the-millennium.

World Economic and Social Survey (2017). "The End of the Golden Age: The Debt Crisis and Developmental Setbacks: Chapter 3." *United Nations*. https://wess.un.org/chapter3/.

5 Climate change, sustainable development, and the limits of green capitalism

Helping poor countries surmount obstacles to development may be less about financial assistance and investment than about helping all of us on this planet to secure stable and sustainable ways of life. Development no doubt requires growth sufficient to raise the poor's standard of living. But growth comes with a price: exploitation of non-renewable resources, environmental degradation, and expenditure of energy that drives up atmospheric temperatures. As for this last cost, we need only recall World Bank President Jim Yong Kim's dire warning that despite our best efforts to moderate global warming, "we could witness the rolling back of decades of development gains and force tens of millions more to live in poverty."[1] It bears repeating that poor people on this planet, most of whom live in areas and engage in occupations most vulnerable to extreme weather events, will be harmed the most by global warming. Their suffering should trouble the conscience of all of us.

In this chapter we will explore the ethics of sustainable development, both as it applies to our current global economy and as it might apply to a more ideal economy. Following the pattern set forth in previous chapters, we begin by asking how major ethical approaches perceive the problem of sustainable development in our current, non-ideal world. Then we assess the potential of that world's dominant economic system, which for lack of a better term I shall designate "global capitalism," to achieve a level of sustainability conformable to our ethical expectations.

Our survey of the public morality of sustainable development appropriately begins with utilitarianism. Aiming to promote public well-being, utilitarian reasoning is the approach that governments are uniquely equipped to implement, given the vast resources and coercive powers that they command. Not coincidentally, utilitarianism as applied by British political economists in the eighteenth and nineteenth centuries first raised the question of sustainability. The most renowned representative of that school who discussed sustainability, Thomas Malthus (1766–1834), questioned whether food production could keep pace with population growth. In more recent years so-called neo-Malthusians have broadened their focus to include the environmental limits to growth in all its aspects. Concerns about resource depletion and global warming complicate utilitarian reasoning about how economic growth might ameliorate global poverty. We cannot simply bank on "green" technology to solve the problem of sustainable growth in time to avoid planetary catastrophe. Public morality imposes duties on governments and citizens to develop such technology, but it is unclear whether the historical tendencies of a capitalist economy as it has evolved up to the present allow governments and citizens enough room to maneuver in this regard.

Another theoretical underpinning of public morality, social contract ethics, raises the all-important question whether (and if so, how) nations of the world can agree on rules that fairly distribute the burdens and benefits of sustainable development. Nations might agree to distribute these burdens and benefits in a way that is mutually acceptable to both developed and developing countries simply out of enlightened self-interest. After all, an environmentally healthy planet is a public good whose sustainability makes life more secure for everyone. But wealthy and powerful nations might also calculate that it is in their best interest to make poorer and weaker nations carry the greater burden of climate change and climate control. Likewise, wealthy individuals within a nation might be reluctant to accept norms of sustainable development that threaten their commercial interests, so long as they can insulate themselves from the harms associated with unsustainable growth. Again, current generations might find it in their interest to shift the burden of implementing sustainable development policies onto future generations. In sum, a purely prudential social contract ethics would not condemn agreements that enabled the wealthiest and most powerful among those living today to extract "concessions" from others who cannot leverage the same bargaining threats.

Libertarian contractarians in the tradition of Locke and Nozick insist that non-coercive agreements incorporate stronger moral side constraints, including basic liberties and rightful access to sustainable living conditions for everyone. Being loath to use government coercion as a remedy for social problems beyond threats to individual liberty, they look instead to voluntary exchanges between producers and consumers. In other words, they see the problem of sustainable development as properly falling within the province of private morality. In their opinion, economic markets are the most efficient means for negotiating solutions that take into account all the social costs and benefits of development. According to them, determining the extent of an industry's property rights – including the right to pollute – boils down to how much consumers and producers are willing to pay for allowing the exercise of that right versus how much pollution-haters are willing to pay for disallowing it. If the parties in question cannot work out an agreeable settlement balancing their interests, which is often the case when they encompass many different communities of interest, courts may assign the primary right to those who are most harmed by the exercise of the other's right, and then allow the latter the option of doing business as usual while compensating those who are harmed. As for public morality, if developed nations got a "head start" in unsustainable industrialization through historical injustice (colonialism, say) then libertarian contractarians would endorse compensating former colonies for this injustice. Compensation might involve permitting developing nations to postpone implementing slow-growth policies that developed nations should impose on themselves; or it might involve helping these countries develop green industries. In the final analysis, libertarian social contract ethicists agree with human rights activists that all persons on this planet have a natural right to live a dignified and sustainable life, free from the unjust constraints imposed by the main perpetrators of environmental devastation.

Welfare contractarians will endorse this right but disagree with their libertarian counterparts about the justice of social inequality. Following the libertarian approach, those who make their demand effective through markets or bargaining are typically the wealthy. Poor people simply do not have the financial resources necessary to buy out polluters or litigate settlements in civil courts. Welfare contractarians therefore argue that government must regulate business on behalf of the least well-off, perhaps by capping the social damage done by industry and then allowing businesses to trade (purchase from each other) carbon- and other pollution credits. International agreements should also prioritize the welfare of the poorest and most vulnerable nations (and peoples). Welfare contractarians, like their libertarian counterparts, would endorse an unequal distribution of burdens in international efforts toward reducing energy consumption. However, their reasoning would not exclusively flow from a principle of compensatory justice. Invoking a principle of impartiality (or reciprocity), they would impose greater sacrifices on developed countries for the sake of distributive justice, or improving the lives of the worst off, regardless of their historical relationship to us.

Human rights advocates insist that forms of development that violate human rights are immoral. In contrast to proponents of utilitarianism and prudential social contract ethics, they reject the idea that basic human rights can be compromised for the sake of maximizing overall or average welfare, or bargained away for the sake of securing a minimal level of physical security. The most pressing challenge for human rights advocates is justifying a human right to sustainable development. As I noted earlier, a community's human right to development depends on securing the human rights of its individual members, and vice versa. These different rights might imply conflicting duties with regard to sustainable development.

Insofar as human rights impose duties on governments to protect equally the dignity of each and every individual subject to their legal power, they have been traditionally understood as falling under the domain of public morality. However, movement has been under way to make non-state entities such as global economic multilaterals and even privately owned transnational corporations their addressees as well. Indeed, we all have personal moral duties not to disrespect the rights of others, foremost among them being the right not to be harmed. So, even though we as individuals might not be burdened with a duty to positively develop the lives of distant others in sustainable ways, we are burdened with a relatively unconditional duty to not harm them. We act unjustly when, by our personal consumption, we contribute to deadly pollution and global warming that asymmetrically harms distant others, and we do nothing to offset that harm.

Communitarian ethics presents a fruitful premise on which to explore such conflicts. Indigenous communities are among those most threatened by unsustainable forms of development, even though they contribute the least to pollution and global warming. The broader communities wherein they reside (nation states) invoke the right to development whenever they promote the building of hydroelectric dams, mining operations, ranches, and farms. Even when such projects benefit the nation as a whole they encroach on the sacred lands of tribal peoples, wreaking havoc with their traditional ways of life. The conflict between communities raises profound questions about the right of cultural communities to preserve their way of life. From a communitarian perspective, this right appears basic. However, cultural communities do not exist in isolation from each other. Intercultural exchanges invariably change cultural identities, so that if cultures survive into the future, they do so by communicating with and adapting to other cultures.

The science of climate change

Two decades from now the Arctic ice cap will no longer be visible from outer space. The Inuit who have inhabited the Arctic for thousands of years have already seen their way of life threatened. Hunters have died for lack of ice shelters. Less floating ice to break up waves makes sea travel precarious and melting permafrost that turns to mushy bogs makes land travel all but impossible. The caribou the Inuit hunt die from ice caused by rain; prevented from eating the lichens that constitute their main food source, their population has dwindled to a few hundred from tens of thousands. The seals and bears the Inuit hunt depend on floating ice for breading and foraging, but fewer and smaller flows that float far beyond land has meant that their populations are now doomed to extinction.

In 2005 the Chair of the Inuit Circumpolar Conference submitted a petition to the Inter-American Commission on Human Rights on behalf of the Inuit of the Arctic regions of the United States and Canada arguing that the impact of global climate change caused by the "acts and omissions" of the United States violated the fundamental rights of the Inuit peoples. The conference noted that

> To Arctic indigenous peoples, climate change is a cultural issue . . . We are a part of the environment and if, as a result of climate change, the species of animals on which we depend are greatly reduced in number or location or even disappear, we as peoples would also become endangered as well.

Of course, the deadly consequences of climate change are being felt everywhere. Rising sea levels will likely submerge the Maldives and other Small Island Developing States (SIDS) completely, even if the two-degree Celsius target set by the 2015 Paris Agreement on climate change is achieved. The long-term projection of a five-meter rise in sea levels portends catastrophic consequences for the one billion people (mainly poor) who inhabit coastal regions that are less than one meter above sea level. Extreme weather events such as droughts and hurricanes have markedly increased and will continue to do so for the indefinite future. Massive food and water shortages are on the rise, along with tropical diseases. Counterbalancing these negative effects are some positive ones, however. Climate change might well increase food yields in the northern latitudes.

Despite these projections, the greatest challenge to reasoning ethically about climate change remains the uncertainty of its trajectory and impact. The *precautionary principle* counsels us to assume the worst possible outcome in devoting scarce resources to combatting climate change and counteracting its effects. At the other end of the spectrum *business as usual* discounts risk entirely on the assumption that technology will save us. A middle approach recommends weighing outcomes in terms of their likelihood, which can be adjusted further by weighing more heavily catastrophic outcomes. Adding to this uncertainty is the temporal dimension for calculating costs and benefits. Should we factor in the harms and benefits that will accrue to future generations? If so, how? In general, the costs for controlling climate change will be borne by present generations, while the benefits will accrue to future generations. And speaking of costs, because the greatest cost of climate change is loss of life, how do we place a monetary value on *that* in calculating how much climate-related loss of life is morally tolerable? And how does economic development impact these calculations? If we presume that future generations will be richer than we are, we who live in the present generation might not think it fair to sacrifice so much of our consumption for their benefit. But that is only one possibility. All things being equal, global warming increases with population growth, so future generations might suffer a catastrophic decline in their standard of living. Population collapse leading to the decline in civilization and even to the eventual extinction of the human species as we know it cannot be ruled out.

We cannot begin to reason ethically about these questions unless we know a little more about the science and economics of climate change. Twenty thousand years ago the earth was five degrees cooler than it is now. The resulting Ice Age caused sea levels to decrease by more than 100 meters. Small fluctuations in temperature can therefore have dramatic effects.

Today's greenhouse effect is caused by atmospheric gases that absorb infrared radiation from a solar-heated earth. Water vapor is the greatest contributor, but the sharp increase in global temperatures over the last 200 years is almost entirely caused by increases in carbon dioxide, methane, ozone, nitrous oxide, and chlorofluorocarbons (CFCs) linked to human activity. The earth's natural carbon cycle depends on the ocean absorbing carbon from the atmosphere (which causes potentially dangerous acidification) and plants absorbing carbon during photosynthesis. Carbon from the ocean gets absorbed by minerals such as limestone and carbon from plants gets absorbed by plant-eating life forms. Carbon oxidizes when it is returned to the air, which happens innocuously when animals breathe and when minerals containing carbon are dissolved; it happens less benignly when plants and their fossilized remnants are burned for clearing or fuel. In the last half-million years, continuing up to the dawn of human industrialization, CO_2 levels fluctuated between 200 and 300 parts per million (ppm). Today that level stands at about 400 ppm.

Methane levels have also sharply risen from pre-industrial levels of 700 ppm to 1,700 ppm today, mainly as a result of farming (especially the production of meat) and natural gas extraction. In addition, large concentrations of methane embedded in glaciers are released during ice melts. Methane is less common than CO_2 (to which it oxidizes in 12 years) but is a much more potent greenhouse gas.

The use of CFCs has been banned since 1987, but this extremely potent green-house gas remains in the atmosphere for a long time. Low-level ozone, unlike high-level ozone, is bad for the planet and has doubled since pre-industrial times. Nitrous oxide levels have increased because of the heavy use of nitrogen fertilizers. Altogether, these secondary greenhouse gases combine with CO_2 to comprise an "effective carbon dioxide concentration" of about 485 ppm (in comparison to the pre-industrial level of 285 ppm). Finally, global warming generates an important positive feedback loop: the creation of larger concentrations of atmospheric water vapor. (The cooling of the atmosphere caused by increased cloud cover pales in comparison.)

The evidence for anthropogenic climate change is incontrovertible. The Inter-governmental Panel on Climate Change (IPCC) that summarizes the work of leading scientists shows that the average temperature of the earth has risen by three-quarters of a degree since 1850 and is currently rising at a rate of about .13 degree per decade. Sea levels have risen 17 centimeters over the last 100 years and are now rising at a rate of 3 centimeters per decade.

Scientists center their predictions of future climate change on the "equilibrium climate sensitivity" number. This number predicts how high the temperature of the earth would rise if the concentration of CO_2 were to double from its pre-industrial level and remain constant. This number is significant because that concentration (currently calculated at 550 ppm) will likely be reached within a few decades from now. The IPCC calculates that there is a 10% chance that temperatures will rise only 1.5%. It estimates that there is a 66% chance that temperatures will rise between 1.4% and 3.8%, and a 5% chance that they will rise six degrees. It also calculates that there is a much smaller probability (one chance in 100) that they will rise 10 degrees. This extremely wide temperature range reflects the complex influences that impact global climate. But a probable increase of at least two or three degrees would endanger the survival of 20–30% of the world's species along with the oceans' coral reef populations. The effect on human population would be deadly. By 2030, between 75 and 250 million people living in Africa will likely face acute water shortages due to drought. The massive displacement of human populations due to coastal flooding was mentioned earlier. According to one estimate, beginning in 2030 1 million people a year will die from the effects of climate change. Furthermore, just slight increases in temperature may produce disproportional effects. Global warming increases disproportionately relative to increases in greenhouse gas emissions; and the effects of global warming increase disproportionately to increases in global warming.

How should we respond to the uncertain increase in temperature and its uncertain effects? The administrations of George W. Bush and now Donald Trump proposed to do nothing. Their recommendation – wait to act until all the information is in – makes sense only if there is no basis for calculating probabilities and the worst possibility is not catastrophic. The opposite, precautionary approach also seems untenable in some of its formulations. As stated in the World Charter for Nature adopted by the UN General Assembly in 1982, one formulation recommends that "where potential adverse effects are not fully understood, the activities should not proceed" (Broome 2012, p. 119). Because we can never fully know the effects of any activity, following this advice would require suspending all forms of production and consumption.

A more balanced response involves maximizing the expected value. Maximizing the expected value involves choosing that option whose likelihood of occurring will yield the best benefit (or yield the least bad harm). A gambling option that yields a 50% chance of winning $100 – whose expected value is $50 – is better than an option that yields a 75% chance of winning $60 – whose expected value is $45 – or an option that yields a 10% chance of winning $400 – whose expected value is $40.

Applying this reasoning to minimizing expected harms is more complicated. Because of the diminishing marginal value of any good, it is more rational to avoid greater risks than to maximize small gains. If my rare violin is valued at $100,000 and there is a 1% chance of it being destroyed during shipping to a buyer, maximizing my expected value from shipping it would require that I pay no more than $1,000 in shipping insurance. However, because the destruction of the violin would yield a catastrophic loss of $100,000, I will be willing to pay more than the expected value of shipping it. Purchasing a $1,050 insurance policy might be rational in light of the insignificant loss of $1,050 in savings versus the significant loss of $100,000.

Calculating the expected value of insuring while factoring in the diminishing marginal value of savings that come from not insuring suggests an analogy with calculating the expected value of insuring against climate change while factoring in the diminishing marginal value of the savings of not insuring against it. Rationality recommends a risk-averse approach to insuring against climate change catastrophe that falls short of the more extreme versions of the precautionary approach while also conservatively hedging against simple maximization of expected benefit. That explains why an unlikely (1%) probability of a truly catastrophic 10-degree temperature increase is much more significant than a likely (66%) probability of a possibly manageable 1.4 to 3.8 degree temperature increase. Of course, the relative significance of each probability depends on assigning a numerical value to the human cost of each expected outcome. How does one put a price tag on human life? On culture and our natural environment? A 10-degree increase in temperature would replicate the earth's climate 200 million years ago, when most of Antarctica was melted and sea levels were 70 meters higher than they are today, swamping the low-lying plains of what are today the world's most fertile lands. Under this scenario, the collapse of human population, the decline of civilization as we know it, and even the extinction of the human species are all possible.

The economics of climate change

From an economics perspective, the disproportionality factor discussed above suggests that mitigating climate change now can produce very great benefits for the future. As a science of costs and benefits, economics aims to promote the least wasteful and most efficient expenditure of resources. In principle, markets efficiently register the costs and benefits of goods and services according to the principle of supply and demand. But climate change is not factored into the cost of production and consumption. It is an externality, or hidden cost of doing business. Its negative side effects might not ever be felt by those who are chiefly responsible for causing them. Therefore, failure to factor these costs into the normal transaction of doing business indicates an inefficient use (or waste) of resources.

One way to factor in the cost of climate change is to tax the emissions that cause it. A carbon tax would be equivalent to the "carbon price," or social cost of carbon, that is to say, the monetary value of the harm it causes to persons. Not surprisingly, economists disagree on what this amount is. Politicians have therefore chosen a different mechanism for assessing the cost of emissions, called "cap and trade." Each country within a cap and trade market – the system has yet to be adopted worldwide, but the EU has done so with some success – is allotted a limited (or capped) number of carbon credits, which it distributes to emission-producing businesses. Businesses who want to emit more than they have been credited have to purchase additional credits from businesses who have emitted less than they have been credited. In effect, the carbon price of an emission is the price it would fetch if traded in a carbon market. If the cap is set very low, there will be fewer carbon credits distributed to businesses and demand for them will be high relative to supply, raising the price of credits. If done properly, the cap will reflect the social cost of carbon, meaning that it will be set sufficiently low to encourage emissions reductions. However, given the politics of cap and trade, negotiators set the cap at a level that they think will stabilize temperatures at some desirable level. But determining what this level is cannot be left to scientists or economists, for what is desirable is a question to be deliberated upon, if not resolved, democratically.

Still, we can speculate about what is desirable. Let us assume that doing business as usual is not desirable, because it allows a few wealthy emitters to benefit at the expense of the world's poor and future generations, which is clearly inefficient (if not unjust). A more desirable option is to set the level of emissions very low, but without demanding that wealthy emitters sacrifice their standard of living. It is more desirable because the world's poor and future generations will benefit from lower temperatures. It is desirable to the rich emitters, because they can be compensated for their cost in reducing emissions. For instance, governments can divert a portion of public tax revenue toward subsidizing the retrofitting of polluting factories with green technology. The present generation can be compensated for helping future generations, by saving less and leaving less for future generations.

Is this the most desirable option? Not if justice matters. It is wrong that persons who are harmed by a person's actions have to pay that person to stop harming them, especially when harm is not mutually inflicted. Nor is the option desirable from the standpoint of efficiency, because it is inefficient to distribute resources to rich persons from persons who have (or will have) fewer of these same resources. The best option thus requires that the rich emitters sacrifice in reducing their emissions. However, as John Broome remarks, pursuing this option is a strategic mistake. It makes the best the enemy of the good. Aiming for efficiency with sacrifice rather than efficiency without sacrifice is to encumber the task of climate change with the much broader task of improving the distribution of resources between nations.[2]

Put simply, wealthy nations will not cap their emissions if doing so requires sacrificing their standard of living. Therefore, for strategic and political reasons it makes sense to *first* pursue the second, less just and less efficient option. After this option has been successfully pursued, the other task of sustainable development – the redistribution of resources between the wealthy and the poor (and future generations) – can be tackled. Ideally, the third option is the best; but given our non-ideal world, the second may have to do for the time being.

Developing for the future and climate change

Development and mitigating the effects of climate change stand to benefit future generations more than the present generation. Yet it is the present generation that will shoulder the cost of these benefits. Is that fair? Is it efficient?

To answer that last question first, we need to think about economics. Investing for climate change has what economists call an opportunity cost: a lost opportunity to invest that money on other things, such as present-day consumption. Some economists think that a dollar invested for enhancing present-day consumption is better spent, or more valuable, than if it were spent on enhancing future well-being, through improving development and controlling the effects of climate change. If we are willing to borrow $100 at 5% interest (at a total cost of $105) to pay for a bag of rice today instead of waiting a year to buy the same bag for $102, it is because we value the rice more today than we will a year from now. The value of rice a year from now should be discounted by 3%. Another way to understand discounting is to recall that economists factor growth into the value of investment. If the average annual return on an investment of $100 is expected to be 5%, or $105, then the persons benefiting from the investment should be expected to pay back a percentage of the $100 in interest (this is needed to insure that the money is not wasted when it could have been spent on other investment opportunities). After deducting, say, 3% interest, the effective amount of the loan is discounted to $97 after the first year. If the loan is not paid back after the first year, the compound interest will continue to discount the value of the loan by some percentage annually.

What this suggests is that we should discount future consumption in comparison to present consumption. To use the above example, we should allot $97 to future consumption of rice for every $100 allotted to present consumption of rice. Another way to look at this is in terms of the diminishing marginal benefit of money. The $100 that can be spent on buying a bag of rice today will buy 5% more rice one year from now (the investment can be expected to grow 5%). But a quantity of rice that is 5% greater than a bag of rice provides a diminishing marginal benefit. For example, if consuming at least a bag of rice suffices to save the life of a starving person, consuming any more rice beyond that amount will produce a benefit that is less than life-saving.

What does all of this have to do with thinking about investing in climate change? *If* we assume that the economy will continue to grow, then it is reasonable to assume that future generations will be better off than the present generation. From this standpoint, economic efficiency dictates that because the present generation is needier than the future generation, we should discount the economic development that benefits future generations and spend proportionally more on the present generation. (Notice, too, that the principle of diminishing marginal benefit implies that the rich today should give more of their wealth to their poor contemporaries. Prioritizing the worst off is both efficient and, from a Rawlsian social contractarian perspective, just, if we view intergenerational investment as a kind of cooperative transaction.)

This argument needs refinement. Currently, economists use the money market to determine interest rates and growth, which they calculate to be around 6%. The market, they maintain, is a democratic method for setting the discount rate of money because it expresses market preferences. However, the problem with this is that market preferences don't tell us much about how we value things. Is a bag of rice today really more valuable to us than a bag of rice tomorrow? True, we prefer to buy the car now because we are impatient and don't want to delay our gratification. But that should not affect our valuation of the car, especially when the preferences of future persons are not counted at all. Perhaps a more democratic valuation of commodities would be reflected in informed deliberation (using speculative or counter-factual reasoning) about their present and future desirability when seen from the perspective of future generations ranging over many possible scenarios.

These options, or possibilities, must factor in the impact of climate change on economic growth. As we have seen, it is within the range of possibility that growth in population and productivity will steeply decline over the next 100 years, so much so that both total and average (per capita) well-being are diminished. In that case, the present generation should not be prioritized and the welfare of the future generation should not be discounted.

The 2007 Stern Review on climate change judiciously acknowledges a fuller range of possibilities and accordingly sets the discount rate at about 1.4%. This is based on aggregating a full range of climactic probabilities and their effects on growth over a span of years. It suggests a middle position between two extremes: utilitarianism, which recognizes no discounting of future welfare at all (and places equal value on the well-being of persons, no matter when and where they live), and prioritarianism, which discounts future well-being – and among some economists, *entirely* discounts future well-being. Whereas utilitarianism would seem to demand great sacrifices in the present for the sake of maximizing future well-being, prioritarianism would seem to dictate the exact opposite. But prioritarian thinking – which discounts the welfare of future persons at a constant rate – also seems counterintuitive in a way that utilitarianism does not. It implies that the death of 1,000 people 1,000 years ago is as bad as the compounded discounted deaths of tens of millions of people today. Indeed, totally discounting future welfare would mean that I should make choices now about my personal welfare that I now know I will regret having made from the standpoint of the future.

So the Stern Review's recommendation about discounting the value of future commodities – but not discounting the value of future welfare – seems a good compromise. And its low discount rate of 1.4% – in comparison to the high discount of 6% as set by the money market – seems right as well. This means that the present generation may have to sacrifice for the sake of ensuring that future generations are able to have on average the same quality of life we have now, but not sacrifice as much as utilitarianism, which does not discount the value of future welfare at all, would demand. Of course, if we believe that the average quality of life on this planet is unacceptably low given the huge numbers who currently live in extreme or severe poverty (or underdevelopment, however that is defined), then we will have to adjust upward the level of sacrifice needed to bring about a fully sustainable and fully developed future.

Now that we understand the economics of discounting, let us return to the economics of sustainable development. Economic growth contributes to population growth until both begin to level out. Population growth, in turn, contributes to climate change. But climate change, in some possible scenarios, slows and even reverses economic growth. This reverses development and increases poverty, which historically leads to higher birth rates as well. So, the problem from the standpoint of an ethics of sustainable development is to achieve a felicitous balance among three interrelated factors: population growth, economic well-being, and climate stability.

Now, we intuitively think that the way to increase well-being is to slow population growth and even, if possible, reverse it. China's one-child-per-family policy, coercive as it may be, seems wise from this perspective: fewer mouths to feed means more left over for everyone else and less pressure to engage in greenhouse gas–producing economic growth. However intuitive that may be, China has been forced by economic realities to abandon that policy. Its population is aging, its rising middle class wants a higher standard of living, and it needs more economic growth – and more young workers – to sustain that growth.

But there is another reason to question China's one-child family. It presumes that adding more future people who fall within a neutral range of well-being – neither poor nor rich – is irrelevant to our understanding of well-being. However, this seems wrong. A policy that harms the well-being of existing people while also adding more people might increase total well-being if the well-being of the newcomers is sufficiently high. If the well-being of the newcomers is on average higher than the well-being of existing people, it will increase average well-being, as well.

These considerations help us to assess how bad a decline in human population might be as a result of climate catastrophe. If you think that valuations of well-being should be neutral with respect to the number of existing people, then the prospects of population collapse should not bother you. However, if you disagree with this view, and believe that, within a range of satisfactory well-being, it is better to have more people than less, then population collapse should surely be considered a catastrophic bad. To begin with, we would have to factor in the absences of people who would have been born had their ancestors not died. Each death means as well the death of a line of descent numbering hundreds of thousands of persons. That would be bad from the standpoint of a utilitarian ethics that prescribes maximizing total global well-being. Second, we would have to factor in the decline in the quality of life caused by wars over scarce resources, the decline in civilization (the arts and sciences) and development, generally. This would be bad from the standpoint of a utilitarian ethics that prescribes maximizing average well-being. Finally, we would have to factor in the possible extinction of the human species. It may be that no species can sustain its population indefinitely. But the imminent extinction of the human species within a relatively short span of 1,000 years must be considered very bad from the standpoint of an existential ethics that values meaningfulness – identifying oneself with a past and future humanity whose existence transcends one's own and is, in some respects, more important than one's own.

Climate change justice

The preceding discussion about the economics of climate change and sustainable development has focused on the ethics of welfare, the province of utilitarianism, not on the ethics of justice. It should be clear by now that welfare is a fraught concept. Total and average utilitarian approaches calculate welfare differently. Prioritarian and marginalist considerations complicate this calculation. Although some of the goods that make up welfare can, in principle, be given a monetary value, others, such as natural beauty, or happiness, cannot. And even those that can, in principle, be given a monetary value, can be assigned that value using different methods, most of them premised on assumptions that can be questioned from this or that perspective.

We will now turn to the other concern regarding the public morality of climate change: justice. We have already encountered it in our discussion of prioritarianism. In that discussion, however, the question about whether distributing resources should be generationally partial was framed in terms of economic efficiency. However, if we think of generations as cooperating with each other over time, then we can also speak about the fairness of the terms of that cooperation. For instance, we can ask whether it is fair that the present generation sacrifice for the future generation (and vice versa). We can ask, in other words, whether the welfare of the present generation should get priority over the welfare of the future generation (and vice versa). Asking these kinds of questions makes intuitive sense when speaking about families. We think it not unjust that parents sacrifice a bit of their time, effort, and resources on their children, with the expectation that their children will do the same for them when they get old. To take an example closer to the topic of the present chapter, we might think that a son or daughter has a moral right to inherit the family farm, but only on condition that he or she maintains it for the next generation. The family analogy is apt for another reason. Some of the demands that children and parents make on each other have less to do with cooperation than with human rights. Although a stranger might permissibly neglect to feed your child, your failing in this capacity would be very wrong (assuming you were capable of doing so), simply because your child has a right to be nourished (if you neglected to feed your child, the duty to feed your child might then fall on an assignable stranger, such as a government agency; if neither of you fulfilled the duty, both of you would be doing wrong).

Let us begin with the approach to justice taken up by social contract ethics. It is perhaps easier to see how justice relates to cooperative schemes that connect members of the same generation. The least morally demanding ethic of cooperation (the variant associated with Hobbes) presumes that nations cooperate exclusively to advance their own people's interest and that it is not unreasonable for them to distribute the burdens and benefits of doing so in a way that acknowledges the privileges of power. It was this understanding of international cooperation that led us to tentatively conclude that the best strategy for getting concerted climate change reform off the ground was not by pursuing the most just or best policy. Because a powerful nation like the United States ought not to be expected to sacrifice its high standard of living for the sake of reducing its very high per capita emission of greenhouse gases, the proper strategy for securing its cooperation in an international climate control effort is to find some way to compensate it, so that it will be motivated to reduce its emissions without having to sacrifice anything. Weaker countries, for instance, might lower their tariffs and even subsidize US businesses so that these businesses recover the cost of retrofitting their productive capacity with greener technologies.

As attractive as this strategy is in the short term, it is not the best policy to pursue in the long run. As the global balance of power shifts, emerging economic powerhouses such as India and China will demand compensation as well, along with Europe and Japan. A collective action problem known as the prisoner's dilemma will threaten to undermine climate change cooperation: in pursuing their nation's self-interest (the avoidance of national sacrifice) powerful countries will extract concessions from poorer countries, making these countries poorer and exacerbating their higher population growth, degradation of natural resources, and so on. The result will be a collective catastrophe – a continuous rise in carbon emissions – that will be the worst possible outcome for all nations.

A more morally demanding ethic of cooperation that descends from the Lockean social contractarian tradition would condemn power-constrained international cooperation as too coercive. This ethic might as well condemn the current climate policy of business as usual as unjustly coercing weaker nations such as the Maldives into abandoning their land and way of life. If wrongful coercion is understood to mean the violation of property rights, then the emission policies of powerful nations violate the property rights of the Maldivians by causing the inundation of their islands. Likewise, any advantage in industrialization that resulted from the wrongful colonial extraction of resources, enslavement of colonial peoples, and so on would also be undeserved when viewed from this Lockean perspective. Therefore, in an exact reversal of what Hobbesian social contract ethics prescribes as reasonable, Lockean contractarianism would prescribe a reverse flow of compensation and sacrifice. Wealthy and powerful nations would be obligated to compensate poorer, less powerful countries for the present, past, and future harms they have (or will have) inflicted upon them. Even if one adopted a "statute of limitations" that forbade punishing presently existing people for the harms inflicted by their ancestors, the unreciprocated harms presently inflicted on poor, weaker nations by wealthy, powerful nations would suffice to obligate the latter to compensate the former.

Of course, compensation – a backward-looking approach to remedying past injustices – would not erase the ongoing harm, extending well into the future, that wealthy, powerful nations inflict on poor, weaker nations. Because Lockean contract theory allows for the unequal distribution of the benefits and burdens of cooperation only on condition that doing so does not threaten the right to life of any person who would thereby be affected, it would require that wealthy, powerful nations undertake considerable sacrifice in altering their current pattern of consumption and production. In this respect it converges with the human rights approach: policies that threaten life itself wrongfully violate or at least render insecure the exercise of a basic human right.

Lockean social contract ethics is libertarian: it condemns actions and policies that wrongfully impede the rights of individuals and nations to freely access goods essential to life. Beyond imposing a negative duty to desist from wrongfully harming others, which it interprets to mean disrespecting others' property rights (including the right to life itself), it does not specify any positive duties, other than the duty to enforce these rights by creating the appropriate legal institutions. Rawlsian social contract theory, by contrast, is egalitarian: it condemns actions and policies that do not also positively assist others in realizing more robust expectations of social cooperation. These expectations stem from viewing as morally undeserved the freedom-constraining circumstances in which individuals and nations find themselves. No individual can be said to deserve his or her genetic endowments and familial inheritance. No nation can be said to "deserve" the land and natural resources it legally controls. Being arbitrarily assigned, these advantages and disadvantages should not impact the distribution of opportunities for well-being, unless allowing them to do so benefits the worst off individuals (or nations).

Rawlsian social contract ethics, at least insofar as it concerns economic distribution, has sometimes been interpreted as a kind of prioritarianism. Rawls's difference principle expressly states that economic inequalities should be arranged so that they benefit the worst off. This is a vague and potentially undemanding principle that Rawls himself sought to strengthen by linking it to the ideal of citizenship within a liberal democracy. So understood, the principle requires a considerable redistribution of wealth, insuring that everyone not only has equal opportunities to become educated and develop themselves as active participants in political life, but that civil and political rights have equal value for each person. In other words, impartiality in reasoning about democratic fairness suggests that everyone should have ample resources enabling them to exercise their rights equally.

As we saw in Chapter 3, Rawls's own understanding of the qualified application of this democratic model of political cooperation to the international arena led him to endorse the idea that each sufficiently developed nation should cooperate with other similarly situated nations in assisting underdeveloped nations (burdened societies) to achieve a decent level of self-sufficiency, or well-orderedness. Cooperation in this endeavor requires that burdens and benefits be apportioned on the basis of each nation's proportional capability. Richer nations, in other words, should assume more of the responsibilities attendant upon fulfilling a positive duty of assistance. Applied to climate change, this understanding of just international cooperation would seem to require that richer nations make greater sacrifices than poorer nations. The duty of richer countries to shoulder proportionally greater burdens of climate control becomes even stronger if we adopt the thinking of those followers of Rawls who have a more cosmopolitan view of global cooperation. To the extent that we perceive ourselves as part of one interconnected human community that transcends borders, we will insist that richer nations shoulder a proportionally greater burden in redistributing assets to poorer nations. For, as a matter of democratic impartiality, everyone inhabiting this planet is entitled to an equal exercise of equally valued rights.

Communitarian ethics, like its social contractarian and utilitarian counterparts, presents us with a variety of ways to think about climate change. The Inuit appeal to communitarian sentiments when they condemn the erosion of their culture and community as a result of climate change. But wealthy emitter nations also appeal to communitarian sentiments when they resist climate change reform. The replacement of carbon industries such as coal mining by green energy technologies presages the end of ways of life that have been passed down within families for many generations. Scaling back economic growth means transforming engrained patterns of cultural consumption and cultural identity as well.

However unlikely it might be, climate catastrophe would doubtless have a severe impact on culture and communal life, unleashing massive conflicts and migrations. It would therefore portend the erosion of those very conditions necessary for morality to flourish. But although culture and community must persist as general prerequisites for an ethical way of life, culture, and community reflect a range of variations. Small indigenous tribes look a lot like extended families. Their cohesion (or solidarity) depends on members being alike in their beliefs and lifestyles. Large nations that have built themselves up through immigration, by contrast, are strikingly multicultural and occupationally complex. In modern Western societies, people's communal bounds are informal and contractual; they perceive themselves as individuals, first and foremost, who are free to choose their vocations, associations, and beliefs as they see fit. Such large-scale associations of loosely connected, mobile individuals may be less vulnerable to cultural and communal uprooting than their indigenous counterparts.

No doubt, both kinds of societies represent extremes along the spectrum of communitarian bounding. From a moral perspective, both exhibit distinctive virtues and vices that have proven to be functionally adaptive in their own way: individualism/self-centeredness and collectivism/group-centeredness. If neither can claim privileged moral status, then the disappearance of one or the other cannot be considered bad as such. In saying this we do not mean to imply moral or developmental relativism. All societies should allow for a reasonable range of individual assertion and communal belonging.

The disappearance of a cultural way of life is bad for those who are its last practitioners. From a more impartial point of view, the disappearance of a cultural way of life means the loss of a strand of meaning and knowledge. But the death of any particular cultural community – either through assimilation, fusion, transformation, or attrition – is a fate that will befall it sooner or later in the course of mingling with other cultures. What should concern us morally is not this natural disappearance of a cultural way of life over a protracted period of intercourse with other cultural communities. What should concern us is the coercive destruction of a cultural way of life caused by external violence perpetrated by another cultural way of life. The destruction of indigenous communities by the external imposition of a rapacious, unsustainable consumer culture, whose practitioners are mainly affluent persons inhabiting industrial societies, constitutes a serious breach of communitarian ethics and arguably a violation of human rights.

Private morality and climate change

Governments have public moral duties to advance the welfare of their own people and act justly toward other people. As individuals, we too have personal duties to advance the welfare of other *persons* while acting justly toward *them*. A utilitarian like Singer, who invokes marginalist thinking, argues that the rich should make extraordinary sacrifices on behalf of the poor. However, as a matter of fact, our capacity to improve the welfare of distant others – especially foreigners with whom we have no personal connection – might be quite limited. Therefore our duty to improve their welfare might also be quite limited.

The same does not apply regarding our duties of justice toward them. According to recent World Health Organization figures, if I live in a developed industrial nation, my personal carbon footprint over a lifetime – 800 tons – will result in lowering another person's lifespan by six months. I say another person's lifespan because the vast majority of people who are harmed by the exorbitant emissions caused by my personal lifestyle contribute but a miniscule fraction to global warming in comparison to my own contribution. If one were to place a monetary cost on the harm each of us living in an affluent society does in a lifetime it would be between $19,000 and $65,000.

Of course, my personal contribution to the total harm is also quite miniscule. Living in a rich country, it might amount to only one-half of a billionth of a degree increase over my lifetime. But combined with the minuscule contributions of several billion people in my situation, it adds up to several degrees or more of temperature increase. Even if I actually caused no harm – which is not true – my risking harm would be wrong. The carbon emissions my consumption causes are unjust if (to quote climate economist and philosopher John Broome): "The harm they do results from an action of [mine]; it is serious; it is not accidental; [I] do not make restitution; it is not fully reciprocated; and [I] could easily reduce it."[3] So, I should not emit any more greenhouse gas unless I compensate for doing so.

It might be thought that bequeathing my material wealth to those who will mainly be harmed, future people, is compensation enough. But this inheritance, which will mainly benefit family and friends, will not benefit poor strangers enough to cancel out the harm that is likely to befall them by my action. And it will not erase the wrongfulness of violating their human right to an unpolluted, sustainable environment.

How should I reduce my carbon footprint? Using only green energy, cutting out dietary meat, and ceasing to use carbon fuel-powered transportation seems like the most effective way. Aside from adopting a vegan diet, these lifestyle changes are very hard (and practically speaking, impossible) for most of us to make. More importantly, it might not be efficient. In a country that implements cap and trade, switching to solar panels will not affect your country's total emissions in the near future, because the energy provider using less fossil fuel will sell its emission credits to another company, thereby enabling that company to emit more. Importantly, this objection does not apply to industries, such as the air transportation industry, whose emissions are not capped. If enough people join with me in not using air transportation, the number of flights will be reduced. By parity of reasoning, switching to solar panels might cause the government to lower its carbon cap if enough people follow your suit. Most importantly, we should try to switch to a greener lifestyle so that we personally do not act unjustly, even if the total harm done remains as before.

John Broome suggests that a more effective way to compensate for our carbon emission is to *offset* it. One way to do this is by contributing money to projects that preserve and grow green spaces (tropical forests, for example) that remove carbon dioxide from the atmosphere. Most of these projects exist in developing countries that still have large tracts of green space, which the countries in question often feel pressured to develop *unsustainably*.[4] Developing countries that do not yet have large electrical grids powered by fossil fuel are ripe for solar-, wind-, and water-generated electricity (Broome mentions something as simple as installing efficient stoves in Africa that don't burn wood). So money can be donated to subsidizing the purchasing of green technologies in developing countries.

Reputable companies charge around $10 to offset a ton of CO_2, but the Stern Review places the harm caused by a ton of emissions to be between $25 and $65 (and Broome himself thinks the cost is higher). Taking the lower figure, we would have to pay $100–$150 annually to offset an annual carbon footprint of 10–15 tons. Could that money produce more good spent on poverty relief? Very possibly. But we cannot compensate for harming people in one respect by doing more good for them in another. If it is worse to harm someone than to not help them, then it is wrong to break someone's leg even if the compensation exceeds the cost of medical and psychological recovery. It follows that diverting money away from fulfilling one's minimum duty to offset (to not harm) to the fulfillment of a less imperative duty to help is normally wrong. I say "normally wrong" because if the harm from emitting comes with no personal benefit to the emitter but benefits others in need, then it might be excused. In the final analysis, however, spending money on offsets has the added benefit of redirecting money from wealthy, developed countries to poor, developing countries, where it will be spent on employing workers and relieving poverty.

Is capitalism compatible with sustainable development?

Most discussions about the economics of sustainable development, including the one outlined above, presume that the economic framework for decision-making will be based largely, but not exclusively, on principles associated with a market economy. In general, markets are an efficient way to determine the costs of goods, services, labor, and capital. But, as we have seen, they do not factor in costs involving the exhaustion and degradation of resources and the production of pollution and greenhouse gases.

Capitalism is the reigning market system on this planet today. There have also been experimental attempts to introduce markets into socialism, most notably in China, Cuba, and the former Yugoslavia. We will discuss how one such model might work shortly. The main difference between capitalism and socialism, therefore, is not the presence of markets, nor is it the presence of profit-oriented businesses. Rather, the main difference between capitalism and socialism is private ownership of productive capacity and finance capital. Economic systems in which private ownership of productive and capital assets prevail are predominantly capitalist.

Does the presence of capitalism rather than socialism make a difference in bringing about sustainable development in the future? Would a market socialist economy be more efficient than a capitalist economy? That is to say, would it more likely reduce poverty and extreme inequality – and develop human capabilities all around – while also limiting bad growth and climate change?

The classical Marxist critique of capitalism as a system for reducing endemic poverty revolves around the necessity of unemployment in a capitalist economy. Competitive advantage achieved through cost-cutting reductions in employee wages and benefits – the chief purpose of labor-saving technology – creates a tendency toward unemployment, which in turn functions as the ultimate threat in disciplining workers' wage demands. Moreover, modern monetary policy dictates a level of "natural unemployment," which it defines as the lowest sustainable unemployment rate (LSUR) compatible with a rate of inflation sufficient to encourage levels of saving conducive to affordable borrowing and steady investment. The structural entrenchment of unemployment in a capitalist economy for the above reasons explains why wage income lags behind investment income, thereby over time producing the sorts of business cycles (overproduction/under-consumption) at the center of Marx's diagnosis of capitalism's crisis tendencies. The most important way domestic capitalist economies mitigate these crisis tendencies is by expanding their markets abroad into less developed regions of the world – exploiting cheap foreign labor while driving out foreign competitors, who lack the technological advantages associated with efficient, large-scale economies. Small producers, shop owners, and subsistence farmers who lose out in this competitive struggle join the ranks of the unemployed, or if they are lucky, find employment in low-paying sweatshops. Again, thanks to a very large and growing number of the world's unemployed in the southern hemisphere, multinational retailers at the top of the chain of production can squeeze local subcontractors below them to offer their services for the cheapest price possible, setting one against the other in a desperate rush to the bottom, where the lowliest laborer who is willing to work for less resides.

To be sure, it is in the interest of the investment class to ensure that global consumption keeps pace with global production, just as it is in the interest of each business owner to ensure that other business owners hire enough well-paid workers to buy the commodities he or she produces. But nothing in the history of capitalism (or in its competitive logic) suggests that business owners can solve their "prisoner's dilemma." Enter the welfare state and the credit system. The state rescues business owners from their dilemma by setting minimum wage and income levels, and providing unemployment and disability compensation insurance and retirement plans. These policies, along with borrowing on credit, guarantee that workers, as well as investors, have enough income to press their consumer demand – so long as mounting debt does not instigate a critical default in repayment.

Despite these modestly successful strategies of crisis management, capitalism works against poverty reduction in a way Marx did *not* foresee. The growth dynamic of capitalism, driven by the cost-efficiencies associate with economies of scale, encourages ever-greater resource depletion and energy consumption. Absent a technological miracle, the resulting increase in global temperatures will bring in its train more extreme weather events, flooding, and desertification that will disproportionately harm the world's poorest.

Defenders of a green, sustainable capitalism look for salvation in government regulation. Underlying this vision of reformed capitalism is a faith that citizens, elected officials, and business leaders will come to embrace a community-based, stakeholder conception of corporate obligations. Can this ethos curb the greed and fear that motivate private investors to want to grow their businesses in unsustainable ways?

Despite antitrust legislation and business failure as normal restraints on capital growth, a healthy capitalist economy must be a growing economy in order to encourage private investors to play a relatively risk-free, positive sum game of investment. But history shows us that any capitalist economy capable of motivating a steady rate of investment necessary for averting long-term recession will perforce grow exponentially. A modest 3% per year growth rate (the average rate the US economy grew during the twentieth century) doubled consumption every 24 years and led to a 16-fold increase in consumption over the course of a century. A low annual rate of 1.2–1.4% – the growth rate the Stern Review's economic analysis of climate change projected would be necessary to avoid "major disruption to economic and social activity . . . on a scale similar to those associated with the great wars and economic depression of the first half of the twentieth century" – would still double consumption every 60 years.[8]

Case study: "green capitalism" and solar energy in Ouarzazate, Morocco[1]

Does green capitalism undermine sustainable community development?

In 2010, the king of Morocco announced a solar energy mega-project that was designed to provide electricity to over 1 million Moroccans, reduce the country's energy imports, and potentially export this clean energy to the European Union in the future.[5] The first phase of the project, named Noor 1, was fully operational by 2016; a massive solar energy plant covered an area of 15 million square feet near the country's southern city known as "the door to the desert," Ouarzazate. Morocco's energy needs are expanding by 7% a year, and the 330 days of sunshine will ensure a renewable source of energy. Recognizing this initiative to be on the path of "green capitalism," the European Union lent 60% of the $9 billion in capital for the project, while the World Bank, African Bank of Development, l'Agence Française de Developpement, and KfW Bankengruppe provided the remaining amount. The plan is for the plant to generate 14% of the country's total energy needs by 2020, and along with renewable wind and water sources, to generate over 50% of the country's total energy requirements by the year 2030, similar to the renewable energy goals of the United States (under the Obama administration) and many member nations of the European Union.

Not only did the project help meet Morocco's growing energy needs, but also it provided new roads, expanded the water grid to 33 nearby villages, and employed approximately 2,000 workers in the plant's construction. The supporters of the project maintain that this is an example of "green capitalism" at its best. Yet the reactions from some activist groups and critics have focused on the fact that the land the Ouarzazate solar plant was built on was community land the government had assessed as marginalized and underutilized and therefore was purchased for an eighth of its value, that the money paid for the land was not dispersed directly to benefit local populations, and that local communities were told and not asked to participate in a discussion of its location.[6] What has come to be described as "green grabbing,"[7] critics argued that although the land was purportedly appropriated from local communities specifically for environmental goals and sustainable purposes, it is nonetheless rooted in the privatization and commoditization of nature; the government sold the solar power plant to the private company Moroccan Agency for Solar Energy (MASEN). "Historical popular sovereignty over land" was essentially ignored, and "green capitalism" has resulted in dispossession of local communities from their own land. Critics of the project conclude by arguing that local engagement and sustainable livelihoods cannot be summarily dismissed when addressing issues that involve the collective public good.

Rebutting the notion of a no-growth capitalist economy doesn't eliminate the possibility of sustainable growth. Heavily taxing gasoline could lower gasoline consumption and provide revenues for capturing carbon emissions without slowing economic growth so long as governments stimulated consumer demand by cutting income taxes and compensated for job loss in the petroleum sector by subsidizing growth in other (more eco-friendly) sectors. But as David Schweickart convincingly argues, faith in the capacity of regulated capitalism to *quickly* transform itself into a sustainably growing economy capable of averting scientific predictions of global climate catastrophe is not supported by historical evidence, which rather shows that radical reform only follows on the heels of economic collapse. Capitalist growth has mainly benefited wealthy countries – the average income gap between rich and poor countries has grown from 3 to 1 in 1820 to 70 to 1 in 1990 – and has trickled down very unevenly to the poor, for structural reasons that I mentioned earlier. So there is no guarantee that sustainable capitalist growth, were it achievable in time to avert an ecological disaster that will profoundly harm the vast majority of the global poor (if no one else), would trickle down to the developing world. In the words of Schweickart, defenders of green capitalism urge us to make a bad Pascalian "wager": against all historical evidence, one must assume that the bare possibility of unending incremental gains in "happiness" through eternal growth in consumption is worth the risk of courting a more probable outcome – infernal planetary misery for most everyone.[9]

There is another problem with this wager. Defenders of "green" capitalism invoke an older model of state-regulated capitalism that appears to have been rendered increasingly redundant by today's neoliberal capitalism. Capitalism places the natural and social systems on which it relies at critical risk, but, more importantly, it places the political system that could lower this risk – through government regulation – at critical risk. Today, a new kind of capitalism based on currency speculation, free trade, financial and fiscal austerity, and other neoliberal policies imposes stringent limits on what governments can do to protect their domestic economies from capital flight and foreign capture. Forced to privatize, outsource, and downsize public services, cash-strapped governments no longer manage their domestic environments in a way that is publicly accountable to their own citizens.

In sum, capitalism has structural defects that make it unlikely that both global poverty and global environmental/ecological damage can be significantly reduced *at the same time*. The promise of green capitalism depends on the capacity of government to use a combination of positive and negative incentives to steer the greed and fear of private investors toward sustainable forms of growth that will benefit all. Today's capitalism undermines the fiscal capacity of government to do this. In any case, investors can simply avoid taxes or refuse subsidies by moving their capital to other countries whose package of negative and positive incentives they deem to be more profitable, if not necessarily greener.

Nothing I have said is meant to suggest that capitalism will succumb to its crisis tendencies. It has proven resilient, thanks to political and legal reform. Working within its domain, we should strive to garner political support for green policies that also grow underdeveloped economies. Private-public partnerships guided by a stakeholder ethos (see Chapter 7) play a vital role here. That the new era of capitalism has cast such a pall on the possibility of averting an impending catastrophe through immediate reform and transformed ethos does not refute the possibility of future reform, post-apocalypse.

Socialist reform?

Is there an alternative model of market economy that, in theory at least, would more likely reduce poverty, environmental/ecological damage, and social and political inequality better than reformed capitalism? Recall the fundamental root of capitalism's crisis tendency: the separation of privately owned capital from socially exploited labor and publicly shared resources (political power and nature). By releasing capital from this relationship, transferring it from private to public stewardship, it becomes possible to use it more efficiently, for the good of all, and by the democratic consent of all.

The comparative advantages of democratic socialism over democratically reformed capitalism in achieving a more just and sustainable world have been thoroughly detailed by Schweickart. The economy in question retains many features of a capitalist economy: markets in goods and services, corporations, entrepreneurs, and even venture capitalists. In Schweickart's model, however, most capital assets are publicly owned and dispensed by central banks to entrepreneurs or other persons seeking to start up or expand businesses. Public investment funds are generated by a use tax on capital assets, such as machinery, buildings, and land. Importantly, loans are dispensed to regional banks on the basis of population size and developmental needs; entrepreneurs must convince citizen advisory boards of the profitability of their undertaking as well as of its potential for green development. Venture capitalists are permitted to start businesses and hire workers for a wage as well. However, wage labor does not obtain in worker-managed firms, where profits are distributed to workers on the basis of criteria – skill level, hourly contribution, etc. – chosen by them.

The most intriguing feature of this model is its sustainability. Like their capitalist counterparts, businesses in a market socialist economy are profit-driven; they compete to maintain or increase their market share. But unlike capitalist firms, which maximize profits by replacing costly workers with labor-saving technologies, worker-managed firms are generally loath to fire one of their own, unless doing so is necessary to stay in business. In any case, structural unemployment is no longer required in an economy where rents and interest have been abolished and inflation can be controlled by expanding production to meet growing demand. Furthermore, whereas capitalist firms have an incentive to grow – greater productivity means greater profits – worker-managed firms do not. Because profits are shared among workers, adding more workers normally does not translate into larger shares, unless a greater economy of scale results in significant efficiency and cost saving.

But how would firms in a local democratic socialist economy protect themselves from the kind of cutthroat competition that currently reigns supreme in our global capitalist economy? Here Schweickart recommends that we adopt a variation of import substitution of the sort I discussed in Chapter 3. On one hand, tariffs would be imposed on highly discounted imports from developing countries; on the other hand, revenue generated from these tariffs would be remanded back to these countries for use in developing their economies. As wages and production standards rise in these countries, the need for protective tariffs diminishes, and import substitution can be relaxed. Because democratic socialist economies are protected from cutthroat foreign competition, they can afford to share their technical expertise with the developing world for mutual benefit.

The greatest contrast between capitalism and the socialist model I have outlined above is worker democracy. Capitalism, after all, is a system of class domination in which those who own controlling shares of businesses dictate terms of investment, production, and employment to the rest of us. No wonder that persons who spend their lives taking orders from those who employ them develop deferential attitudes to those higher up in the chain of command while kicking those below them. Eliminating this element of coercion from our economic lives and encouraging everyone to participate in decisions regarding investment, production, and employment would make for a more just economy.

Infusing stakeholder business ethics with democracy might not solve all problems associated with a market economy but it would mitigate them better than reformed capitalism. Justice demands that all parties to the social contract shift from a one-sided focus on maximizing personal gains – which is the natural default of any market system, capitalist or socialist – to a broader focus on the common good, with a preference for solutions that maximize the condition of the worst off.[10]

Summary

This chapter addresses the intersection of two kinds of economics: developmental and environmental. Drawing from the science and economics of climate change, it argues that development and climate control are inseparable. Given current predictions, our best efforts at climate control will not forestall temperature increases that will likely kill a million people a year by 2030. Such predictions do not rule out the catastrophic collapse of human populations.

Despite these dire predictions, much could be done by governments and individuals to significantly reduce emissions and lower the chance of widespread human suffering. Although the growth dynamics of capitalism work against poverty reduction and climate control, a socialist alternative that might offer a better chance for bringing about sustainable development will take years to evolve.

In the meantime, governments and individuals have moral duties to make the world a more just and better place. Governments have a far greater duty to make the world a better place given their resources. They should not discount the welfare of future generations on the shaky assumption that economic growth will continue unabated. Maximizing well-being – or minimizing the risk of global misery – might therefore require sacrificing present consumption for future gains.

Ideally, international justice might require that developed nations sacrifice more than developing nations. This duty becomes more imperative to the extent that the former have harmed the latter. Insofar as exorbitantly high levels of consumption violate the human rights of poor people, rich people owe them compensation. Practically speaking, however, getting rich people and the governments that act on their behalf to acknowledge this wrong is hard. So, international cooperation toward sustainable development will initially defer to the national self-interests of powerful nations. Compensating these nations for climate control costs will likely be the only way to motivate their cooperation in global climate control.

Regardless of how their governments act, individuals must acknowledge their personal contribution to global emissions and try to make restitution for their harm. Insofar as this harm is serious, non-accidental, unreciprocated, and capable of remediation, persons enjoying an affluent lifestyle should compensate those who are asymmetrically harmed – the global poor. The best way to do this is by altering one's diet and offsetting one's emissions by donating to forest-preservation or green technology programs in the developing world.

Questions for discussion

1   Do you think that market solutions to the problem of climate change, such as cap-and-trade, are plausible solutions? What other solutions might there be?
2   Do wealthier, more industrialized nations have a moral obligation to provide funds/green technology to aid in the development of developing nations? Why or why not?
3   How do you view the problem of future generations? Do we have special obligations to future generations to provide them with a habitable planet? How much should we be allowed to privilege the present over the future?
4   Do you think that Schweickart's market socialist model can adequately address many of the issues of climate change? What are the positives and negatives of this model?
5   Can we rely on technological innovation from so-called "green capitalists" to save us? Do we have to fundamentally change the way we live? If so, in what respect do we need to adapt? If not, why not?

Notes

1   Kim (2013).
2   Broome (2012, p. 47).
3   See Broome (2012, pp. 78–79). Broome mentions a theoretical objection, based on an argument developed by Derek Parfit in *Reasons and Persons* (Oxford: Oxford University Press, 1984), Chapter 16, that purports to show that no one living three or four generations from now can justly claim to be harmed by actions done by the present generation. The argument goes like this:

  • If the present generation acts to reduce its carbon print, this will produce a ripple effect changing future events, including the identities of future persons.

- The future persons who will exist if we do not reduce our carbon footprint are not the same persons who will exist if we do reduce our carbon footprint.
- Future persons who will exist if we do not reduce our carbon print cannot complain about not having a better life because they would not have existed at all if we had acted to reduce our carbon print.

Broome concedes that this argument has some force when applied to the emissions of a whole generation but less force when applied to the emissions of a single person, whose reduction of emissions now will not have much of a ripple effect on the identities of future persons, many of whom will be the same persons regardless of whether he or she reduces his or her emissions (Broome op. cit., pp. 63–64).

4   Broome, however, wonders whether programs such as Reducing Emissions from Deforestation and Forest Degradation (REDD), which is supported by the UNFCCC, really are efficient. Under this program, companies are paid not to develop forested land. But how do we know that this payment really *adds* to offsets? It doesn't if the forested land in question was never going to be developed anyway or the company will just develop a different patch of forest in exchange for not developing the patch targeted for preservation. Broome therefore recommends donating to smaller offsetting companies that have been independently certified.

5   Summarized from Sandrine Ceurstemont, "The Colossal African Solar Farm that Could Power Europe." November 29, 2016, at www.bbc.com

6   Taken from Hamza Hamouchene, "The Solar Plant in Morocco: Triumphal 'Green' Capitalism and the Privatization of Nature." *Jadaliyya*, March 23, 2016, at www.jadaliyya.com/Details/33115/The-Ouarzazate-Solar-Plant-in-Morocco-Triumphal-%60Green%60-Capitalism-and-the-Privatization-of-Nature.

7   J. Fairhead et al. (2012, pp. 237–264).

8   Stern (2007), cited in Schweickart (2009, p. 563). Chapter 10 of the review ("Macroeconomic Models of Cost") put forth a range of growth projections that might be required to stabilize the current output of CO_2 at 450 parts per million; business as usual might require a 3.4% *decrease* in GDP; rapid transition to green energy, the use of steep carbon taxes to subsidize growth in other sectors, the efficient use of carbon trading, etc. might comport with an a 3.9% *increase* in GDP. Furthermore, the cost of compensating for the damage done by global warming will also cut into GDP.

9   Schweickart (op. cit., pp. 568–570).

10 As I noted above, if justice requires prioritizing the worst off, then it might require that the present generation of affluent people sacrifice some of their consumption for the sake of less affluent people living in the present and future. Although it may be wrong to penalize the generation of affluent persons born after 1990 for the sins of their forefathers, it may be more wrong to require developing countries to scale back development to meet CO_2 reduction targets.

Suggested reading

John Broome (2012). *Climate Matters: Ethics in a Warming World.* New York: W.W. Norton.

This relatively short book written by the famous Oxford philosopher and economist manages to make the intersection of complex economic ideas and ethics accessible to the layperson. Chapter 5 of our book draws most of its treatment of the science and economics of climate change from Broome's short masterpiece.

Naomi Klein (2015). *This Changes Everything: Capitalism vs. The Climate.* New York: Simon & Schuster.

Klein's book not only draws a clear line between current economic policy and climate change, but she also presents a direction forwards for dealing with the problem of climate change.

Ernst Friedrich Schumacher (1973). *Small Is Beautiful: A Study of Economics As If People Mattered*. New York: HarperCollins.

Schumacher's book puts forth a system of local, sustainable development built on appropriate technology as a solution to the 1973 energy crisis. Its content is largely applicable today in thinking about ways of promoting sustainable, climate change–resistant technologies.

David Schweickart (2011). *After Capitalism*, rev. edition. Lanham: Rowman and Littlefield.

Schweickart's short book makes a compelling case, based on both economics and ethics, for the greater justice and sustainability of a market socialist economy composed of worker-managed companies.

Online Source and Visual Media

Jared P. Scott and Kelly Nyks (Producers) with Jared P. Scott (Director) (2016). *The Age of Consequences* [Motion Picture]. United States: PF Pictures.

This documentary links climate change to many of the developing issues concerning the Syrian conflict and the current European refugee crisis. It paints a harrowing picture of the conflicts that already have developed out of climate-related migration and points toward the possibility of more to come.

References

Broome, John (2012). *Climate Matters: Ethics in a Warming World*. New York: W.W. Norton.

Fairhead, James, Melissa Leach and Ian Scoones (2012). "Green Grabbing: A New Appropriation of Nature?" *Journal of Peasant Studies* 39(2).

Kim, Jim Yong (2013). "Op-Ed: Ending Poverty Includes Tackling Climate Change." *The World Bank*. www.worldbank.org/en/news/opinion/2013/07/10/op-ed-ending-poverty-includes-tackling-climate-change.

Schweickart, David (2009). "Is Sustainable Capitalism an Oxymoron?" *Perspectives on Global Development and Technology* 8.

Stern, Nicholas (2007). *The Economics of Climate Change*. Cambridge: Cambridge University Press.

6 Immigration and development

Development requires economic welfare, social recognition, and political empowerment for its realization and robust exercise. Poverty threatens all three conditions. To escape from it, migration is sometimes the only option.

But migration is not always the best option. Besides depriving poor communities of skilled workers, migration negatively impacts the development of the migrants themselves. Enhancement of welfare from better-paying jobs often comes at the expense of social recognition and empowerment. When parents migrate abroad for gainful employment and leave their families behind, their children are deprived of loving relationships they need for development. Migrants also suffer loss of citizenship rights in their country of destination as well as loss of social respect and esteem. A worse fate befalls undocumented migrants and victims of trafficking.[1]

The view that many migrants are blameless victims of harsh political and economic circumstances was officially adopted by the 193 nations who signed the 2016 New York Declaration for Refugees and Migrants, which culminated the September 19, 2016 United Nations Summit on Addressing Large Movements of Refugees and Migrants – the first of its kind in the 71-year history of the UN. The Declaration declares "solidarity with, and support for, the millions of people in different parts of the world who, *for reasons beyond their control, are forced to uproot themselves and their families from their home*" (l.8 – my stress). The Declaration continues by acknowledging "a *shared responsibility* to manage large movements of refugees and migrants" for *humanitarian reasons* and to "address [their] root causes" (l.11–12).

The Declaration contradicts prevailing policies regarding the duties that governments have toward migrants. Official humanitarian law holds that governments have at most an unspecified duty to rescue selected persons fleeing *political* oppression by offering them temporary sanctuary, and says nothing about persons fleeing civil wars, economic insecurity, and environments devastated by pollution, coastal flooding, and catastrophic weather-related events. Fulfillment of such an unspecified duty of political rescue is left to the discretion of governments acting on the wishes of their citizens. This *communitarian* view contradicts the *cosmopolitan* duty to respect the human rights of all persons to migrate freely.

This chapter surveys a range of communitarian and cosmopolitan arguments in assessing governments' duties toward migrants. These arguments can be situated along two axes. The first axis concerns the distinction between ideal and non-ideal theory we discussed in Chapter 3. Ideal theory, you will recall, encompasses the moral duties that would obtain in an ideal world. Depending on how one imagines such a world, the current moral dilemmas associated with migration would probably cease to exist. Rawls imagined that in an ideal world nations would be morally permitted to be more restrictive in their immigration and refugee policies, simply because there would no longer be desperate persons fleeing crushing poverty and civil violence in their countries of origin. Cosmopolitan thinkers disagree with Rawls's belief that sovereign nations should persist in an ideal world, in part because they think that sovereign states are unlikely to cooperate in solving global poverty and climate change. They surmise that in an ideal world what we today regard as sovereign states would become subordinate territories within a single world state, preferably structured along the lines of a federal democracy. In this ideal state migration would be unrestricted because political borders separating administrative jurisdictions such as provinces and cities would be open.

Philosophers have argued over which of these ideal worlds is preferable. Communitarians like Michael Walzer, whom Rawls cites, maintain that a world state or any world of open borders is both practically impossible and morally undesirable. It is practically impossible because human beings are essentially territorial animals; our security – beginning with family and extending outward – depends on occupying a space providing vital resources that can be closed to outsiders. If we were to tear down the walls separating national borders, smaller communities within nations would simply erect their own walls, becoming so many petty fortresses. Open borders are morally undesirable as well. Unrestricted mobility makes for a society of strangers; under these conditions, administrative bodies would not feel any sense of loyalty to their subjects and subjects would not feel any sense of loyalty to the state. Neither would care deeply about the welfare of the other, and communal bonds of solidarity and caring would give way to a society of atomized individuals who only cared for their immediate families. Cosmopolitans, for their part, argue that communal tribalism of any kind prevents people from appreciating each person's basic dignity and humanity. They place their faith in the spread of rational enlightenment and humanism, and note that history shows a propensity toward overcoming tribalism. Most importantly, they deny that communities will disappear or weaken with the passing of restrictive borders.

We will leave aside the debate, which I have already discussed in Chapter 3, over whether or not restrictive borders are ideally desirable. Suffice it to say, both communitarians and cosmopolitans make compelling cases for their respective ideals. In this chapter, we will see how communitarian and cosmopolitan arguments might apply to our non-ideal world. As it is currently structured, that world appears to be almost entirely ordered along communitarian principles. Almost everyone takes it for granted that states have a sovereign right and duty to regulate their borders more or less as their citizens see fit and mainly for their benefit. But that is only partly true. Cosmopolitans can point to the existence of international humanitarian law. The Geneva Convention on Refugees (1951) legally binds signatory states. Even if this treaty is not enforceable, it shows that most people acknowledge cosmopolitan moral limits to any state's right to refuse entry to some persons.

The balancing of sovereignty rights and human rights in current legal and moral practice touches on the second axis along which communitarian and cosmopolitan arguments can be situated. Communitarian and cosmopolitan arguments refer to the two sets of moral duties we have highlighted so far concerning goodness and justice. Communitarians and cosmopolitans understand these values in markedly different ways. Communitarians emphasize the goodness of stable communities of shared identity rather than the goodness of aggregate material prosperity and physical well-being. Cosmopolitans of a utilitarian bent reverse this emphasis. And, whereas communitarians emphasize the justice of democracy, or collective self-governance exercised by people over their local communities, cosmopolitans emphasize the justice of human rights and transnational duties of cooperation between individuals.

Despite stressing different aspects of goodness and justice, it is wrong to see communitarians and cosmopolitans as proposing diametrically opposed views about the ethics of migration in our non-ideal world. Neither communitarians nor cosmopolitans endorse closed borders because even communitarians acknowledge a duty to assist some refugees by permitting them to immigrate to a safe haven. Conversely neither communitarians nor cosmopolitans endorse open borders because unrestricted migration threatens security and, along with it, the secure enjoyment of human rights.

Human migration

Before examining how communitarians and cosmopolitans address the ethical dilemmas posed by migration in our non-ideal world, we must first get a sense of the magnitude of immigration today. People migrate for many reasons. Given the emotional and material cost of transplanting oneself and possibly one's family from one place to another, the decision to migrate is often fraught with great anxiety and uncertainty. Here we are speaking not about relatively affluent people who migrate to be with their spouses, to experience the thrill of a different life, or to get ahead. We are speaking about people who migrate out of necessity – to procure their own survival or the survival of their families.

Most migrants transplant themselves for economic reasons. Some do so for political reasons. Humanitarian law draws a sharp distinction between these two kinds of migrants, although in reality they overlap. International law recognizes a claim to enter a foreign safe haven by migrants seeking refuge from political oppression. It does not recognize a similar claim by migrants fleeing extreme poverty, many of whom must enter their chosen safe haven illegally. It matters not that their government has abysmally failed in protecting them from poverty and its offspring: violence, substance abuse, disease, ignorance, and underdevelopment. Criminal neglect falls outside the definition of political persecution. So the most desperate economic refugees enter illegally and therefore suffer the greatest kind of developmental marginalization: criminalization. (A similar stigma attaches to the 13 million "stateless" persons who are currently denied legal status within their country of birth.)[2] In order to see why their law-breaking should not be criminalized and their legal status normalized, I recommend that we turn to the fate of political refugees, especially those who enter a foreign safe haven as asylum seekers, whose entry into sanctuary states often skirts normal legal avenues for processing petitions.

Before developing the analogy between economic and political refugees, I would like to remind the reader of the enormity of today's refugee crisis. This crisis is not simply about numbers, but reflects the failure of states and international relief agencies to resolve a legal tension between rights of sovereignty and human rights of refugees. This tension pervades all discussions regarding the ethics of immigration.

Today about 3% of the world's population (around 250 million persons) are migrants. This percentage has remained constant despite population growth, principally because of the increase in the number of countries and restrictive borders. Some 91 million move between developing countries, 86 million move from developing to advanced countries, and another 73 million move between advanced countries or from advanced countries to developing countries. Most migrants are poor, originating from developing countries, and move for economic reasons.[3]

Turning to refugees, or migrants who migrate due to conflict or persecution, the UN High Commissioner for Refugees (UNHCR) recently reported that 2016 witnessed the largest surge of forcibly displaced persons ever recorded – 65.6 million (25.5 million seeking refuge outside their country), surpassing the 50 million refugees at the end of World War II (UNHCR 2016).[4] The addition of 20 million forcibly displaced persons since 2000 has been spurred by drug wars in Mexico and Central America and by civil conflicts in Europe, Southeast Asia, sub-Saharan Africa (origin of one-third of all refugees), and the Middle East (chiefly in war-torn Syria, origin of one-fifth of all refugees). Approximately 90% of refugees migrate to safe havens in poor developing countries that can least afford to support them (Turkey now hosts more refugees than any other country, with 2.7 million, followed by Pakistan, with Lebanon recording the highest concentration of refugees, roughly 25% of its population). By contrast, the world's wealthiest nations, including the United States, Australia, and member states of the EU, under pressure from citizens who are hostile to immigrants, are devising ways to keep out and contain the unparalleled wave of refugees.[5]

This disparity is not surprising. The Geneva Convention on Refugees designates the first foreign safe haven a refugee enters upon exiting his or her country of origin as having primary legal custodianship over that refugee. Such havens are typically adjacent to refugees' countries of origin and, like them, are often poor and institutionally weak. Furthermore, the non-refoulement provision of the Convention prohibits states from repatriating foreign arrivals, regardless of whether they meet the stringent definition of a refugee or asylum seeker, if doing so would place their lives and liberties in jeopardy. To circumvent this responsibility, wealthy countries, which are typically not adjacent to the countries emitting refugees, do everything in their power to prevent refugees from entering their territory, from building walls and intercepting smuggling vessels, to setting up border checks in foreign as well as domestic ports. The incentive to block entrance is further strengthened by the moral presumption prevalent among wealthy democracies that refugees must not be detained in camps beyond a reasonable time and should be resettled as normal residents.

Current law thus conspires to ensure that the burdens for receiving and resettling refugees will not be equitable, despite the fact that all nations share responsibility for a state system that legally sanctions disparate treatment of the world's peoples. Thus, having witnessed a 51% increase in the number of refugees seeking asylum since 2013, Europe has put in abeyance plans to admit refugees in a manner equitable to member states (in effect, modifying the "first safe haven" provision of the Geneva Convention) due to strong resistance from its eastern flank, with the latter responding by setting up more border checkpoints, fences, and detention centers. Even more controversial, however, is a recent agreement between Turkey and the EU that permits the EU to send new migrants (chiefly from Syria and the Middle East) arriving in Greece to Turkey, a country whose own human rights record is so bad that one out of five Turkish citizens who apply for asylum in the EU are granted it by European countries.

Humanitarian concerns have taken a backseat to politics. The increase in the number of refugees drowning in transit from North Africa and the Middle East to Italy during the first four months of 2015 increased 15-fold (to about 1,600) over the same period a year earlier after Italy cancelled its costly search and rescue program (Mare Nostrum) because of fear that it would encourage more illicit smuggling (the program is credited with having saved more than 150,000 lives in 2014). Meanwhile, EU plans to blow up empty smuggling vessels have been resisted by the UN, and the disastrous capsizing of a smuggling boat with loss of 900 lives has subsequently forced the EU to renew its search and rescue programs.

Europe hopes to build political resolve for rescuing refugees by getting the United States, Canada, and Australia to agree on hosting some of them. But the kind of multination cooperation that led to the resettlement of over 2.5 million Vietnamese refugees after the Vietnam War will be hard to replicate in the current anti-immigrant climate. The Australian government is hostile to the idea that it should provide safe haven to the more than 25,000 refugees – most of them poor Bangladeshis and Rohingya Muslims, whose citizenship status has been revoked by the Myanmar government (in 2017 an estimated 800,000 Rohingya have been driven from their homes in Myanmar to Bangladesh by Myanmar's military). While many of the Malaysian and Indonesian smuggling vessels on which they flee are denied entry and left to drift with the expected tragic consequences, those refugees that make it to land are either immediately repatriated (the fate of most Bangladeshis) or are kept in sparse camps awaiting UN processing of asylum requests that can take months.

The same resistance to refugee resettlement pervades public opinion in the United States, as was recently documented by the 2016 election of Donald Trump.

Resistance was partly fueled by widespread fear that Muslim refugees pose significantly greater security risks than other groups.

More pertinent to my argument is American resistance to resettling Central American migrants fleeing regional violence. This crisis illustrates the legal challenges that attend an evolving definition of asylum seeker while highlighting moral duties to compensate migrants who are fleeing from hardship caused in part by the government to which they are now appealing for sanctuary.

Case study: the Central American refugee crisis

Do rich countries have compensatory duties to admit refugees?

In 2014, 70,000 children (most of them unaccompanied by an adult caretaker) streamed across the southern border of the United States fleeing violence and economic chaos in Honduras, El Salvador, and Guatemala. The violence – mainly from government security forces exercising a free hand (*mano dura*) and the drug gangs they are attacking – was abetted by US foreign policy. Among the major gangs reaping terror were MS-13 and Calle 18, which were formed in Los Angeles, the home of many Salvadoran refugees fleeing the Central American wars of the 1980s. Denied legal refugee status (in sharp contrast to Nicaraguan refugees, whose Sandinista government the Reagan administration was trying to overthrow), Salvadoran refugees and the children they brought with them formed their own underground drug businesses, which they exported to other American cities, and a decade later were deported in large numbers back to their ancestral homeland, where they began terrorizing Salvadorans.

Economic and political refugees

The Obama and Trump administrations' response to the migration of unaccompanied children has wavered between treating them as illegal economic opportunists and legal refugees from conflict. This uncertainty reflects changes in domestic and international law. In years past, states could refuse sanctuary if they determined that a migrant's claim to political persecution did not rise to a level calling for emergency rescue. In recent years, however, *endangerment*, and not just political persecution, has been added to the list of factors obligating states to open their doors to refugees.

Indeed, an argument can be made that endangerment should replace persecution – which sometimes can be relatively mild – as the most salient consideration in defining refugee status. Many countries already allow entry to persons fleeing natural disasters, civil wars, and threats of violence from which they cannot be protected by their own government. The United States, for example, allows persons fleeing from domestic violence and other forms of endangerment to apply for "temporary protected status" if their own government will not act to remedy the danger. Under this provision, at least some Central American migrants fleeing gang warfare have been granted relief.

This looser practice of migrant protection also accords with the UNHCR's "extended definition" of a refugee as anyone outside their country of residence who faces "serious and indiscriminate threats to life, physical integrity or freedom resulting from generalized violence or events seriously disturbing public order" and other "man-made disasters."[6] Threats to life, physical integrity, or freedom resulting from events seriously disturbing public order can include severe, life-threatening poverty. Hence, under this broader definition of refugee, persons fleeing poverty or regions devastated by climate change should qualify as refugees.

This change in the institutional practice of who counts as a refugee supports the argument that economic refugees should be given the same protections as political refugees. It might be objected that this consideration would be relevant only for economic refugees who migrate legally. But the (il)legality of migration has no bearing on the moral merits of whether or not a refugee should be granted sanctuary. Immanent endangerment provides a particularly compelling reason why persons fleeing political persecution must sometimes forgo the formality of applying for asylum (or a transit visa) and enter a foreign port illegally. Lack of trust and desperation may further compel such persons to lie to border officials and asylum judges regarding the exact reasons for their entry. As Joseph Carens notes, such "illegal" behavior is no more reprehensible than what some Jews did when they sought to flee German-occupied territory during WWII using false identification.[7]

The expansion of the legal definition of refugee to include persons who enter a country illegally and request protection from economic as well as political endangerment is supported by the fact that governments violate the human rights of their subjects by deliberately or negligently not protecting their vital needs. If the recent genocidal wars in the Horn of Africa have taught us anything, it is that governments can kill unwanted minorities under their jurisdiction by simply not rescuing them from starvation caused by natural disasters.[8] A government's failure to protect the rights of its own inhabitants to access food when it can do so alone or with the help of outside agencies amounts to criminal neglect.

To be sure, neediness and failure to protect against it are scalar concepts. Does the Mexican government's failure to protect its citizens against drug wars and police- and military-sponsored violence constitute criminal negligence? Does its failure to cushion the economic dislocations caused by the privatization of communal farming lands (*ejidos*) and the North American Free Trade Agreement (NAFTA)? When does failure to protect reach the point of criminality (equivalent to violating a human right) as distinct from some less culpable and less actionable form of negligence? When does a migrant fleeing economic hardship caused by his own government become a "political" refugee and not an economic opportunist?

A factor complicating our consideration of the refugee status of Mexican nationals seeking safe haven in the United States is that liability for human rights deficits extends across political jurisdictions. If policies adopted by the United States government contribute to these deficits, then the United States arguably has a very strong duty to repair the harm it has caused, and one way it can do that is to acknowledge the refugee status of undocumented Mexican migrants. It is hard to deny that the government of the United States shares some liability with the Mexican government for putting vulnerable Mexicans at risk for human rights deprivations. US domestic and foreign drug policy has arguably contributed to maintaining a black market in illicit drugs that feeds the cartels and gangs that profit from it; building a wall along the southern frontier has only exacerbated turf wars between gangs seeking ways around it. Lax regulation of gun purchasing and registration in the US facilitates a ready supply of illegal arms across the border. US-trained and -armed security forces in Central America sometimes work clandestinely with the very drug cartels they are supposed to be fighting against and routinely violate the civil rights of civilians during the course of "doing their job." Finally, US government sponsorship of and support for NAFTA, CAFTA-DR, and other free trade agreements that have been in force in the region has contributed to economic stagnation and increased levels of poverty for some Mexican communities, both of which feed corruption and the underground drug economy.

Migrants fleeing natural catastrophes unrelated to civil strife also count as political and economic refugees whenever failure to provide them relief stems from avoidable government "negligence" that in a world of enormous concentrations of wealth can only be described as transnational in scope. Indeed, virtually all migrants fleeing destitution can be so counted, once we assume that most governments, multinational corporations, and global economic multilaterals share liability for international trade agreements, resource extraction privileges, and lending and borrowing conventions that cause their destitution.[9]

Migration and development: the communitarian perspective

Now that we have some understanding about the ever-expanding legal duties that governments have toward political refugees – which perhaps should include many migrants who have hitherto been treated as economic opportunists – let us examine the moral duties that governments have toward migrants, especially, the most desperate migrants who are in need of rescue.

Communitarian ethicists endorse the extensive right of a sovereign people to decide whom to admit as temporary or permanent members of their national community. Moreover, to recall what was said in Chapter 3, they insist on this right as a necessary condition for the moral development of the community's members, whose value system and solidarity can be weakened by the importation of foreign culture and people. However, communitarian ethicists do attach some conditions to the exercise of this right. To begin with, they concede that its exercise is limited by the duty of emergency rescue noted above. How a nation decides to implement this positive duty of beneficence is itself conditional. It depends on a nation's resources and, equally important from a communitarian perspective, its cultural identity. The decision about which needy outsiders to admit and for how long depends on the majority within the admitting country.

All things being equal, the duty to rescue large numbers of people that might stress resources and cultural bonds is less binding than the duty to rescue fewer numbers who do not impose this burden. Communitarians accordingly find morally problematic a situation where developing nations possessing scarce resources and fragile political communities bear the brunt of resettling refugees. Again, the duty to rescue people with whom the majority shares some cultural tie – be it of national origin, religion, or ideology – is stronger than the duty to rescue people for whom the majority has little affinity. This explains why Israel has a stronger duty to rescue Jews fleeing oppression than other groups; and it explains why the United States has a stronger duty to rescue persons fleeing persecution from its ideological enemies than persons who profess open hostility to its constitutional values. Conversely, it explains why communitarian-minded political scientists such as Samuel Huntington III worry about what they perceive (wrongly, in our opinion) to be the divisive and subversive impact of so-called Hispanic migration (both legal and illegal) on American values of hard work, ambition, and respect for the rule of law.

Finally, once an asylum seeker has already entered the country, it is worse to repatriate her if conditions in her home country are bad than to have refused her entry in the first place. To refuse admission to someone fleeing persecution does not make her condition worse off than it already is; but to hand someone back to her oppressors *is* to make her worse off than she now is, and amounts to collaborating with human rights violators.

The last example suggests that duties of beneficence are not the only duties that communitarians recognize as applicable to migrants. Communitarians also acknowledge that duties of justice sometimes apply. In the above example, it is wrong to repatriate an asylum seeker if that means harming her. Communitarians also recognize contractarian duties toward refugees. The United States sought the support of many South Vietnamese during the Vietnam War. When the South Vietnamese government fell the United States had a duty to protect its supporters by offering them asylum in the United States. Another contractarian duty recognized by communitarians obligates a country to allow immigrants in good standing who have resided in their host country for a sufficient amount of time to sponsor foreign members of their family for immigration. This permission should normally be granted to immigrants seeking to be reunited with their spouses, parents, and children. Reasonable concerns about "chain immigration" extending to more distant relatives might justify restricting the right to just immediate family members. Because communitarians esteem contribution to the community, they might also endorse granting even undocumented members in good standing amnesty and a pathway toward citizenship. All of these duties, it should be noted, can advance the development of both host populations and migrants: migrants and hosts mutually enrich each other's moral and technical aptitudes.

Finally, communitarians should recognize duties of compensatory justice. If a country's policies have significantly harmed another country's people, then that country owes these people compensation. In the case of so-called climate refugees such as the inhabitants of Small Island Developing Nations discussed in

Chapter 5, the minimum compensation due to them, once their land has become inundated, is immigration. Because affluent countries have contributed disproportionately to climate change, they have an especially strong obligation to resettle climate refugees.

Another duty of justice that Michael Walzer discusses in his communitarian account of immigration can best be understood in terms of Lockean social contract theory. Walzer sensibly notes that it is wrong for a country to settle a territory by evicting its native population. Especially notorious cases of wrongful migration occurred in the Americas, Africa, and Australia. In the case of Australia, wrongful migration was compounded by a further injustice. Australia (like the United States) sought to preserve its predominantly "white" identity by limiting immigration to certain classes of Europeans. Although Walzer concedes that "white" Australians were entitled on communitarian grounds to erect an exclusively white enclave, he emphatically denies that they were entitled to oppress native aborigines or prevent needy Asians from settling the vast tract of unoccupied Australia to advance their own development. It would have been morally better had they simply eliminated their racist immigration quotas (as they and their American counterparts eventually did later in the twentieth century).

In sum, a communitarian ethics of immigration places the burden of proof on migrants. They must persuade citizens of a host country that they will not burden that country's resources or identity, or in any way "lower" their level of development. In claiming priority, they must also show some affinity with these citizens. If they cannot demonstrate cultural affinity, they can claim priority by demonstrating the injustice of denying them entry according to the criteria mentioned above. Without appealing to a potential host country's duties of justice toward them, it is hard to see how, on communitarian grounds, economic refugees could make a strong case for admission to a wealthy country. The strongest case they might make would be based on a claim of compensatory justice. Economic refugees from Africa, for instance, can advance this claim against former European colonial powers that oppressed their ancestors and despoiled their homeland. The same might be said of Mexicans migrating to parts of the United States that had been taken from Mexico in what many regard as an unjust war of conquest.

Most problematic about communitarian ethics is its assumption that the cultural identity of a community determines its moral code. If that code happens to be racist (and more specifically, white supremacist) as it once was for the majority of Americans and Australians throughout much of the twentieth century, then desperate migrants falling outside the "white" spectrum would not be welcome. However, one might also argue that there are aspects of American and Australian cultural identity – specifically, the endorsement of liberalism and humanism – that contradict racism. Although this more rationalistic, Enlightenment heritage might comport with excluding prospective migrants who had a demonstrable antagonism to liberal toleration, it would not comport with exclusions based on religion, race, ethnicity, gender, sexual orientation, and most political ideologies.

The preceding objection relates to a further difficulty with communitarian approaches to immigration. If a national community officially endorses human rights in its constitution, including the right of legal inhabitants to live and work wherever they please, then it is hard to see how they can deny this same human right to outsiders. Such a right cannot be restricted for economic or cultural reasons, but only for the sake of protecting other human rights. Restrictive covenants preventing blacks from moving into white neighborhoods in the United States were declared unconstitutional for this very reason (when not motivated by racism, whites living in these neighborhoods were worried that allowing blacks to move in would lower the value of their homes). So, how can restrictions against foreign migrants – based on similar "cultural" and economic considerations – be justified? At best, such restrictions might be justified for the sake of securing the domestic enforcement of other human rights.[10] In the final analysis, efforts by states to keep needy persons from fully exercising their human right to self-preservation by migrating seem doomed to failure. (Efforts by states such as Romania to keep needy parents from exercising their human right to emigrate in search of employment, on the grounds that doing so deprives the children they leave behind of caring relationships, seem just as futile and also violate a fundamental human right). As national borders become more porous and national identities become more multicultural, it is hard to sustain the idea that the national communities of today's affluent nations are as closed and homogeneous as many communitarians maintain. To paraphrase Joseph Carens, people living in El Paso, Texas may have more in common with people living in Juarez, Mexico (which sits across the border from El Paso) than they have with people in Anchorage, Alaska. The kind of hyper-stable community that communitarians believe is necessary for caring attachments (see Chapter 3) might not be so necessary after all, or at least might not require restrictive borders.

Migration and development: cosmopolitanism and utilitarianism

As a general ethical theory, communitarianism endorses a qualified moral relativism: it asserts that the diverse, sometimes overlapping, sometimes conflicting ethical cultures subscribed to by the world's vast plethora of national communities are the touchstones for what is good and just. These cultures all seem to agree that national communities are bound by a duty of rescue, which they can sometimes satisfy by admitting desperate migrants into their midst. They also apparently agree that friends should be accorded preferential treatment, partners in joint collaboration for common ends should be treated fairly, and that harms should be compensated. But even societies that endorse human rights also endorse a partial favoritism when it comes to the treatment of "insiders," whoever they might be: family, friends, associates, fellow co-nationals, and members of one's "tribe."

Cosmopolitan ethical approaches don't draw a distinction between insiders and outsiders. They appeal to ostensibly universal norms that mandate treating all persons impartially, no matter the relationship in which they happen to stand to us. Human rights approaches, when not applied to the rights of the community, are generally cosmopolitan: all individuals possess equal dignity simply in virtue of their humanity. Therefore, they should be accorded the same human rights and be treated the same way, regardless of nationality or communal membership. Utilitarianism is another cosmopolitan approach. It asserts that each person's well-being counts no more and no less than any other person's well-being.

In principle utilitarianism is agnostic with respect to standards of well-being. Jeremy Bentham adopted a subjective standard: what is preferred is what is good. John Stuart Mill, like the capability theorists we have examined in this book, adopted an objective standard: what conduces to the all-around development of human faculties – which, for Mill, presupposed liberty and individuality – is what is good. We needn't take a position on what any particular person's good is so long as we agree on an assortment of *primary* goods, or goods (to paraphrase Rawls) that anyone needs in order to realize/develop his or her own conception of the good.

Chief among these primary goods is income. It is therefore no accident that utilitarian ethicists working within the field of development known as political economy – they would include Adam Smith, David Ricardo, Thomas Malthus, James Mill and his son and John Stuart Mill – were inclined to equate well-being with income and global well-being with aggregate wealth.

What do economists have to say about the relationship between migration and wealth? As we have already seen in Chapters 3 and 5, the principle of marginal utility in most circumstances appears to favor an equal distribution of wealth. In theory, this could be accomplished by either redistributing income across borders (from rich to poor people) or by redistributing people across borders (from poor nations to rich nations). Therefore, utilitarian-minded economists generally favor relatively unrestricted migration as the most efficient immigration policy for development, just as they favor unrestricted trade and investment for the same reason.

Remittances from migrants back to their country of origin constitutes and important source of income for developing countries. Remittances undoubtedly enhance the welfare of migrants' families residing in these countries. They thereby diminish the very poverty that causes migration in the first place. Officially declared remittances alone (not counting informal transfers) amounted to $436 billion in 2015, a 14-fold increase over the level recorded for 1990, with India (over $70 billion) and China ($64 billion) being the major beneficiaries (the relevant figure for Mexico was $27 billion, an amount exceeding Mexico's revenue from oil exports). Remittances account for between 20% and 50% of GDP in developing countries such as Tajikistan (49%), Nepal (25%), Haiti (21%), Tonga (24%), and Gambia (20%) (Goldin 2016, p. 148). Earlier studies showed that a modest 3% increase in the workforce of developed countries from adding workers laboring in developing countries would result in additional remittances of up to $100 billion to developing countries (the World Bank estimated that this sum would be more than double that amount during the period from 2005 to 2015). Increasing remittances by 10% correlates with reducing the portion living below $1 a day by 3%.

A possible developmental downside to economic migration is the potential for immigrants to take jobs away from domestic workers. However, evidence shows that migrant-generated consumer demand actually drives job growth, often at higher skill levels and in sectors of production that do not employ migrants.[11]

Looking at economic migration from the opposite side of the ledger, governments of developing countries encourage the exportation of domestic labor to the developed world not only to take advantage of remittances but to mitigate domestic discontent caused by poverty, joblessness, and lack of social services (the latter often stemming from government diversion of tax revenue toward debt payment). Working with corporations in the developed world, they have sought to expand the WTO's Mode 4 program, which regulates the global flow of skilled workers, executives, independent contractors (medical professionals, engineers, etc.), to include construction workers, domestic workers, and less skilled laborers. The WTO strongly opposes regulating conditions of employment and insists that these be determined in accordance with voluntary standards set forth by the International Labor Organization (ILO). Organizations such as Migrant Rights International and National Network for Immigrant and Refugee Rights justifiably oppose Mode 4 as an extension of guest worker programs that cause brain drain from the developing world and exploit "temporary" workers whose rights to movement and unionization are curtailed and who are vulnerable to deportation upon the termination of their jobs. Mode 4 also runs afoul of the UN International Convention on the Protection of the Rights of All Migrant Workers and Members of Their Families (1990), which extends basic human rights to all migrant workers (documented and undocumented), supports family reunification, mandates rights to employment and education equal to those possessed by citizens of the host country, and prohibits collective deportation.

Migration and development: the social contract perspective

We have already noted how social contract duties constrain communitarian immigration policies. Contributing members of the community should be allowed to sponsor immediate family for immigration; foreigner refugees who have borne risks on our behalf should be ranked high among those to whom we grant asylum; and extra-territorials whom we've wrongly harmed should be compensated, if need be, by admission to our community.

Prudential contractarian ethicists will find nothing wrong with a nation's tailoring its immigration policies to favor the interests of its citizens above (and even in total disregard of) the interests of outsiders, constrained only by some prudential norms. If it is in the interest of a nation to import skilled foreign laborers, it will be in its interest to entice them to come, perhaps by allowing them to sponsor immediate family for immigration. If guest workers are willing to migrate and work for lower wages than full-fledged members of the community, prudential contractarians would find nothing wrong with that. Contractual consent, circumstantially coerced as it might be, suffices to legitimate the justice of such exploitative relationships.

Prudential contractarian ethics thus accepts immigration policies that advance the development of the rich and powerful ahead of the development of the poor and weak. Libertarian contractarian ethics would not accept such policies. To begin with, libertarian ethicists would object in principle to immigration policies that restrict an individual's natural right to freely migrate across national borders in pursuit of self-preservation unless it could be shown that the exercise of that right conflicted with the natural freedom of other persons. To paraphrase this libertarian principle: Freedom can be limited only for the sake of freedom.

Libertarian immigration policies might benefit the poor by making it easier for them to immigrate to developed countries. If businesses in one country and workers in another country wanted to contract with each other for mutual benefit, the state would have no moral grounds on which to stand in preventing them from doing so; both parties would be exercising their innate right to dispose over their own private property – a right that governments must protect but not limit. (Alternatively, businesses should be free to offshore production and outsource labor rather than import labor from abroad.)

Although libertarian ethics might promote development through unrestricted commerce in labor, goods, and capital, there is no guarantee that it would. Communitarians and welfare contractarians would be among the first to dispute the benefits of free market transactions for developing poor people, as we saw in Chapter 3. Unrestricted property rights also entitle owners to discriminate against minorities – as occurred when businesses in the American South refused to serve (or hire) blacks.

Welfare contractarians therefore object to unregulated property rights. Because they endow the state with expansive regulatory powers to procure equal opportunity and welfare for all, they remain ambivalent about the justice of unrestricted migration. Rawls cites Walzer's communitarian objection to such an ideal. But followers of Rawls such as Joseph Carens disagree. Persons' national origins have the greatest impact on their life opportunities. Being neither deserved nor undeserved, they should not have such an impact. Impartial reasoning behind a veil of ignorance – in this case, imagining ourselves to be one of the world's unlucky – therefore inclines one to accept a global application of Rawls's two principles of justice: global cooperation between persons should be structured so as to endow each person with equal liberty while at the same time maximizing the economic condition of the worst off. Although the latter (difference) principle could be implemented by redistributing wealth rather than people, the former (liberty) principle would seem to endorse ideally a world of unrestricted freedom of movement.

Summary

This chapter shows that human migration has a significant impact on development. But the effects of migration are ambivalent. Poor and rich countries alike – as well as the migrants and their families – are both benefited and harmed. Perhaps the least ambivalent benefit of migration is economic. Utilitarian ethicists who narrowly focus on this aspect of development can point to studies showing that migrants reap substantial gains in income without costing jobs for workers in their host countries. Much of what they earn is sent back to their countries of origin, where it contributes to family income. By all indications, labor migration helps ease unemployment in these countries while generating remittances that lower poverty.

If we leave aside economic gains, the overall benefit of migration to development is less certain. Communitarian ethicists point to potential costs associated with "brain drain," the decimation of poor communities of workers, the separation of family members, the uprooting of people from their communities and traditional ways of life, and the creation of social cleavages.

Justice concerns arise as well. At the beginning of this chapter we questioned the current legal distinction separating political and economic refugees. This distinction – which has led to the criminalization of many undocumented economic refugees – increasingly finds little support in actual legal practice. Without this distinction, many undocumented economic refugees would be regarded in the same light as undocumented political refugees, or asylum seekers, who enter refuge countries illegally with the expectation that they will receive at least temporary protection from the life-threatening circumstances they are fleeing.

Refugee law raises additional justice concerns pertaining to the principles of first entry and resettlement. Developing countries typically bear the costs of housing large numbers of refugees, often in camps that function like prisons. Efforts to devise more equitable ways of admitting and resettling refugees have begun in the EU but have not gone far. Because the causes that drive economic and political refugees from their homelands are also international, it makes sense for the international community to resolve on a humanitarian procedure for distributing refugees that does not unfairly burden developing countries.

Human rights norms support this endeavor; so do social contractarian principles. Contractarian principles exclusively tailored toward advancing national interests seem to contribute little support for this undertaking. Nevertheless, it might be in the enlightened self-interest of rich nations to ease the refugee crisis plaguing poor countries through economic and immigration policies. Unemployment in the developing world causes social unrest that can affect the developed world (the rise of international terrorism has economic as well as ideological causes). So, decreasing unemployment in poor countries through economic aid or more open immigration policy might be the right thing to do as a matter of national self-interest.

Libertarian contractarianism appeals to more robust moral principles than its prudential counterpart that more directly endorse individual development through open immigration policy. The natural right of any individual to freely pursue his or her self-preservation limits the extent to which restrictions on immigration in the name of national interest are justified. The history of unjust colonial expropriation of property and people also undermines the legitimacy of restrictive borders, and may well require that former "owners" of colonies compensate former colonial peoples with generous immigration policies.

Finally, welfare contractarians will endorse more egalitarian global policies that minimally bring all nations to a level of independent functioning and sustainable development and maximally prioritize the well-being of the worst off (be they individuals or communities). Whether restrictive or open immigration policies should be a part of implementing a global difference principle (in Rawls's sense of the term) remains unclear. Attacking the root causes of economic and political migration – civil conflict, poverty, climate change, and inequality – could advance global development better than migration itself.

Questions for discussion

1   Which of the two theories (communitarian or cosmopolitan) do you find most convincing with respect to open borders in an *ideal* world? Do you agree with the communitarian ideal world in which sovereign states can limit immigration flow, or do you agree with the cosmopolitan ideal world of an open flow of immigration across federal democracies?
2   Should economic refugees be guaranteed the same levels of protection as political refugees? What potential problems would this produce? What problems does it solve?
3   Do wealthier nations have a responsibility to admit more or less refugees than they typically do now? Why or why not?
4   What does the language of the 2016 UN New York Declaration for Refugees and Migrants suggest that states must do to address refugee crises? Does this declaration conflict with a state's right of sovereignty? If it does conflict, what should be prioritized – sovereignty or the UN declaration?
5   Given the complex causal sources of climate change and migration, can we pinpoint a discrete class of climate refugees, on one side, and blameworthy nations, on the other?

Notes

1   Many of these victims are slaves, whose number today – 35 million – is greater than the equivalent number during the Atlantic Slave Trade two centuries ago. India (14.5 million), sub-Saharan Africa (5.6 million), and China (3.2 million) account for most of them (Goldin 2016, p. 146).
2   Rohingya Muslims and Haitians, whose legal status has been denied by the Myanmar and Dominican governments, respectively, stand out as especially egregious examples of statelessness.
3   Goldin (op. cit., p. 146).
4   Syria is the origin of 3.9 million refugees, followed by Afghanistan at 2.6 million and Somalia at 1.1 million. Palestinians constitute the largest group of refugees at 5.1 million.
5   1.7 million persons applied for asylum or refugee status in 2014. Leading countries receiving applications were Russia (275,000), Germany (173,000), and the United States (121,000). Only 105,000 were admitted for resettlement in 26 countries. The United States was the recipient of 73,000 of them (UNHCR 2014).
6   UNHCR Resettlement Handbook, Chapter 3.2.2; Procedures and Criteria for Determining Refugee Status.
7   Carens (2013, pp. 210–211).
8   In January 2010 the Centre for Research on Epidemiology of Disasters published an article in *The Lancet* estimating that between 178,000 and 461,500 excess deaths had occurred in the

Darfur region, mainly as a result of starvation and disease caused by the civil war between the Omar al-Bashir–led Sudanese government and non-Arab Muslim rebels, which began in 2003 and continued until 2010. The UN estimates that that close to three million persons have been displaced (many by means of coerced migrations) in what the International Criminal Court describes as mass genocide and other crimes against humanity perpetrated under the auspices of the Bashir government.

9 Pogge (2008).
10 Miller (2016, pp. 52–55).
11 Ottaviano and Peri (2011).

Suggested reading

Hildegard Bedarff and Cord Jakobeit (2017). "Climate Change, Migration, and Displacement: The Underestimated Disaster." *Greenpeace Germany*. www.greenpeace.de/sites/www.greenpeace.de/files/20170524-greenpeace-studie-climate-change-migration-displacement-engl.pdf.

Greenpeace's report gives a detailed analysis of reasons for migration due to climate change, typical decision-making processes of those migrating, as well as numerous case studies of climate change induce migration

Joseph Carens (2013). *The Ethics of Immigration*. Oxford: Oxford University Press.

Carens's book argues for a relatively broad conception of migrant rights and ultimately contends that developing an open border policy, while maintaining the sovereignty of states, is morally necessary. As a whole, the book attempts to tackle many of the issues we have discussed in this chapter.

David Miller (2016). *Strangers in Our Midst: The Political Philosophy of Immigration*. Cambridge, MA: Harvard University Press.

Miller's book presents numerous problems facing both migrants and host societies. He ultimately suggests that there are dual responsibilities of host societies and migrants to help integrate into their host societies.

Kieran Oberman (2013). "Can Brain Drain Justify Immigration Restrictions?" *Ethics* 123(3): 427–455.

Oberman argues that there are some reasons why the concern of "brain drain" may justifiably limit immigration restriction, but he maintains that this is justifiable in only a small number of cases.

Michael Walzer (1983). *Spheres of Justice: A Defense of Pluralism and Equality*. New York: Basic Books.

Walzer's chapter, "Membership," is the classic benchmark for subsequent discussions on the ethics of immigration.

World Bank Group (2017). "Migration and Remittances: Recent Developments and Outlook. Migration and Development." *Brief No. 28*. Washington, DC: World Bank. https://openknowledge.worldbank.org/handle/10986/28444.

The World Bank Group's brief gives an up-to-date, detailed picture of migration and remittance flows in recent years. This is an especially good resource for those concerned with the economic costs and benefits of migration with respect to remittances.

Online Source and Visual Media

Steph Ching and Ellen Martinez (Directors & Producers) (2016). *After Spring* [Motion Picture]. United States: After Spring LLC.

This documentary portrays a case study of the lives of nearly 80,000 Syrian refugees in the Zaatari Refugee Camp in Jordan.

References

Carens, Joseph (2013). *The Ethics of Immigration*. Oxford: Oxford University Press.

Goldin, Ian (2016). *The Pursuit of Development: Economic Growth, Social Change, and Ideas*. Oxford: Oxford University Press.

Miller, David (2016). *Strangers in Our Midst: The Political Philosophy of Immigration*. Cambridge, MA: Harvard University Press.

Ottaviano, Gianmarco I. P. and Giovanni Peri (2011) "Rethinking the Effect of Immigration on Wages." *Journal of the European Economic Association* 10(1): 152–197.

Pogge, Thomas (2008). *World Poverty and Human Rights*, 2nd edition. Cambridge: Polity Press.

United Nations High Commissioner for Refugees (UNHCR) Global Trends (2016). http:www. unhcr.org/en-us/556725e69.pdf#zoom=95.

7 Transnational corporations

We live in a global marketplace. Sitting in the comfort of your home in front of your computer in Chicago, or using your iPhone while walking your dog in London's Hyde Park, you can purchase leather handbags from Casablanca in Morocco. From your office in Shanghai, you can search and apply for a mortgage to purchase property on the coast of Costa Rica. In Nairobi, Kenya you can walk into a local Uchumi supermarket and buy toothpaste made by Procter & Gamble, chocolate by Nestlé, coffee makers by Mr. Coffee, and batteries by Energizer Canada. The car you purchased in Los Angeles might have been assembled at a plant in Durham, North Carolina, but its various parts will have come from manufacturing facilities in Japan, Mexico, South Korea, and other locations in the United States. This process of economic globalization has allowed us to purchase products from our local markets that have originated from places around the world.

Since the end of World War II, international commerce has been driven by multinational corporations (MNCs) (also known as transnational corporations (TNCs)). A TNC is defined as a private business (either family-owned or publicly traded on one of the world's stock exchanges), that conducts business activity in local offices or through local representatives, operates a local manufacturing or assembly plant, or has a distribution network in at least two or more countries. Although the vast majority of TNCs are based in industrialized or Western nations, such as Ford in the United States, Mitsubishi in Japan, and Unilever in The Netherlands, just to mention a few, there are a growing number of TNCs located in developing countries, such as Alibaba in China and Tata Holdings in India. These new TNCs from developing countries might change the nature of how such large organizations do their business, and we will return to them at a later point in this chapter.

The obvious reason that a corporation plans to expand overseas and becomes a multinational corporation is to increase its profitability. This can be achieved in a number of different ways, of course, depending upon the company's available resources, vision for the future, and long-term strategic plan (i.e., whether to establish a subsidiary, enter into licensing agreements, arrange a joint venture, or perhaps just provide a capital investment). Initially, management might decide to sell the corporation's products overseas in order to gain a foothold in the local consumer market for cars, personal care products, or electronic equipment. As its market share grows over the years, and depending upon its strategic plan, management might then decide to establish a local manufacturing facility for its product. Doing so involves a host of related issues such as whether or not labor costs are less expensive, whether or not the government within the host nation will provide tax incentives, and whether or not general infrastructure costs related to operations, such as electricity, transportation, communications, and construction, are cost effective. Clearly, a large number of multinational organizations have been successful at navigating these challenges and have developed into prosperous, multibillion-dollar global businesses.

As we have become more sophisticated consumers, however, it is natural that we have also become more aware of, and willing to investigate into, the nature and implications of our international economic transactions, including those related to and involving TNCs. There is a growing worldwide consciousness, especially in the industrialized nations, that acting solely out of economic self-interest, or reaching the best economic deal for oneself, is not always the most advantageous for everyone involved. Yet this concern seems to be in direct conflict with one of the bedrock principles of the free market system that defines the purpose of the TNC as a business – to make a profit. The tension between how global economic transactions ought to be conducted by TNCs and the goal of maximizing the profitability of a business raises complicated ethical challenges. For example, should a TNC based in Europe or the United States be subject to the same environmental regulatory guidelines while operating in a country overseas? When a multinational pharmaceutical company conducts clinical trials for a new drug in the slum of a developing country, such as Kibera Slum in Nairobi, is the TNC legally bound by the same requirements in providing an "informed consent" agreement as it is in its home country? More generally, TNCs have the capacity to bring large amounts of capital investment into a developing country that is poverty-stricken, debt-ridden, and dependent upon such investment. The economic inequities and disparities between the wealthy, industrialized nations and developing nations struggling to lift their populace out of poverty become even more striking when TNCs make agreements that benefit wealthy nation consumers at the expense of low-paid workers who toil abroad in deplorable conditions. Thus the traditional ethical question arises as to whether or not sweatshops are acceptable TNC operations if they provide access to high-demand products at significantly lower cost.

The ethical ramifications of TNC operations in developing countries are complex, nuanced, and not altogether straightforward. When a TNC establishes its business overseas, the company's goal is to use its personnel and other resources to build its operations in order to expand its market reach and increase its profit. A TNC, strictly speaking, is not directly interested in development issues except insofar as it helps or hinders its ability to make a profit. Nonetheless, we can still ask one of the most controversial questions in this book: Do TNCs have a role in development, and what are the ethical implications of that role?

The role and responsibility of a corporation

At the present time, liberal or what is sometimes called neoliberal economic policy dominates the global economic order. This includes the traditional concepts of profit, free trade, market liberalization, laissez-faire, privatization, and the free flow of capital investment. These ideas were originally articulated by Adam Smith in his *Wealth of Nations*, written during the late eighteenth century. One of the most important and influential reiterations of Smith's overall approach to economic theory has come from Milton Friedman, the author of *Freedom and Capitalism* and the article, "The Responsibility of Business is to Increase its Profits."[1] Friedman's position is worth reviewing in summary not only because he is an unapologetic proponent of liberal economic theory but for his thinking about the social responsibility of business, which has been a lightning rod for the ongoing debate about corporations and economic morality.

According to Friedman, free markets are a necessity, not a luxury; there is an intrinsic connection between economic freedom and political freedom, and the free market system serves as the basis for both personal and political liberty.[2] The invisible hand operating in free markets for the provision of goods, labor, services, and information offers the best and greatest protection of personal liberty. For example, Winston Churchill was prohibited from talking against the rise of Hitler in Germany previous to the outbreak of WWII by the government-owned and operated British Broadcasting Corporation (BBC) because it considered his position alarmist and too controversial, but Friedman believes that this would not have happened if it had been privately owned. Fundamentally, economic progress is made by people and not governments; the high standard of living achieved in democracies is directly related to the ingenuity, creativity, and independence of working individuals and not through regulatory policies or protective efforts of a government. Thus government interventions that promulgate import quotas, subsidies to farmers, rent control, minimum wages, regulation of industries such as the banking or investment industry, as well as the licensing of occupations, public housing, and forcing people to pay into social security are all instances of excessive – and unjustifiable – government regulation. Friedman assumes that there should be equal rights and equal opportunities, but not equality of wealth. For him, the purpose of the capitalist and free market system is to enable freedom of the individual – what an individual does with that economic freedom is his own business.

> There is one and only one social responsibility of business – to use resources and engage in activities designed to increase its profits so long as it stays within the rules of the game, which is to say, engages in open and free competition without deception or fraud.

This quotation complements Friedman's libertarian contractarian views in its stress on the social responsibility of business, which is, of course, an extension of his economic theory and directly applicable to the conduct of TNCs.

The role of a CEO within a corporation is singular and without exception: to increase profits. The focus on increasing profits is also reflective of the overriding responsibility of the CEO, namely, that the CEO's sole responsibility is to the shareholders of the firm. Issues that include executive and employee wage scale and bonuses, minority employment opportunities and gender equity, community outreach and obligations, the treatment accorded to customers as well as vendors, and the recognition of and commitment to certain environmental guidelines or standards are all of secondary importance. Friedman goes so far as to say that a CEO who concerns him/herself with these considerations and sets aside funding for them is, in fact, committing theft. He/she is stealing from the profits that are owed to the shareholders of the corporation. Accordingly, Friedman's argument concludes that the corporation, managed and given direction by its CEO, must be single-minded about the pursuit of profits and therefore has no social responsibility whatsoever.

There is no doubt that Friedman's teachings have had a key role in shaping perception about a company's social responsibility, and that his ideas have been of continuing influence as exemplified in the economic assumptions that underlie the Washington Consensus described earlier in this book. Yet the criticism of this orthodox view of free market economics, that the only responsibility a law-abiding business has is to maximize profits for the shareholders is, according to some entrepreneurs and business owners, not altogether wrong but too narrow. Before Friedman died in 2006, John Mackey, the founder and original CEO of Whole Foods, Inc., engaged in a debate[3] with him that has led to a distinctively alternative framework for understanding the social responsibility of a corporation. Mackey argues that there is not one but six stakeholders of importance to the operations of any business, including investors or stockholders, of course, but also including customers, employees, vendors, local communities, and the environment.

Mackey argues it is the entrepreneur, founder of a business, or the CEO who is ultimately responsible for the company's vision, strategic plan and for directing and managing operations – not investors; it is the former who has the right to and responsibility for defining the purpose of the firm. The company's leader sets company strategy, negotiates terms of production, supervises vendor contracts, etc., and all that goes into establishing and managing a business. There is no disagreement with Friedman's assertion that a company must create value for stockholders. But Mackey's approach to what this means is not part of mainstream economic thinking. Mackey argues that founders or even CEOs set an amount to which an investor either agrees or not for establishing a business or expanding operations domestically or overseas. If the investor agrees with the founder's or CEO's strategy, then the investor provides capital or buys stock, and if he does not agree, then there is no capital investment or stock purchased by the potential investor. Investors hold stock voluntarily in a public company and if they disagree with the direction of the firm or the decisions of the CEO they can either sell their investment or submit a resolution to be voted upon at the shareholders' meeting.

According to Mackey, it is not a sleight of hand for an entrepreneur or CEO to say that philanthropy is good for business. At Whole Foods stores across the

United States, he implemented what was called a "5% Day" where the company donates 5% of a store's total sales to a local community not-for-profit organization. Groups that had large membership lists were identified, contacted, and then encouraged to shop that day at a Whole Foods store. This resulted in a twofold benefit: the first was that more people shopped at Whole Foods, and second, the donation to the community not-for-profit was increased by the new customers. This innovative approach to what constitutes a broader stakeholder base speaks for itself; starting with a mere $45,000 in capital and with $250,000 in total sales the first year, by 2005 the company had sales of $4.6 billion, net profit of over $60 million, and a market capitalization of $8 billion.

Not one investor objected to the idea of a 5% day at Whole Foods stores. So Mackey raises the following question: How is theft committed by the CEO if the policy was established, all investors had approved without any objections, including the venture capital firms that had provided capital, and the policy itself was well publicized even before its implementation? The CEO is not stealing from the shareholders but rather involving a much larger group of stakeholders in the benefits of a free market system. What has been overlooked, and is perhaps the more important question and a broader one is this: Why give to the local community at all? What does philanthropy have to do with running a business?

What Friedman and indeed what most orthodox neoliberal economists have overlooked, underappreciated, or just ignored in Adam Smith's work is his theory of moral sentiments.[4] Smith argues that the moral considerations of sympathy, empathy, friendship, love, and desire for approval are equally important components of human nature as is self-interest. The capacity for caring for other people is part and parcel of human nature, and we are not or should not be egocentric, as we were as children. The effects of capitalism and the free market system point beyond mere self-interest. What would this look like in the current global economic context? According to Mackey, the business model of Whole Foods is an answer. Value is not only for investors of capital or shareholders of stock, but for a broader understanding of what comprises a larger, more inclusive group of stakeholders. If companies created by entrepreneurs or managed by CEOs can have broader goals than the maximization of profits for shareholders, then policies involving benefits to local community not-for-profit organizations, enhanced customer services and vendor relations, and adherence to environmental guidelines, are not just hypocritical devices or cloaking mechanisms for increasing profits. Mackey agrees that Friedman is right insofar as social responsibility should not be coerced from a business, and that profit making is intrinsically important to a free society. The important point for Mackey is that not all businesses have only this sole purpose.

Legal barriers to corporate social responsibility (CSR)

Governments within developing countries have historically been at a disadvantage when bargaining or negotiating with TNCs. During the 1960s and 1970s, national governments in South America, for example, entered into mineral extraction contracts with TNCs by offering tax incentives and other favorable investment agreements. The assumption was that the TNC would grow its profits unencumbered by government interference, and that the government would be able to put more resources into country development due to the financial benefits accrued from the TNC investment. However, more often than not, after a few years these governments came to the realization that the TNC profits were increasing at dizzying rates while the spillover of financial advantages to the developing country were less than satisfactory or minimal.[5] The result was a wave of government pressure and attempted regulations on the operations of the TNCs in their country which often led to the nationalization of the US- or European-owned local investment. The concerns of governments in developing countries culminated in the formation of the Group of 77 countries within the UN, which demanded that developing countries be treated more equitably within the global economic system, and that TNCs be subject not merely to oversight but that their investments and operations in developing countries be regulated. The Draft Code of Conduct on Transnational Corporations (1974) was an attempt to address these issues, and to discuss and formalize the oversights and regulations proposed by developing countries. Pressured by TNCs and their respective developed nation governments, discussion about the Draft Code proposals were slowed and ultimately abandoned.[6]

At the same time, TNCs were also hard at work protecting their rights and investments in developing countries, as well as circumscribing their obligations. The attempt to regulate foreign investment and the operations of TNCs in countries throughout South America, Asia, and sub-Saharan Africa by governments who wanted to bring them into concert with the goals of development was met with a proliferation of international investment agreements (IIAs), which were ostensibly designed to provide a process that balanced the interests of TNCs and their investments and the regulatory policies of developing nations, but in essence favored the interests of TNCs.[7] By 2009 there were numerous cases brought by TNCs in developed countries against developing countries, with the majority of the latter on the losing side of arbitration decisions. Governments in developing countries have focused on refining the arbitration process for international investment disputes by clarifying the language of contracts, rights, and obligations of TNCs operating within their borders. Yet making this work for the purpose of aligning the interests of TNCs and developing country policies related to poverty alleviation or environmental protections, for example, was challenging to say the least. Not surprisingly, efforts by developing countries advocating for the revision or replacement of international arbitrations rules established by the International Centre for Settlement of Investment Disputes (ICSID), the International Chamber of Commerce (ICC), and the United Nations Commission on International Trade Law (UNCITRAL) have had little success.[8]

Although not normally considered as such by management in TNCs, the concept of corporate social responsibility has developed into another potential self-aggrandizing defense for TNCs in circumventing the legally enforced regulation of international investment wanted by developing countries. The idea behind corporate social responsibility that has developed from the 1990s to the present is that domestic corporations and TNCs can establish their own codes of conduct that eschew any need for government regulation and legal enforcement. These *moral* codes of conduct that describe and sometimes even enumerate a firm's responsibility in regard to child labor, human rights, and environmental protections, for example, are *voluntary* obligations or duties which "are not binding as a result of previous legislative or judicial intervention."[9] In fact, a quick and short perusal of the generally formulated numerous and diverse codes of corporate social responsibility, including such high-profile ones as the OECD Guidelines for Multinational Enterprises (2011), the British Ethical Trading Initiative Base Code (2014), the UN Global Compact, and the more company-specific codes of conduct as promulgated by TNCs such as British Petroleum, Coca-Cola Corporation, Walmart, Canon, Nestlé, and Novartis, to name just a few, will verify the voluntary nature of these codes. The UN Global Compact[10] has 10 principles which define "a principled approach to doing business. This means operating in ways that, at a minimum, meet fundamental responsibilities in the areas of human rights, labor, environment and anti-corruption" (UN Global Compact Website 2018). The formulation of these ten principles is instructive: "businesses *should* support and respect the protection of internationally proclaimed human rights"; "businesses *should* uphold the freedom of association and . . . the right to collective bargaining"; "businesses *should* support a precautionary approach to environmental challenges"; "businesses *should* work against corruption in all its forms."

The formulation of these codes of corporate social responsibility is important since it reveals different levels of voluntary commitment, yet all avoid the overriding issue of binding legal enforcement. Except in a very few cases, such as the University of Wisconsin's suit against Adidas in relation to the production of apparel that led to compensation for 2,700 local workers in Indonesia,[11] it has been virtually impossible to successfully bring suit against a TNC for infringement of human rights, violation of labor laws, and environmental catastrophes in developing countries. Examples such as Shell Oil in the Niger Delta, Coca-Cola in India, and Walmart in Bangladesh are more typical of the resistance of TNCs to act in compliance with local laws applicable to their overseas operations and suppliers. Nowhere is this more obvious than in the vague language used in contractual agreements between TNCs and their overseas suppliers, specifically in the structure of supply chain links related to local labor. To be blunt, the literature and discussion of codes of corporate social responsibility focus almost exclusively on what ought to be done, or what is desirable, and not on the legal enforcement of what is viable or even possible.[12]

Case study: Walmart in Bangladesh

Can transnational corporations be trusted to put worker safety ahead of profits?

On November 24, 2012 a fire broke out in the Tazreen factory in Bangladesh.[13] Hundreds of workers were trapped in the building because the exit doors had been locked. For people working on the upper floors in the building, windows were the only way to escape the fire. More than 100 workers sustained major head and back injuries by jumping out third- and fourth-story windows in their attempt to save themselves from the fire, and 112 were killed. Less than one year later, on April 24, 2013, a commercial building named Rana Plaza, eight stories in height, collapsed and caught fire. More than 2,500 workers were injured and 1,139 killed. Located as well in Bangladesh, it is widely regarded as one of the worst accidents in a textile factory. Ready Made Garments (RMGs), the kind produced by the workers in both Tazreen and Rana Plaza, contributed to 81% of Bangladesh's export earnings in 2014–2015, including RMG trousers, jackets, and t-shirts; 61% of the country's RMG products were exported to the European Union, while 21% of RMG products were exported to the US. Both the Tazreen and Rana Plaza textile factories produced garments for Walmart, Gap, German discount store KIK, Sears, and El Corte Ingles, a department store chain located and based in Spain.

In 2013, a collaboration among approximately 200 clothing brands and retailers, as well as trade unions and advocacy groups, signed the Accord on Fire and Building Safety in Bangladesh, which was drafted to ensure safety standards for textile factories in the RMG industry. The accord is a legally binding agreement that requires multinational brands and retailers to work with trade unions to ensure that necessary repairs and building upgrades are identified and complete, and that workers have rights that protect them from dangerous workplace conditions. Walmart refused to sign the accord, and instead formed the Alliance for Bangladesh Worker Safety (ABWS) along with Gap.[14] The ABWS is based on a voluntary, rather than a contractual or legal, commitment to improving worker safety, and Walmart began to focus on worker training programs in fire safety. In 2014, Walmart announced that it was contributing $3 million to BRAC, an international NGO working in Bangladesh to assist workers impacted by the Tazreen and Rana Plaza tragedies. Of that amount, $1 million went to the Rana Plaza Donors Trust Fund, $250,000 went to the Tazreen Claims Administration Trust, and the remaining amount to BRAC for its work in responding to textile factory accidents in Bangladesh.

Walmart's supply chain network includes approximately 280 textile factories that produce RMG in Bangladesh. Walmart has neither provided nor reported on the list of these factories and their locations with which it has no subcontracts. This is a way of regularly conducting business with informal and unregulated textile factories, which number in the thousands located in the country. In 2015, the Accord on Fire and Building Safety in Bangladesh, the Alliance for Bangladesh Worker Safety, and the International Labour Organizations (ILO) reported that 3,425 safety inspections had been carried out in textile factories throughout Bangladesh, but that only eight facilities had passed the final safety inspection.

Compounding this issue is the weakness of legal systems in most developing countries. Nigeria is a good example. Shell Oil has been drilling and extracting oil in the Niger Delta for many years. A local ethnic group, the Ogale, argued that its 40,000-strong community had been devastated for years by oil spills which Shell had never cleaned up or provided equitable compensation for the destruction of the community's environment. Over the years, the Nigerian National Assembly has passed laws that require legal compliance and punishment for offenses related to discharge of hazardous material.[15] Section 30 of The National Environmental Standards and Regulations Enforcement Agency (Establishment) Act of 2007 provided for the agency's legal authority to engage in the right of seizure if environmental offenses were found to have been committed. The Harmful Waste Act (part of the Special Criminal Provisions Act), provides for the protection of public health in sections 234–248, as well as enumerates a long list of offenses related to the disposal, transportation, sale, and storage of harmful waste that are categorized as criminal. But the act includes diplomatic immunity for foreign nationals who are prosecuted for some of the offenses as described in the legislation, and individuals or local groups and communities are restricted in their ability to bring suit against environmental offenses committed by TNCs like Shell Oil. Another problem is the lack of zeal in government prosecutors to bring suit against TNCs. Delay, corruption, and a willingness to accept monetary compensation in lieu of strict enforcement of laws related to environmental offenses have resulted in a lack of confidence in the legal system to protect the Nigerian citizenry. The Ogale, along with another ethnic group, the Bille, finally decided that they would receive no justice from the Nigerian court systems and decided to bring suit against Shell Oil in the United Kingdom since Shell Oil is a UK-based TNC. Shell Oil argued in response that the company and its Nigerian subsidiary, Shell Petroleum Development Company (SPDC), was not liable and that the UK court had no jurisdiction in this matter. In 2017, Britain's High Court ruled in favor of Shell Oil: "[T]here is simply no connection whatsoever between this jurisdiction and the claims brought by the claimants, who are Nigerian citizens, for breaches of statutory duty and/ or in common law for acts and omissions in Nigeria, by a Nigerian company."[16]

Not surprisingly, Shell Oil has a robust and detailed description of their corporate social responsibility in Shell General Business Principles and Group Code of Conduct.[17] This is a voluntary code of conduct, even though Shell's Implementation of the Voluntary Principles of Security and Human Rights on its website states that local subsidiaries, suppliers, and contractors must comply with all locally applicable laws. However, in the legal suits brought against the company, just like Walmart in Bangladesh, TNCs argue that the supplier employees or local subsidiary employees are not – strictly speaking – parent-company employees, and so the parent TNC is not liable for any illegal activities committed by the suppliers in breach of local labor law. Similarly, although it subscribes to the corporate social responsibility (CSR) principles of the UN's Global Compact, from 2000 to 2008 Coca-Cola vigorously denied and fought the accusations brought against it for having pesticide residue in its dozen or so produced drinks in India, causing water shortages in the communities around its local production facilities, as well as the pollution of local water resources. In 2006, an Indian NGO had provided the government with confirmation of the existence of pesticides in locally produced Coca-Cola drinks, but the attempt by the Bureau of Indian Standards to implement a higher standard based on those required by the European Union for all carbonated drinks was mired and ultimately lost in government machinations.[18]

It is not an overstatement to conclude that TNCs are fully cognizant of the weaknesses of legal systems in the developing countries where they conduct operations and it is not atypical for TNCs to place their operations in countries where regulations, enforcement, and the legal system are most weak. Often overlooked within this analysis is the reason why legal systems in developing countries are weak and ineffectual. The main reason is historical: regulations and their enforcement require strong and stable, incorruptible and viable, legal procedures and institutions. In most developing countries these procedures and institutions have not had time to develop and coalesce into a strong legal system. The United Kingdom's tradition of common law starts with the Magna Carta in 1214, and the concept of case precedent so important in the American legal system has a history of over 200 years. In contrast, a faculty of law was not started until 1961 at Strathmore University in Nairobi, Kenya, the first law school in Kenya, while a second faculty of law was established at the University of Nairobi (Kenya) in 1970. The University of Lagos, located in the capital of Nigeria, established a faculty of law in 1962 with three Englishmen and two Nigerians. The first law school in all of Asia was formed in 1855, the Government Law College, at the University of Bombay (now Mumbai). A college of law was founded during the 1820s at the University of Haiti, but its effectiveness as an educational institution has been plagued for many years by the fact that the majority of faculty (including law professors) work on a part-time basis, have an hourly based wage scale, and thus have minimal time for meaningful contact with students. Books are expensive and at a premium, and other education resources are generally lacking. Add to this a component of unparalleled bribery and government influence over the judiciary, and the result is a legal system in Haiti that lacks integrity. Strengthening both the legal education and legal systems in developing countries in order to address the scope, breadth, application, and enforcement of legally binding regulations on TNCs is key to preventing egregious damage to local communities through environmental damage and weak child labor laws. Yet although there are currently numerous partnerships between law schools in the West and those in developing countries, the current condition of these legal systems will take many years to strengthen.

Keeping TNCs honest

As a result of the bad publicity from the sordid examples above that have been collected by investigative reports by developed-nation journalists, international watchdog groups, local NGOs, and a growing number of activist consumers, TNCs have embraced codes of CSR in order to not only rebuild and enhance their public reputation, but to address the economic damage that resulted in loss of consumer confidence (e.g., Coca-Cola's 40% drop in sales in India and a resulting drop in worldwide annual sales of 15% in 2003 were specifically due to the damaging publicity from the pesticide debacle).[19] In fact, both Coca-Cola and Walmart have developed into model examples of TNCs that have accepted, implemented, and provided ongoing monitoring and evaluation of their success in meeting CSR principles and quantifiable goals in their annual reports, and they regularly publish and update sustainability reports on their company websites. In India, Coca-Cola has crafted numerous initiatives to improve water conditions and water management effectiveness in collaboration with international NGOs, local NGOs and community groups, and government agencies. Walmart has updated and strengthened its policies in relation to labor conditions in Bangladesh and worked with Maquila Solidarity Network, an NGO whose advice was taken to implement a no-tolerance child labor policy for its retail supply chain. Even Shell Oil has initiated numerous community development programs within the Delta region in recent years, including a microcredit project, 27 health clinics, and educational scholarships for approximately 17,000 children. The growing power of publicity surrounding its operations in the Niger Delta also convinced the company that it was in its best self-interest to finally settle with the family of the internationally recognized author and environmental activist Ken Saro-Wiwa, who was hanged in the mid-1990s along with eight others of a minority ethnic group located in the Delta region, on trumped up charges in which both management at Shell and the Nigerian government were complicit.

The importance of international and local NGOs, investigative reports by journalists, and the role of media activists to publicize and pressure TNCs to accept and adhere to voluntary codes of CSR in light of the lack of successful legal recourse in developing countries cannot be underestimated. Increasingly over the years, certain NGOs such as Worldwatch.org have focused on whether or not TNCs adhere to the principles and codes of conduct as stated on their websites and annual and sustainability reports. Similarly investigative journalists from *Time, Newsweek, The New York Times, The Guardian, Bloomberg*, and *The Telegraph* have provided detailed reports on the operations of the giant TNCs such as Walmart, Shell Oil, British Petroleum, Apple, Coca-Cola, and Nike, as well as many others, and their adherence to CSR. The oversight of NGOs in conjunction with investigative reports have helped to clarify the moral issues related to specific TNC abuses for the general public and especially for consumers. As consumers become more educated about the operations of TNCs, they have developed a crucial role for themselves in holding TNCs responsible by the fact of their purchasing power. Improved labor conditions at Nike or Walmart supplier facilities in developing countries can be attributed to the massive pressure put on TNCs by developed-nation consumers once they have access to well-documented information of damage or mistreatment. And consumer influence is enhanced by media activism, exemplified by documentaries such as *Flow: For Love of Water*, and by the proliferation of information disseminated on the Internet that focuses on the operations and practices of TNCs. The alacrity with which the Internet spreads investigative reports on TNCs has contributed to the quick response by NGOs and consumers to hold them accountable and has fostered adherence to their principles and codes of CSR. In lieu of accepting legally binding regulation imposed by the governments of developing countries, CSR can be regarded as a touchstone for a TNC's conduct overseas – and it is public scrutiny that is the key to maintaining a credible level of adherence to CSR principles, codes of conduct, and sustainability goals. Negative publicity and the consequent damage to the reputation of TNCs, not to mention the potential economic damage, has led to the realization that with a worldwide communications network such as it now exists and the likelihood of not being able to avoid public scrutiny, they can no longer act with impunity. In other words, the local communities in developing countries within which the TNC conducts its operations cannot be ignored.[20]

On the other hand, NGOs, social activists, and consumers must also pay attention to Friedman's notion that the business of business is business, and that making a profit is central to the operation of any business, and that if management is not attentive to this basic fact, bankruptcy is the result. They must accept the fact that, by definition, TNCs are not responsible for development – they are not responsible for addressing the myriad social problems that confront a developing country. Profit is the basic reason a TNC is in business and expands overseas. Within this narrow framework for understanding the purpose of a TNC Friedman is correct. Yet, as indicated above, it is undeniable that their operations have a wide-ranging effect on the local communities where they work. And it is a misplaced assumption that markets correct themselves and can, in turn, address issues related to human rights abuses, child labor, unfair wages, and environmental spoilage. Market forces are not a reliable solution for social problems.[21] The current structure of the global neoliberal economic system is not neutral; at the present time its trade policies, labor laws, protection against land reforms, and other protectionist policies favor TNCs. Some legal systems in developing countries are strong enough to provide opposition to the unbridled operations of TNCs; those that are not cannot. And it does not look likely in the near or even distant future that legal systems in most developing countries will have the ability to enforce compliance of social responsibility codes of conduct. Nonetheless, the moral force of adhering to CSR standards is slowly, incrementally growing due to the relentless efforts by civil society, journalists, and consumers to publicize moral lapses in TNC non-compliance.

Conclusion

At a minimum, therefore, it is in a TNC's enlightened self-interest to be a good community partner and give attention to the numerous stakeholders that are impacted by its local operations. Within this minimal adherence to CSR, one can argue that they should ascribe to a policy of "do no harm" where the protection of safe water resources, fairness in labor practices, and the prevention of environmental degradation are good examples. At best, they can follow Mackey's model and take on a proactive role in their voluntary adherence to the principles and codes of conduct of their stated CSR by reaching out to communities to implement meaningful and useful stakeholder relations that result in improved health, education, and human rights. Whatever strategy regarding CSR the management of a TNC decides to embark upon, TNCs can be bad or good for developing countries. This can only be determined on a case-by-case basis. The health of local markets in a developing country can be affected by TNC abuse, but TNC conduct is not the sole decisive factor. TNC and government agreements, contracts, corruption, civil society, and local social movements are mitigating factors. Fairness, equity, and justice are a result of an interplay among numerous actors.

A new development has occurred on the global scene, namely, the appearance of emerging, developing-country multinationals, that suggests a new way of thinking about CSR.[22] The experience and understanding of local conditions and context within management of these developing country TNCs has the potential to transform adherence to and legal enforcement of CSR. One of the largest cosmetics company in Brazil, Natura Cosmeticos, has become a leader in biodiversity conservation, and collaborates with indigenous communities in Amazonia to gather raw materials for its products. The firm is a founding member of the Union for Ethical BioTrade. Narayana Hrudayalaya Private Ltd., a rapidly growing healthcare firm in India, has provided cardiac care and treatment to poor communities throughout the country, and the Tata Group in India has built numerous schools in underserved communities. Management at these firms reason that since the government is unable to provide basic services such as healthcare, education, and protection of the environment, it is the responsibility of the private sector to meet and fulfill the social needs of an ever-increasing but poor population that can neither advocate nor protect itself. In contrast to the shareholder model of the TNCs in developed countries that still holds its narrow and restrictive influence, and despite their foot-dragging reluctance to acknowledging a broader concept of corporate social responsibility that is in their own strategic self-interest, Mackey's vision of a stakeholder model of CSR is coming to fruition in developing countries.

Questions for discussion

1   Do you agree with Friedman's or Mackey's view on corporate social responsibility? Is there simply a duty to produce profit for shareholders, or does responsibility extend beyond this? Why? Are there other models as well?

2   Think about your own consumption. What is your role as a consumer? Should you have a say in the way in which products are produced? What can you do as a consumer to combat the problems facing those in developing countries?

3   What are the positive and negative effects of globalization and the spread of transnational corporations? Does the good outweigh the bad, or vice versa?

Notes

1 Friedman (1970).
2 See also Friedman (1962).
3 See Friedman et al. (2005).
4 See Smith et al. (1790).
5 Haslem et al. (2012, p. 204).
6 Ibid., p. 208.
7 UNCTAD (2010, pp. 18–23).
8 Haslam et al. (op. cit.).
9 Smits (2017, p. 102).
10 See *The Ten Principles of the UN Global Compact*, at www.unglobalcompact.org/what-is-gc/mission/principles.
11 Smits (op. cit., p. 98).
12 Ibid., p. 100.
13 This case study is taken from Bhattacharjee (2016).
14 See www.walmart.com
15 Mordi et al. (2012, p. 3).
16 Vaughan (2017).
17 www.shell.com
18 Cellido Torres et al. (2012, p. 55).
19 Ibid.
20 Vives (2008, p. 7).
21 Ibid., p. 20.
22 World Economic Forum (2015).

Suggested reading

Milton Friedman (2002). *Capitalism and Freedom*, fortieth anniversary edition. Chicago: Chicago University Press.

This book explores, among other things, Friedman's notion that the only responsibility of a business is to maximize profits for its shareholders.

Milton Friedman, John Mackey and Thurman John Rodgers (2005). "Rethinking the Social Responsibility of Business." *Reason*, October 2005 issue. https://reason.com/archives/2005/10/01/rethinking-the-social-responsi.

This debate, as described in this chapter, outlines the differing conceptions of business as put forth by both Friedman and Mackey.

Markus Giesler and Ela Veresiu (2014). "Creating the Responsible Consumer: Moralistic Governance Regimes and Consumer Subjectivity." *Journal of Consumer Research* 41(October): 849–867.

Giesler and Veresiu's work outlines the need to help develop consumers into moral subjects. As such, consumers then have the ability and moral knowledge to make ethical consumption decisions, with the eventual goal of ending unethical business practices.

Michael Hopkins (2008). *Corporate Social Responsibility and International Development: Is Business the Solution?* Abingdon: Routledge.

Hopkins's book addresses the concept of corporate social responsibility, especially with respect to businesses and NGOs responsibilities to lower, and ultimately eradicate, poverty.

United Nations (2011). "Guiding Principles for Business and Human Rights: Implementing the United Nations 'Protect, Respect and Remedy' Framework." *United Nations Global Compact*. www.unglobalcompact.org/library/2.

This UN report outlines certain guidelines for international standards of business with respect to human rights.

References

Bhattacharjee, Shikha Silliman (2016). "Precarious Work in the Walmart Global Value Chain, 2016." *Workers Voices From the Global Supply Chain, A Report to the ILO 2016.* https://asia.floorwage.org/workersvoices/reports/precarious-work-in-the-walmart-global-value-chain.

Cedillo Torres, Cristina A. et al. (2012). "Four Case Studies on Corporate Social Responsibility: Do Conflicts Affect a Company's Corporate Social Responsibility Policy?" *Utrecht Law Review* 8(3): 51–73.

Friedman, Milton (1962). *Capitalism and Freedom*. Chicago: University of Chicago Press.

Friedman, Milton (1970). "The Responsibility of Business is to Increase its Profits." *New York Times*, September 14, 1970.

Friedman, Milton, John Mackey and T.J. Rodgers (2005). "Rethinking the Social Responsibility of Business: A Reasoned Debate Featuring Milton Friedman, Whole Foods' John Mackey, and Cyprus Semiconductor's TJ Rodgers." *Reason* (October 2005): 29–37.

Haslam, Peter, Schafter, Jessica and Pierre Beaudet (2012). *Introduction to International Development*, 2nd edition. Oxford: Oxford University Press.

Mordi, Chima, Iroye Samuel Opeyemi, Mordi and Ibiyinka Stella Ojo (2012). "Corporate Social Responsibility and the Legal Regulations in Nigeria." *Corporate Social Responsibility and the Legal Regulation in Nigeria. Economic Insights – Trends and Challenges* LXIV(1): 1–8.

Smith, Adam (1790). *The Theory of Moral Sentiments*. Library of Economics and Liberty. www.econlib.org/Smith/smMS.html.

Smits, Jan M. (2017). "Enforcing Corporate Social Responsibility Codes Under Private Law: On the Disciplining Power of Legal Doctrine." *Indiana Journal of Global Legal Studies* 24(1) (Winter 2017).

UNCTAD (2010). "World Investment Report 2010: Investing in a Low-Carbon Economy." *United Nations Conference on Trade and Development*. unctad.org

United Nations Global Compact. www.unglobalcompact.org

Vaughan, Adam (2017). "Nigerian Oil Pollution Claims Against Shell Cannot Be Heard in UK, Court Rules." *The Guardian*, January 26, 2017. www.theguardian.com/business/2017/jan/26/nigerian-oil-pollution-shell-uk-corporations.

Vives, Antonio (2008). "Corporate Social Responsibility: The Role of Law and Markets and the Case of Developing Countries." 83 *Chicago-Kent Law Review*. 199.

World Economic Forum (2015). "How Emerging Multinationals Are Embracing Social Responsibility." *Knowledge@Wharton*, INSEAD Knowledge. http://knowledge.wharton.upenn.edu/article/why-emerging-multinationals-are-embracing-social-responsibility/.

8 The development practitioner

Most development practitioners who work in areas such as sub-Saharan Africa, Central and South America, and East Asia, for example, don't think of and don't write about their fieldwork experiences in terms of those issues related to private morality, as described in the introduction to this book.[1] And, most importantly, except for egregious issues such as corruption and the misuse of donor funds (which are in the arena of public morality), relevant data points included in their formal analysis and assessment of indicators, outcomes, financial sustainability, or impact statements of development programs do not ordinarily incorporate the development practitioner's analysis of ethical problems related to the success or failure of a program.

Aid management has developed its own universal language; known as "logframes," it is a methodological tool all NGOs, small or large, use in program development, planning, implementation, management, and evaluation. Logframes are essential for donor funding; hence the use of logframes as a methodological tool dominates the provision of what is considered good development. Logframes can go through many manifestations and modifications before their final version and, as they are revised going up the ladder of an NGO bureaucratic hierarchy that requires the logframe to be altered to meet the specific priorities of the government donor or a larger funding source such as UNICEF, it is often the case that the final proposal looks nothing like the ideas and metrics within the original logframe that had been developed in participation with local partners and community input.[2] The requirement of the overriding majority of donor agencies to provide statistical data and analysis, whether of disbursed funds or indicators, such as catchment population reached, precludes the inclusion of ethical problems or consequences that result from a logframe. Granted, those who fund donor agencies, or the board of directors that approves the allocation of funds, argue that it is impractical to evaluate program development in a timely manner without a methodology that focuses on statistical summaries. But these narrative reports and anecdotal evidence ordinarily are written to support the statistical results, and are not usually regarded as determining factors in the methodological process of monitoring and evaluation. Thus what could be and sometimes are the issues that determine the success and failure of a development program are undervalued in the process of development itself.

We believe that the experiences of development practitioners in the implementation and management of development programs is a necessary and sufficient condition for programmatic success. Too much of the time grassroots ethical conundrums of aid workers are therefore relegated to a status of "interesting connection" or "insightful observation." The invaluable experience of the development practitioner is written mostly in the form of personal reflections in a daily diary at night or over the weekend for a later time of reflection; yet the interactions of a practitioner with a local rural-based ward education officer who works for the government, for example, who does not hold the same views as local teachers and community members who sit on a library committee, could result in significant problems for determining the community's responsibility to provide resources for a community-based library, whose success depends on providing much-needed access to textbooks for primary and secondary school students.

It is not merely unfortunate but counterproductive that the people who are closest to development programs that are implemented, and who have become acquainted with the social, political, ethnic, and cultural context that underlies the involvement of local community members and those who benefit by the program, do not have the venues to convey their grassroots experiences and observations, either with each other, or to people who would be most interested.[3] Thus there is a dearth of writing on the analysis of ethical concerns from those people directly affiliated and working in the field of development.[4] In not a few instances when implementing or managing a development program, what to do or not to do is an ethical issue, not merely a practical one; development practitioners must not overlook that what is frequently considered a local barrier is in fact an ethical problem that can undermine the implementation of the most carefully vetted and designed program.

Some of the most important ethical issues listed below are most familiar to the development practitioner who has spent extensive time in fieldwork. Unless one has taken advanced coursework in an international development program, it is not intended as criticism to say that the majority of aid workers have no formal orientation to help them navigate potential solutions to grassroots ethical problems that affect their providing successful program assistance.[5]

In order to facilitate and move this discussion forward, we suggest that the private morality of a development practitioner might be oriented or guided by a consequentialist or utilitarian approach that involves a cost-benefit analysis that calculates the aggregate advantages and disadvantages to a local community for example, or perhaps employs a social contract framework for analyzing and determining considerations such as equitable cooperation between donor agencies and local community-based organizations (CBOs) regarding symmetries of power in decision-making authority, alterations to the design or implementation of the program, and dispersal and use of donor funding. The first thought on everyone's mind when the development officers from a donor agency meet with the elders of a local community is this: How can the unequal power and resources between the donor agency and the community be addressed so that true collaboration results in successful development?

Communitarian ethics, already discussed in detail in Chapter 3, focuses on local religious values and cultural and ethnic identities that forge unity, social cohesion, and solidarity within communities. Thus the framework of ethical reasoning that might be most appropriate for the development practitioner is one that involves building and relying upon relationships of trust throughout a community that one is in collaboration with to alleviate poverty or improve access to educational resources.

Since the 1990s there has been attention given to the fact that development practitioners are confronted with moral problems in the course of their fieldwork, but it is during the last 10–15 years especially that there has been an acknowledgement and concern that grassroots or local context related to ethical issues such as vehicle use, time of visits, power relations, compensation, brain drain, local expectations, and differing perspectives on aid all have fundamental and far-reaching consequences for the success or failure of development programs. Below we identify and describe some of the most important ethical issues that challenge the development practitioner:

1   *Appearances Matter*
    One of the most overlooked examples of a lack of sensitivity and understanding of local feeling is the vehicle use by most NGOs that work in developing countries throughout the world. It is incomprehensible and inexcusable that young expat program officers from international donor agencies who arrive in a rural setting to discuss with community members the implementation of a safe water program, for example, are not cognizant of the symbolism of their large Toyota Land Cruiser upon their arrival. For the majority of the poor in rural areas who make less than $1.50 per day, the appearance of an oversized, white vehicle with the NGO's name emblazoned in large black English letters on its side is an emphatic representation of separation from local communities and context, Western intervention, the imposition of external and non-contextual advice, and the display of wealth; this vehicle contributes to the palpable distinction between "us" and "them."

2   *Honest Assessment*
    It should be no surprise that expert foreigners who arrive in large vehicles for short-time visits to provide program monitoring and management advice are viewed with skepticism by community members. When a foreign program officer from a large donor agency comes to visit a development program once or twice a year for a period of 2–4 hours during an afternoon, one who is even conversant with local language skills (which is not always the case), it is not possible to understand the local context of issues that are involved in making the program a success or failure. Over the years, it has been the commitment of large donor agencies to hire local personnel to manage local development programs and, as a result, the short visits by foreign program officers has been largely addressed. Yet this sometimes has the unintended consequences of local personnel that are hired by the donor agency telling their management (foreign country directors) of what they think management wants to hear.

3   *Power and Participation*

Fraught with complexity and nuance in the development world are the power relations related to assumptions about donor/recipient relationships. When the American or European development practitioner arrives in a poor, rural setting in a large, white Toyota Land Cruiser, the symbols of wealth, privilege, and power are immediately impressed upon the local population. Perhaps most important is the symbol of differentiation. There is no minimizing the fact that the development practitioner has arrived to help those who are less fortunate. This difference can become a chasm of misunderstanding and miscommunication and can undermine the most well-crafted development program if the practitioner is not cognizant about the relationships of power, gender, ethnic history, and current political context. We have already discussed the harmful effect of colonialism and its impact. This history is not dead – the imposition of a foreign language, of labor laws, of land acquisition, of the diminution and even destruction of culture, religion, political organization, and ethnic lifestyles lives in the memory and perceptions of many, many citizens of former colonies. And it is naïve to think this is in the past and not relevant to the success and failure of development programs. Local communities therefore must participate in the design, management, and evaluation of local development programs. This is currently an issue that international NGOs agree upon, namely, that participation by local community members is one of the effective methods of ensuring the cultural sustainability of a program.

Yet the control and dispersal of funds is what symbolizes the differentiation most. Many international NGOs are reluctant to provide direct funding or put money in the hands of program participants (except for microlending initiatives). It is true that most people in poor remote rural areas and urban slums in developing countries have never seen, much less had to manage, a grant of US$1,000. It is not uncommon that, once having received such a grant to purchase a zipper machine for school uniforms, for example, the recipient disappears with the money. Since they have never seen such a large amount of money before and do not have the skills to manage it, there should be no surprise in its misuse. On occasion, the recipient might think that a donor is not hurt by the disappearance of this money; and it should not be surprising that the recipient might even think that the US$1,000 is life-transforming for him and his household. This is reason enough, according to international NGOs, for the development practitioner in the course of fieldwork not to provide direct funding either to individuals or local community-based organizations. But this is precisely what is at issue in the donor/recipient relationship: to what degree is the international NGO and development practitioner willing to engage and trust in local community members to determine the use of, and subsequently disperse, funding for a program? In the final analysis, it is not always the development practitioner that determines the continuation of a development program in light of misuse of funds, or in the evaluation and assessment of a local community's readiness to engage successfully in moving a development program forward. NGO country directors rely heavily on statistical program reports and accounting discrepancies. Yet in certain cases the advice of the aid worker can sometimes be a decisive factor, and this responsibility is unlike any the development practitioner has ever experienced before: Is a community ready and capable of participating in, and effectively collaborating on, a development program?

4   *Pay Equity*

There has been a growing concern about the disparity in pay scale between country directors and program officers from the US or Europe and local staff who work for NGOs in developing countries. Articles by foreign staff who work for donor agencies in West Africa, for example, have complained about the injustice related to the differential allocation of daily compensation for hotel costs. Whereas foreign program officers are allocated a certain amount of money to stay at good hotels during field visits, local staff are provide less funding to stay at what is typically described as, for example, an "African hotel." Complaints have also surfaced about the significant difference in pay inequity between expats and local staff. A foreign aid worker who receives, say, $3,000 per month, plus living and transportation allowances, is contrasted with a local staff member who ordinarily receives approximately half that salary or less for comparable work-related responsibilities, and also receives no living or much reduced transportation allowances. The complaint, as it has been described by both foreign staff and local staff who work side by side, is that the work of local staff is not valued as highly as the work of the foreign development practitioner, that local staff are treated unjustly by the NGO, and that this inequity ultimately contributes to the brain drain of local talent to depart for jobs in Europe or the US where they are paid fairly for their work. More and more foreign program officers working for NGOs are bringing this issue to the attention of the development industry. Clearly, equal pay for equal work ought to guide each and every NGO's employment wage scale. Although an important ethical issue, we believe that there is another similar though not identical issue related to wages that is of greater consequence, and one that has not been given much attention at all.

Compensation of local workers (secretaries, social workers, public health workers, etc.) who work for international NGOs skews local salaries and draws the best of those individuals that might be of more benefit working within the public sector of their own country. For example, a woman in Nairobi, Kenya with a few years experience and a diploma in front office and administration can expect to earn between Ksh100,000 and Ksh130,000 per month (approximately US$100–$130) as a secretary for an international NGO. In contrast, the average salary for a woman with some college receives less as a secretary in a local corporation or firm with the same responsibilities. Similarly, social workers who are employed by international NGOs earn significantly more than the average monthly salary range of between Ksh12,879–Ksh29,930 for social workers. In fact, within Kenya 70% of local workers in the international NGO sector earn more than Ksh100,000 per month than their counterparts in the business sector and government. The result is obvious and similar to the problem above: the most qualified and talented individuals gravitate toward international NGO employment; the best and brightest of a nation's workforce are thus working for international NGOs rather than for national, regional, or local goals. Of course, one might argue that these goals coincide. This issue is an extremely important one, and one that international NGOs have not investigated or attended to thoroughly.

5   *Brain Drain*

Extraction of local individuals for development work elsewhere than their local community has become a widespread and commonly accepted practice. Large donor agencies and NGOs regularly hire local individuals to help monitor and manage local program development. These men and women are identified in their communities as leaders and catalysts for change, have completed secondary school, know the local language as well as English, and have some nascent experience or acquaintance with development work, for example, acting as the secretary of a community-based organization. The NGO hires the individual with the most promise, then trains that person to fulfill the requirements of what is needed to move a development program forward.

Over a period of two to three years the individual is provided with additional training, given the opportunity to travel to the capital of the country for various workshops and to meet other individuals hired by the NGO in the same circumstance and for the same purpose, and meet foreign development professionals from the NGO as well. If that individual performs well, and is considered efficient and effective at his/her job, there is a likelihood that the person is transferred from his original community either to the capital and given more management responsibilities, or even to another country to implement a similar development program. In certain instances, a highly talented local person's career track might start from his/her community in Western Senegal with an international NGO, continue to Dakar with additional responsibilities, be identified by another international NGO and transferred to work as a program advisor in Sweden, then on to New York as the director of an international program for the culmination of a career. Only the best have achieved this. But one must pause and ask the following question: Is this the most effective use of such a person? It is the Western assumption that this track is not only the accepted but the most desirable career path. But wouldn't it have been better for the individual to remain in his/her own community where their talent could have been put to its most effective use? Has the NGO unknowingly and naively plucked out the person who can best assist his own community? It is expected that the international NGO community will argue to the contrary: the above-described career path enables development work to be most effective. Yet, one could argue that this is counterproductive to development work in that it drains the most talented individuals from their own country that needs them most.

6   *Pitfalls of Volunteerism*
The use of volunteers has become a recurring theme of how large and small NGOs from developed countries are able to market their organizations to those individuals who want to provide hands-on assistance to poor people overseas. The unquestioned assumption is that this enables foreign volunteers to use their skills (or even those who can only do manual labor) not only to help poor people, but also provide testimonials to the good work of the organization they are volunteering for, and hopefully bring additional funding to that organization. Yet when volunteers from developed countries arrive to help build, paint, stock a library in a slum, this takes away the opportunity of locals to earn money for this type of manual labor, which is usually the only type of work many residents of a slum are qualified for. Granted, the NGO saves money in labor costs, but the risk is to alienate and breed animosity against the NGO for not hiring local labor. The result can be that the library is not considered to be part of the local community, and when an act of random violence occurs due to political unrest, for example, the library might find itself without anyone in the slum willing to protect it from looting, significant damage, or even destruction.

The use of volunteer foreign medical personnel in remote rural areas to staff a dispensary or medical center that lacks qualified medical personnel also raises concerns. Even though these medical volunteers provide much needed assistance (with foreign medical or nursing students giving injections) such volunteers should never be seen or understood to replace the need for training local medical personnel to staff a developing country's medical infrastructure; except for conditions that are defined as short-term, foreign volunteerism should never become the norm rather than a focus on training for local personnel.

7   *Urban Versus Rural Challenges*
Development programs must be established with the assessment and understanding of specific contexts and this involves how the development practitioner presents the program of his/her donor agency. Nowhere is this more true than in the difference between urban slums and rural areas. The phenomenal and unprecedented growth of slums in Nairobi (Kenya, East Africa), Abijan (Ivory Coast), Mumbai (India), and São Paulo (Brazil) appear to be unabated. Millions of people over the past 30 years, whether due to the failure of a farm, the death of a spouse, the search for a job, destitution, or even the traditional emigration routes from rural to urban settings, are swelling the slums of developing countries on an untold scale. Lack of employment opportunities, poor sanitation that gives rise to cholera outbreaks, inadequate shelter, unsafe drinking water, a high incidence of HIV infection, and violence currently plague second- and third-generation slum dwellers around the world. Add the fact that in certain slums there is a mix of different ethnic groups

and nationalities where, for example, Somalis live next to Luo and Kikuyu in Kibera slum (Nairobi), with different first languages, social values, purposes of living in the slum, and family structures, the challenge to providing programs that meet basic needs such as sanitation and safe water, and social services such as alcohol addiction and domestic violence, seem insurmountable. It should be no surprise that people living within the slums each have their own distinct expectations of what might be forthcoming when the development practitioner arrives. The identification of these varying perspectives and expectations, whether realistic or unrealistic, is the responsibility of the development practitioner. Lacking an astute understanding of the contextual nuances of these issues will lead to the certain failure of any intervention of assistance, whatever might be the theoretical framework that is at the basis of that intervention. This is just one instance of where the theoretical framework for development must converge with practical considerations.

Rural areas in developing countries also have their own specific conditions and context. As of 2012, the majority of people in developing countries still live in rural areas engaged in agricultural activities and animal husbandry. (But the gap between urban and rural populations is closing fast.) Challenges such as drought, the distance a member of the household has to walk to access water for drinking and cooking, the distance to access medical care, and the burden of diseases such as malaria and typhoid all contribute to the unique context of rural development. Yet at the core of rural development is the overriding presence and centrality of the village, the elders, the social cohesion of women working in the fields and the community as a whole. It should be obvious that the rural context is different than the slum experience, and that the development practitioner must attune his approach to these different contexts and the individuals living within them accordingly. The development practitioner must be aware of nuance within these contexts as well, and not interpret local intentions and perspectives in the same light. It is not uncommon for local women's groups and individuals that perceive potential benefits from a program to tell the development practitioner what they think he/she wants to hear. Behind these remarks are the intentions and perspectives of people who live in dire circumstances and poverty, but each with their own perspective. These intentions and perspectives must be evaluated carefully in order to understand what might affect the success of the program. On the other hand, the development practitioner must be aware of the difference between his/her own notion of development as opposed to the traditionally accepted responsibility within village communities to take care of orphans, for example. Western assumptions about best practices in the urban and rural contexts of development are not "one size fits all" and can possibly result in major miscommunications regarding program participation and sustainability. The development practitioner also has the obligation not to mislead or overpromise potential advantages of the program to the local population – not to raise expectations that might not be fulfilled. Thus what one conveys to an urban population as opposed to a rural population has to be specific to the context and clear in specific expectations, benefits, and potential burdens. Occasionally, the enthusiasm of a development practitioner sometimes leads to a lack of clear communication on these issues. Local interpreters can also be overly positive and misrepresent the benefits to the community, and this brings us back to the importance of a development practitioner's fluency in the local language.

8   *Authentic Development Needs*

The relation between development and globalization has been a focal point of academics, World Bank analysts, and government officials from around the globe since the turn of the twenty-first century. On the one hand, it has been argued that globalization – understood according to the World Bank as the integration of national economies into the free market system and the attendant sustained economic growth, expanding free trade, capital flow, deregulation of industries, and the free flow of information not merely related to strategic economic interests and intellectual property rights – has been instrumental in reducing poverty in China and East Asia and transforming local political contexts. On the other hand, it has been argued that globalization has not been the panacea for addressing development issues and worldwide social injustices. The World Bank perspective and the implementation of neoliberal economic policy has misinterpreted the conditions that gave rise to the China and East Asia "economic miracle" and the reduction of poverty in that part of the globe. In fact, economic growth and liberalized trade, increasing exports, and multinational corporate direct investment in developing countries exists side by side with absolute poverty, lack of food security, and high unemployment. This topic comes down to, once again, a workable definition of what constitutes development. We have already been clear on this issue – we argue that the capability approach is the most reasonable, sensible, and practical theoretical framework for not only understanding development but implementing an ethically sensitive and responsible practical fieldwork approach.

What has been overlooked in the debate about the relation between development and globalization, and the specific advantages and disadvantages of globalization related to the poor, are the needs of the poor themselves. What if the assumptions about the benefits of globalization are wrong? Specifically, what if the majority of the global poor, even if they were able to double their income of US$1.90 per day, would not think it of importance to purchase a washing machine and dryer, a television rather than a radio, a microwave oven (regardless of the fact of whether they have access to electricity), or personal care products such as hair gel, deodorant, and toothpaste? What if these assumptions are all wrong? What if the global poor are focused upon and just as concerned as we in the West are about the welfare of our households? What if the global poor are more concerned about food security – buying enough food for three meals per day rather than just one, and having enough left over to plan for another day of three meals? What if the global poor are more concerned about having enough money to purchase a required school uniform so that their children can attend the local government school? What if the global poor are more concerned about having enough money to pay for a user fee required by the government to take their children to the local dispensary or clinic for treatment of malaria? What if the broader issue of unreflective and naïve Western assumptions about the benefits of globalization – the needs, wants, priorities, and desire for a Western lifestyle based on accumulation and consumption specifically as the West defines it, is not what the global poor want? Here is where the development practitioner can give orientation and advice to donor agencies regarding the indicators, goals, and impact of development programs. It is only through the lengthy acquaintance with and understanding of local context and what globalization might mean for the poor in a particular context that development can be authentic and consequently successful.

9   *Appropriate Technology*
A 2012 report indicated that only 14.9% of rural and urban households surveyed in Uganda had access to the electricity grid,[6] and that the current president, Yoweri Museveni, had nonetheless decided that he will not implement a comprehensive peri-urban and rural electrification infrastructure project. This decision has many implications for development, some straightforward and some not. Of course, one obvious implication is that many Ugandans are unable to use electrical products and equipment; charging a cell phone becomes a challenge, and the regular use of computers with access to the Internet is relegated to visiting the nearest available cybercafé, or if one is fortunate enough, to access a computer and Internet at work because your workplace has a generator and adequate fuel to operate it. Refrigeration for vaccines in rural hospitals, for example, is not available because government facilities do not have enough funding to purchase fuel for its generator to run every day (which gives rise to the need for cold-chain logistical experts from donor agencies or consulting firms to deliver the polio vaccine – costing millions of dollars).

The solution to the above problem lies in what has been called "appropriate technology" in which local knowledge and expertise devise local solutions that are contextually appropriate and significantly less expensive, do not require electricity and technical training to operate, and can be easily transferred from one area to another with minimal effort. Developed to assist poor local communities at the grassroots level, such examples of appropriate technology include vaccines that do not require refrigeration, solar ovens for cooking, stationary bike stands that charge cell phones, drip irrigation techniques, safe water ceramic containers, and many, many more that all development practitioners with fieldwork experience are acquainted with. This is where the development practitioner can collaborate with local program officers and advisors most effectively to provide context-specific appropriate technology.

As important as these contextual technologies might be, however, they are only of limited effect and do not address the fundamental issue of inequity, of equal access to information and communication technology that has been proven to change not only individual lives but the history of nations. Cell phone technology and the proliferation of its use in developing countries, such as women having the ability to pay bills and transfer money on inexpensive cell phones, are undoubtedly impactful. Yet appropriate technologies only go so far – even though they somewhat ease the burden of poverty and in the case of the cell phone bring hitherto distant individuals and communities into closer communication – they do not contribute to bridging what has been termed the "digital divide,"[7] namely, those who have access to and those who do not have access to the use of information and communications technology, and this of course includes access to and use of the Internet.

If we believe in the capabilities approach, then those who have access to information and communications technology, such as the wealth and financial elite in all countries, the political class, corporate and business centers, and personnel in universities, have access to information that enables them to make informed and better decisions, allows them to follow social and political movements, and also discuss those with others while not being limited to geographical or travel constraints. Meanwhile others, such as those poor who live in rural areas and urban slums, are excluded from accessing such information and are unable to make informed decisions and are thus unable to fully participate in the decisions, for example, that determine the future course of their political governance.

Thus we come full circle to the Ugandan president's decision not to build the infrastructure needed for a countrywide urban and rural electrification program. The glaring barrier to providing the urban and rural poor access to information and communication technology is affordability. It is unrealistic to expect the poor to pay for satellite-based programs that provide Internet access to rural areas and urban slums that are beyond their capacity to afford. Of all the structural injustices that development is confronted with, this is one of the most important. The development practitioner can assess whether universal service (providing communications services within an affordable price) or universal access, where people have reasonable access to a cyber-café or telephone center, is most appropriate for that area. Without this effort, the political and social ramifications of the digital divide will remain in effect, and the poor will remain without the knowledge, opportunity, and ability to participate in and to make informed decisions related to their own welfare.

10 *Corruption*

In Tanzania, corruption occurs at many levels: in the ostensible form of police checks for cars, the ubiquitous public *dala dala*, and lorry insurance along the main roads, or in the form of veterinarian fees charged by government officials in rural areas, or in the form of surcharge fees for the release of containers on the docks at Dar es Salaam. Most research done on the issue of corruption focuses on policy solutions, e.g. transparency, partnership vetting, community involvement, etc., from which the development practitioner receives minimal direction for moral problems confronted at the grassroots level. If an animal husbandry program is designed to benefit the lower-income families in a particular rural location, and then local government officials disburse half of the program resources to their relatives and local elites, does the development practitioner recommend the continuation of the program that has benefited 50% of the catchment population, or recommend the discontinuation of the program due to the blatant nepotism of local government officials? On the one hand, if the decision is to continue the program, then the international donor NGO risks losing its integrity and garnering a reputation for "looking the other way" and having "deep pockets" that ignores the moral issue at hand. If, on the other hand, the recommendation is to discontinue the program, then the result is to withdraw resources from the poorest people who need it most. These are the horns of a genuine moral dilemma that no policy-level recommendation can easily answer. One thing for the development practitioner to keep in mind, though, is that continuing the program will cultivate an expectation that all future donor NGOs will also "look the other way" and accept the costs associated with it.

Case study: a small NGO vs. land grabbers

Can appropriate technology help combat corruption?

According to Transparency International,[8] one out of two people living in sub-Saharan Africa is confronted with corruption when dealing with land-related issues. This type of corruption can take many different forms: elders within a community can misuse their customary authority and approve of illegal land grabs; secret deals between government officials and land developers can result in the displacement of farmers and their households; in order to secure their election, a politician can sanction the approval of title deeds to specific ethnic groups and communities. In addition, youth in rural areas lose opportunities for employment due to corruption related to land issues and are forced to migrate to urban centers where jobs are even more competitive.

In 2017, a small NGO was founded with the intention of providing a football (soccer) field for the local tribal community, which had traditionally owned, lived upon, and managed the land in Eastern Cape, South Africa, for hundreds if not thousands of years. The founder of the NGO, functioning as his own development practitioner, described the situation as follows: "A government department intervened and claimed ownership of the land allocated for the field. I later found out that officials had sold this land to a local businessman so he could develop it for his own commercial interests. This is not an isolated incident and these vulnerable communities need better tools to protect their most valuable asset. The problem is the lack of a proper land registry and transparency around local land ownership."

Faced with an obvious case of corrupt land-grabbing, the young man approached a tech start-up firm in Ghana that had developed decentralized electronic ledgers that were tamper-proof and used to record land title deeds. The Ghanaian firm agreed to make an on-site visit and provided technology to help the community survey the land; by employing a user-friendly electronic format to collect data, the community is able to confirm land ownership.

11 *Cultural Etiquette and Being Humble*

Far too often in the past, the development practitioner or the donor agency consultant, has swooped into the local community with a Toyota Land Cruiser, shaken hands with the village chief or the medical or education officer of the local ward, given a two-hour lecture in English (with a translator echoing the general meaning) to local community representatives about the design, management, and proposed outcomes of a program identified for their area, and then hopped back into the Land Cruiser to return to his hotel in the capital. Fortunately, occurrences such as this are fading away, and there is an awareness that effective development programs have to respect cultural contexts. In a fundamental way this includes treating local people as equals in the decision-making process that involves their own community; this includes the willingness of the development practitioner to be open to negotiations on a wide range of topics and issues related to the implementation and management of a program; it involves listening to local partners and communities and not assuming that the knowledge base from the West is superior to or more effective in designing solutions to local area problems – whatever those problems might be.

A challenging aspect of development work involves the identification and hiring of an individual to represent a donor agency in the field and to work closely with individuals and communities who live their lives in searing poverty. Many well-intentioned people from the US and Europe are attracted to the seeming romantic and adventurous life of the selfless aid worker that is often portrayed inaccurately. Development work involves long hours, harsh working conditions, and the ability – not attended to in most donor agency hiring – of the prospective development practitioner to sit across from an individual or a group of people who are not only poor, but with whom he/she has nothing in common but one thing – namely, a shared common humanity. Bridging this gulf is what the majority of people who have lived in the comfort of their own rich countries, surrounded and raised in a bountiful cultural, intellectual, scientific, and political milieu, cannot do. Yet this is precisely what is required of the development practitioner for implementing an ethically knowledgeable and sensitive approach to programs whose success is dependent upon understanding the context of issues of a cultural, political, religious, ethnic, and social nature at the local or grassroots level.

12 *Theory and Practice*

However attractive and appropriate communitarian ethics (or any other theory that is used as a reference point for ethical decision-making) might be to a development practitioner, there are limits to its application. Should local customs and identities, and traditional roles and values always be respected, even when these customs and traditions continue patriarchal gender subordination? In Tanzania, when a husband dies without a written will, property inheritance comes to the forefront. Elders of a particular ethnicity, for example, adhere to customary law, which circumscribes inheritance issues in relation to ethnic customs, identity, and traditions. A Masai woman who marries a Chagga man is not going to inherit her husband's home and property; rather it will go to the first-born son, or be divided among the children and other family relatives. A wife can be dispossessed, and recourse to statutory law that protects women's inheritance rights is summarily resisted by male elders. A wife can press her case in a court of law, but then risks being ostracized by the community as well as her husband's children and family relatives. The paradox of respecting local and ethnic customs which include patriarchal social structures that conflict with women's empowerment and restrict their right to development is a crucial ethical consideration for development practitioners – with no easy solution.

13   *Case Studies and Context Sensitivity*
The importance of case studies for development ethics and development work cannot be underestimated. This is true of what is described as "anecdotal evidence" as well. This is where the development practitioner can provide a unique contribution to development ethics, for it is in the conduct of fieldwork that the practitioner will be confronted with the ambiguities, nuances, conflicting values, and ethical problems that make development work one of the most challenging of all endeavors.[9] Participating in a library committee meeting, for example, comprised of local government personnel, teachers, principals, and local community members, conducted in a poor, under-resourced, remote rural setting, with an agenda of how to resource and develop the library for both primary and secondary school students in the area, brings to the forefront where potential ethical fault lines lie. Attentiveness, documentation, and accurate description of such a meeting itself, when crafted carefully as a case study, can lead to invaluable data and insight into what constitutes the successful development of a remote, rural community library. It is important to note here that this cannot be captured by focusing on the collection of statistical data related to the number of children and youth using library resources. The difference in levels of education might indicate not only a difference in values between educators and local community members, but a difference in the perception and social value of a community library built in that area; for some teachers, 1,000 books might be more than enough of a resource for community members, whereas for other teachers the goal of 5,000 books might be the minimum for what constitutes adequate resources for a library; the symmetry or asymmetry of power relations among and between the ward education officer, principals of schools, and community members might be either smooth or fractious depending upon the personal relationship between individuals, their ethnicity, their family background, income levels, and their education; disagreements within the library committee meeting might mask the deep-seated animosities that individuals have for each other which affect the development of the library. The more the development practitioner is familiar with the context of this meeting, the more instructive the case study and the lessons learned that result from this experience.

Summary

The achievement of development goals is influenced by development processes and the fieldwork approach to achieve those goals. The rights of local populations, whether infants, children, youth, women or men, take precedence over organizational objectives. Development practitioners have the responsibility to conduct themselves morally in their fieldwork. Yet this is mitigated by the lack of framework for conducting oneself morally in the field when the practitioner has been given loose or indistinct guidelines, especially when confronted with a thorny, on-the-ground moral problem. We believe it is the intention of most NGOs that the formal processes of checks and balances, conflict of interest policies, and employee codes of conduct help provide a measure of clarity to guide fieldwork from an ethical perspective. Yet NGO organizational policies and fieldwork approaches don't always translate into ethical frameworks for what is done in the field, but rather gravitate by default to those processes which produce successful impact reports and what practically works best from the NGO's perspective, as determined by their organizational mission statement, vision, objectives, and goals.

The issues confronting the development practitioner in the field, and the reference point for their ethical reasoning, require much more analysis and discussion. We hope to have provided "food for thought," so to speak, and to have sparked an interest in pursuing these topics so that development work can be even more effective in benefiting those people around the world who need it most.

Questions for discussion

1   Do you agree with the authors' description of "logframes" as a methodological tool for assessing development work?
2   How should development practitioners include local communities in their work? What are some of the ethical issues they might confront?
3   What is a context-driven approach to development work? How does this affect the development practitioner's fieldwork?

Notes

1   By development practitioner we mean those individuals from the industrial or developed nations who work or volunteer on a long-term basis to work and live in a developing country, and who work closely with local community groups, elders, and local government personnel to assist in the implementation, management, and provision of resources for development programs.
2   Wallace (2004).
3   See Waite (2017). Ms. Waite, a former policy officer at WaterAid, is one of the individuals at the forefront of a nascent movement to bring attention to the ethical issues confronting the development practitioner.
4   Horton and Roche (2010); an interesting and sometimes provocative exchange between development practitioners and philosophers.
5   Typical of the approach of most NGOs, international financial institutions, and government aid agencies is the focus on credible evaluations and reports as to whether or not aid works. As such, the emphasis is on policy recommendations at the institutional or organizational level: see Oxfam America's policy suggestions to Congress in "To Fight Corruption, Localize Aid," at www.oxfamamerica.org; *Civil Society and Aid Effectiveness: Findings, Recommendation, and Good Practice.* Paris: OECD Publishing, 2010; and also the *Accra Agenda for Action, in the Evaluation in Development Agencies.* Paris: OECD Publishing, 2010, which discusses the results when, in 2008, donors and

governments agreed to working more closely with civil society organizations to make aid more effective through numerous policy suggestions.

6 *Uganda Rural-Urban Electricity Survey 2012*, compiled by the Uganda Bureau of Statistics.
7 Haslam et al. (2012, p. 482).
8 Taken from Transparency International (2017).
9 In a section of a report published by ActionAid entitled "Ethical Sharing," the NGO provides a telling example of context-sensitive development when community participants discuss their fears about what the development practitioner can reveal or share about them with local elites, such as their experiences of deprivation, that might lead to reprisals against them and their families; see Buckles (2016).

Suggested reading

There is not a significant amount of research or literature focusing on the development practitioner; the sources below are a beginning.

Des Gasper (2006). "What Is the Point of Development Ethics?" *Ethics and Economics* 4(2): 1. http://ethique-economique.net/

Des Gasper (2012). "Development Ethics – Why? What? How? A Formulation of the Field." *Journal of Global Ethics* 8(1): 117–135.

Keith Horton and Chris Roche (eds.) (2010). *Ethical Questions and International NGOs: An Exchange Between Philosophers and NGOs* (Library of Ethics and Applied Philosophy 23). Dordrecht: Springer Science+Business Media B.V.

References

Buckles, Daniel (2016). "Perspectives on Transparency Practices at Actionaid: A Participatory Inquiry." *Action Aid International and SAS2 Dialogue*. www.actionaid.org/sites/files/actionaid/transparency-study-actionaid_-_final.pdf.

Haslam, Peter, Jessica Schafter and Pierre Beaudet (2012). *Introduction to International Development*, 2nd edition. Oxford: Oxford University Press.

Horton, Keith and Chris Roche (eds.) (2010). *Ethical Questions and International NGOs: An Exchange Between Philosophers and NGOs*. Dordrecht: Springer Science+Business Media B.V.

Transparency International (2017). "Young Change Makers Using Tech To Solve Land Corruption." *Transparency International*. http://blog.transparency.org/2017/02/06/young-change-make, rs-using-tech-to-solve-land-corruption/.

Waite, Robyn (2017). "Bringing Morality and Ethics to the Forefront of NGOs' Legitimacy." *WaterAid*, 22 February 2017. https://washmatters.wateraid.org/blog/bringing-morality-and-ethics-to-the-forefront-of-ngos-legitimacy.

Wallace, Tina (2004). "NGO Dilemmas: Trojan Horses for Global Development." *Socialist Register*. www.socialistregister.com/index.php/srv/article/viewFile/5818/2714.

9 Personal duties

Personal giving and the obligation to assist

Why are there so many poor people when we live in a world of abundance? The movie *The End of Poverty?* (2007) begins with this provocative question. The film then attempts a somewhat scholarly and detailed analysis (as much as can be done in an hour-and-47-minute film) of why much of the global south remains poor. The "structural violence" committed against the poor, in the form of burdensome taxes, lack of debt relief, unfair trade and tariff policies, lack of land reform, and unequal resource allocation are acts of social injustice promulgated by the continuing influence of a 500-year old economic system that is fundamentally capitalistic. Colonialism, it is argued in the film, is the natural accompaniment to the capitalist economic system, which reached its apogee in the occupation of most of Africa, India, parts of Asia and South America in the nineteenth and early twentieth centuries. And yet, even after the political fight for and independence of these countries, they continue to remain under the economic heel of their former colonial masters. The neoliberal policies, especially those of the Washington Consensus in the 1980s, including structural adjustment programs, privatization of local industries, unrestricted flow of capital, and the insistence of little if any government intervention and regulation of a free market economy, was a strategy put in place to address the poverty of developing nations. Yet it was only when the national economies of Asia rejected these policies, closed their trade doors, and developed their own industries and business sectors behind tariffs that the "Asian Miracle" enabled those countries to compete internationally and lifted hundreds of millions of people out of poverty.

The film's specific analyses and resulting conclusions are, of course, controversial. Perhaps, one might even be dismissive of the film's argument and striking visual imagery of the many faces of hopeless poverty and casually offer the proverbial response: well yes, but "the poor will always be with us." Yet, does this platitude release us from responding to the basic needs of others? What should be our response to the need for shelter, food security, healthcare and education for millions of poor people around the globe? Do we have a duty to assist or do we have a moral obligation to refrain from assisting? Undoubtedly, this is one of the most challenging and debated questions in the field of ethics today.

The argument against aid

Garrett Hardin's article "Lifeboat Ethics"[1] is one of the strongest and most influential arguments against the provision of assistance to people in distant lands. Before delving into his arguments, however, his Malthusian assumptions require a brief description.

As we touched on in Chapter 1, Thomas Malthus maintained that human beings have intrinsic value. This is a fact that should not be questioned. Moreover, the physical sustenance and nurturing of the human race requires food; protein, carbohydrates, dairy, and agricultural produce, etc. are all necessary for human existence. At the same time, human beings have instinctual drives; the increase in population is proof of the sexual passion that is exhibited throughout human history. According to Malthus, although it is incumbent upon us to recognize these facts, nonetheless, the unrestricted growth of a nation's population can lead to disastrous results. If, as Malthus calculates, the increase in food production is arithmetical, and the increase in population is exponential, then the undeniable conclusion is that the human population will ultimately outrun its food supply. Is Malthus correct?

Extrapolating from his argument and applying it to the example of the Irish potato blight in the nineteenth century seems to provide support for his theory. Due to the English occupation, the possession of the most fertile land by English nobility, trade barriers and consequently, the lack of sufficient nutrients for an adequate diet, approximately 2 million Irish people lived in misery while on and off the edge of malnutrition. Then the potato was introduced from the Americas. Dramatically, the population grew from 2 million to 8 million by 1845. Disaster struck in 1847 with the potato blight and the resulting typhoid that followed. What happened? Two million people died, 2 million people left for the United States in the first great wave of Irish emigration, and 4 million people remained in Ireland till the end of the blight and disease yet living in continued misery. Thus Malthus is correct. When the population of a country increases to a level that the land's food production cannot sustain, the result is disaster in the form of famine and disease.

Hardin's arguments are, as indicated earlier, based on Malthusian assumptions. It is useful to review each of his three arguments in detail since each of them has a discrete lesson to be learned. The argument entitled "Lifeboat Ethics" is revealed through a famous metaphor. Imagine you are on a lifeboat in the middle of a vast expanse of water. The lifeboat has, for example, 15 people in it, with space just enough to sustain the lives of only those already onboard. Now also imagine that there are numerous other people in the water who want to board the lifeboat. What should you do? It is almost certain that the people in water will die if you and your fellow passengers do not allow them onboard your lifeboat. But your lifeboat has limited carrying capacity and cannot take on more people without capsizing and jeopardizing the welfare of the passengers.

The metaphor is quite obvious: the affluent nations (Western Europe, Canada, and the United States) are ensconced in the lifeboat and the people from poor and developing nations are swimming around it trying to get onboard, i.e. trying to emigrate into and access the affluent life of the West. Hardin argues that the affluent nations are required to maintain a safety factor of a healthy margin between the number of people onboard (within an affluent country) and the carrying capacity of that nation. The optimum population, he argues, is below the maximum population carried by the land. Presently, the affluent nations are at the optimum population level, and it would not merely be foolish but self-destructive to allow more people to immigrate into those nations. Accordingly, the affluent nations must adhere to a zero population growth policy, and as well adopt strict immigration policies that won't swamp the boat and endanger the current welfare and lifestyle of its citizens. With some variation, this is the argument used by adherents of building the wall between Mexico and the United States to prevent illegals from south of the border from taking jobs away from Americans, as well as used by certain political parties in Eurozone countries whose platforms include anti-immigration policies as thousands of refugees from Syria and the Middle East, as well as refugees from North Africa, flounder and perish in makeshift boats hoping to survive the crossing of the Mediterranean Sea into the promised land of security and hope for a better life in Europe.

Hardin's second argument, "The Tragedy of the Commons," builds upon his first. Once again, the metaphor is simple and straightforward. There are, for example, 10 dairy farmers who own one cow each that share a common pasture. All farmers reap positive and equal benefits from the shared commons, including a food source for the cows, sufficient water, and enough grazing space. Each farmer also shares equally in the burden to maintain the commons in order to reap equal benefits. Now imagine that one farmer decides that he will add three more cows of his own to the commons. Although he benefits in the short term through his cows' access to the water and the land for grazing, the resources of the common pasture are overused, since there is not enough water and grass to feed all of the cows equally as well. What was one held in common where all shared the advantages and the burdens is subsequently undermined by short-term interest and the wonton overuse of essential and limited resources. The commons is ruined. The lesson to be learned is clear: each nation has the responsibility to and must manage its own commons, i.e. the irreplaceable, limited resources (however that might be defined, whether natural resources such as mineral, or financial reserves, or even essential services provided to that country's own population). For Hardin, however, this admonition is not enough. Consequently, he adds the striking warning that if a nation's leadership fails in doing so, then it must be left to its own misery.

This leads us to Hardin's third argument, "The Ratchet Effect." Too many times in the past 50 years, even though developing countries and their limited resources have been plagued by either government mismanagement or political corruption, the Western nations have not held them responsible and left them to their own misery. Government agencies such as USAID, DANIDA, and SIDA, as well as international NGOs such as Care International, Save the Children, and Doctors Without Borders, have come to help these nations avoid the starvation and destitution that their populations suffer. Once again we return to Hardin's

Malthusian assumptions. Nature, he argues, takes care of the commons; if people in developing countries refuse to constrain their procreative instincts and, as a result, the population increases to a level that the carrying capacity of the country cannot sustain, then nature intervenes and does it for them. Famine and disease are natural outcomes of overpopulation and the misuse or mismanagement of a nation's limited resources.

The ratchet effect is a common occurrence. Altruists from wealthier, foreign nations arrive and survey the appalling conditions of the starvation within a developing country, and decide to provide emergency food aid and medical care to alleviate the hunger and disease affecting millions of people. As a result of these massive efforts, which cost millions of dollars and to which many, many Americans, Europeans, and Canadians contribute their hard-earned money, the population slowly recovers and over a period of time finally stabilizes. Hardin continues his argument by saying that these efforts not only lead to the artificial stabilization of the population, but to a population increase which, in turn, leads to another cycle of famine, starvation, and disease. Thus the situation created by "do-gooders" is recursive – an unending cycle of altruism and then greater misery. Hardin accuses altruists of continuing to raise the level of population without coming to terms with the natural relation of the local population to its environment. Without doubt, Hardin concludes, it is wrong to provide food aid to over-populated, developing countries due to the common occurrence of the ratchet effect and the creation of more and more misery. One need not look too hard in order to focus upon an example that fits into Hardin's "ratchet effect." The travails of Ethiopia and the millions of men, women, and children who have died due to famine and its resultant diseases is a terrifying example of what can be sited in support of Hardin's argument.

In summary, Hardin's arguments can be formalized as follows: (1) aid to the poor in developing countries (poverty alleviation, hunger relief, emergency medical care, etc.) will threaten our own lifeboat and its carrying capacity; in short, the Western nations have only limited resources and those resources should not be given away; (2) providing aid to the poor overseas threatens the welfare of our own descendants, to whom we have overriding prior obligations; and (3) assisting developing countries who cannot or will not manage their own resources effectively results in the fact of increasing misery and suffering due to the ratchet effect. Thus, Hardin concludes that we are morally required NOT to give aid to developing countries.

Hardin's arguments seem to be strong and relevant and not summarily dismissed. It seems reasonable that Europe, Canada, and the United States should focus on assisting their own people and not those whose governments are corrupt and/or inept. Moreover, the responsibility people have in the above countries to the welfare of their own descendants surely takes precedence over providing aid to developing countries where that assistance might not even be effective and can actually contribute more misery. To waste money in such a way would not merely be foolish but imprudent. Yet Hardin's argument, as we have already noted in the introduction, has been largely refuted by the *demographic transition* hypothesis and Kuznet's curve that increasing development and rising income security results in greater equality and lower population growth. Food scarcity is no longer a natural fact due to the Green Revolution of the 1970s, and reliable demographic forecasts predict a leveling out of the worldwide population at approximately 12 billion by the middle of the twenty-first century.

Moreover, Hardin's approach, in addition to his Malthusian assumptions, is based on an unspoken communitarian assumption that underlies his entire theoretical framework, namely, that there is an affluent lifestyle in Western nations that must be protected and sustained regardless of the injustice imposed upon people living in developing countries. And this leads him to gloss over the fact the Western nations that preserve the current global economic order which gives rise to the structural injustices, the "structural violence" against the poor in developing countries, is what the affluent nations are causally responsible for. As already discussed in Chapter 5 in the section on "Private Morality and Climate Change," we have the responsibility as individuals, for example, to not only advance the welfare of distant persons but to act with justice toward them. This involves reducing our carbon footprint by *offsetting* it, by making personal contributions to projects focused on green technology in developing countries that remove carbon dioxide from the earth's atmosphere, which has the result of redirecting money away from developing countries and their reliance on fossil fuels in the transportation industry to developing countries that can then be spent on reducing poverty.

The argument to assist

The most important, influential, and far-reaching argument in favor of providing assistance to those overseas who live in poverty has been offered by Peter Singer,[2] the Australian philosopher well known for his support of and adherence to the utilitarian framework and specifically for his arguments in favor of animal rights. Formally presented, the argument is as follows:

i) If we can prevent something bad from happening without sacrificing anything of comparable moral significance, we ought to do it.
ii) Absolute poverty is bad.
iii) There is absolute poverty we can prevent from happening without sacrificing anything of comparable moral significance.
iv) We ought to prevent (that) absolute poverty from happening.

The first premise of this argument is a moral one; of this there is no doubt. In fact, Singer argues that this statement functions as a principle which is unambiguous and uncontroversial: if it is in our power to prevent something bad happening, without thereby sacrificing anything of comparable moral significance, then we ought to do it. The second premise, that absolute poverty is bad, is not realistically going to be challenged. Although it is more controversial, the third premise, formulated precisely and with nuance, deftly avoids the objection that my or your contribution is a mere "drop in the ocean." The argument as constructed does not address whether or not my contribution makes a difference to alleviating absolute poverty as a whole, but whether it prevents "some" poverty. If one agrees with this argument, Singer asserts, it is impossible to avoid concluding that by not contributing more than we do, people in affluent countries are allowing those people in developing nations to suffer from absolute poverty. And Singer emphasizes that this applies not only to governments but also to individuals. We are each individually responsible to do something about this situation when we have the opportunity to do so. It is analogous to the story that Singer uses to illustrate his conclusion: You are sitting on a park bench, eating your lunch and minding your own business. A young woman appears with a baby in a stroller. She decides to go to the toilet some ways away, but since the baby is asleep she is not worried. Yet the baby awakens, becomes traumatized, and falls into a pond with water over the baby's head. Do you have a moral obligation to save that child? Singer's reply is an unambiguous and unhesitating "yes." Since the balance is between your pants or skirt getting wet and saving the life of a child, you are obligated to do so. To restate Singer's principle, if it is in our power to prevent something bad happening, *without thereby sacrificing anything of comparable moral significance*, we ought to do it. This argument has generally been called the obligation to assist. If this principle is correct, then we are led to the conclusion that affluent countries have an obligation to assist those people living in absolute poverty in developing nations, no less than the obligation to save a child who is drowning. The implication, as Singer states it, should be clear and straightforward: assistance to those who are living in absolute poverty is not, as has been conventionally thought, a philanthropic or charitable act which is supererogatory or beyond the call of duty.

A crucial component of Singer's argument can be interpreted as a response to Hardin's idea that we have an overriding responsibility to take care of our own people and focus on the welfare of our own descendants. Singer's response is that distance, nationality, and racial affinity are not morally relevant criteria for our moral obligation to assist the poor. Should whites help poor whites before poor African-Americans? Of course not. What is relevant here involves a clear understanding of the idea of prudence. Prudence demands that one not give away more than one realistically is able to and thereby threaten the welfare or existence of one's family or nation. One cannot assist others if one is destitute. Apart from this, however, our moral obligation to help others is not diminished.

Another of Singer's arguments needs to be included here as well. Almost all of the affluent nations have a moral duty to alleviate poverty because they are causally responsible for the past suffering of hundreds of millions of people and for the hundreds of millions of people who continue to suffer. The following are just a few of the many examples of colonialism and its long-lasting aftereffects:

- The extraction of silver from the mines at Podesi, Bolivia during the seventeenth century enabled Spain to quadruple its reserves, build a navy that expanded its empire around the globe, and defeat the incursions of the Islamic armies on the Iberian peninsula; the result of their extraction of this

irreplaceable mineral resource has left Bolivia one of the poorest countries
with one of the lowest per capita incomes in South America.

- During the Conference of Berlin in 1884–1885, when the European colonial
  powers drew the boundaries for their partition of the African continent, King
  Leopold of Belgium negotiated and was given what is now known as the
  Democratic Republic of Congo. A vast land mass covered by tropical rain
  forest, Congo's waterways were the only practical form of travel during the
  late nineteenth century and for most of the twentieth century as well. The
  impenetrable terrain hid one of the most sought after and valuable resources
  for the development of the modern world: rubber. With his own private army
  in control, Leopold administered the Congo as his personal fiefdom. When
  the local people refused to harvest rubber for him, he resorted to force, initially by incarcerating wives and children, then by amputating hands and
  feet of family members including children, then by forced labor and murder.
  One of the least known genocides to have ever occurred, it is estimated that
  between 6 to 11 million people died under Leopold's reign from 1885 to
  1917 to extract this most precious of raw materials. The result brought untold
  riches to Leopold and the Belgian economy – with a staggering cost in human
  life.[3] With minimal investment in civil infrastructure, education, and healthcare for the local population, Congo still bears the heavy burden of a tradition
  of corruption and underdevelopment that has continued from colonial times
  to the present.
- In 1830, the Dutch implemented the Cultivation System in Java, part of the
  Dutch East Indies, which required peasants to provide one-fifth of their total
  harvest to the Dutch administrative authorities. They were required to grow
  certain crops and remunerated a fixed amount in cash. Since this payment
  was unrelated to any market forces, the remuneration was inadequate by any
  measure. The imposition of the Cultivation System was in addition to a previous land tax of two-fifths of a peasant's annual harvest. By 1850, approximately 19% of the total Dutch state income, and by 1865 a total of 33% of
  the total Dutch state income, was generated by colonial land and tax policies.
  It wasn't until Indonesia participated in what has become known as the Asian
  Economic Miracle of the 1980s and 1990s that the Javanese people began to
  climb out of the poverty imposed during the colonial era.[4]

The dissolution of colonial empires that led to the independence movement
from the late 1940s through the mid-1970s gave rise to hope for the economic
liberation, empowerment, and development of many countries throughout Africa,
Asia, and South America. Yet the transition to the post-colonial era was never
to fulfill that hope. New nation states were left politically and socially disorga-
nized; civil infrastructure, medical infrastructure, and educational systems were
underdeveloped and in certain nations virtually nonexistent; economic models of
development were imposed on new nation states whose structures benefited their
former colonial rulers; the human rights abuses that were commonplace during
colonial administrations became just as regular under the new government elites;

and most significantly, foreign aid became a tool that was interpreted as helping the newly independent nations to become more European, not to develop indigenous markets or industries.

Accordingly, for Singer, the moral obligation to help the poor is based on the historic structural economic injustices that affluent nations continue to take advantage of to improve their own people's lifestyle and which keeps large segments of the population in developing countries in poverty. When we hurt someone, we are responsible for restitution. Here is where the biblical phrase "We are responsible for the sins of our fathers" is applicable. For Singer, there is no denying this immutable fact. And if one argues that a person is not responsible for the actions of his or her ancestors, then Singer will say that one equally has no justifiable claim to the fruits of his or her ancestor's labor, i.e. to the wealth that he or she has inherited. By preserving and participating in the current global economic order, with all of its structural injustices, the affluent nations and their populations are contributing to global poverty.

Let us now leave Singer's arguments for the obligation to assist and turn to another well-known position that supports aid for overseas development and aid to lessen absolute poverty. This argument is based on Isaiah Berlin's book, *Four Essays on Liberty*.[5] Berlin argues that there are such things as what are called "negative rights." These rights are enshrined by the US Bill of Rights and the first 10 amendments therein. For example, the right to religious liberty and worship, the right to free speech, and the right to freedom of assembly are all negative rights since I have the duty to refrain from interfering with your practice of the aforementioned rights; your right to freedom of speech is protected from being contravened by others. In this sense, Berlin argues that rights and duties are correlative; your right to free speech is always guaranteed by my duty not to interfere with the expression of that right.

One of the principles within the United Nations Universal Declaration of Human Rights (1948) posits that there are "positive rights." These positive rights are rights that each individual – no matter their race, ethnicity, gender, geographical location, national identity or religion – possesses by the very fact of their being human. Positive rights include the basic necessities of life, such as shelter, food security, safe water, healthcare, and basic education. Extrapolating from Berlin's analysis of negative rights, one would then argue that positive rights have correlative duties as well. When one asserts a positive right to safe water, for example, it is incumbent upon some person (or country) to fulfill that right; in short, one has a correlative duty if one has the wherewithal to provide safe water to those who assert the right to it. The problem has always been, however, whether or not there are such things as positive rights, not to mention their correlative duties. It is not surprising that positive rights have not always been acknowledged much less even responded to as the fulfillment of a duty.

Does a moral obligation to assist take the place of or should it supersede charity?

To donate or contribute either $10.00 or $10,000,000 to Doctors Without Borders, Save the Children, or Care International is interpreted commonly as a supererogatory

act, one that is categorically different from and goes above and beyond the requirements of an obligation or duty. Most people confronted on the street and asked if
they had a moral obligation to help alleviate absolute poverty in Bangladesh, for
example, would say no. And furthermore, the individual on the street would add
that not giving a contribution is not at all blameworthy; rather, giving anything
should elicit a praiseworthy remark. It is not unlikely or unreasonable, however,
to think that the perspective of the common person on the street will change when
given more information about crushing debt repayments, unfair trade policies,
unjust tax structures, lack of land reform, and the resulting poverty of many people
in developing countries. When all this is explained to the average persons, he or she
might consider charity to be too weak an incentive and too intermittent and unreli-
able in its power to remedy long-term, unjust economic structures that keep a large
portion of the world's population in poverty. Within such a conversation, the person
on the street might be moved or convinced by an appeal to the obligation required
by a commitment to social justice rather than charity. And thus it is not a matter of
charity whether or not to fulfill a social justice obligation in providing some degree
of financial support to a Jesuit priest who devotes 17 years to working with local
people in a barrio in Lima, Peru to improve sanitation, access clean water and electricity, improve food security and shelter, and enhance local educational resources
for thousands of households. From this perspective, one is not providing charity,
but contributing to the glimmerings of reversing long-standing social injustices.
Similarly, involvement in development programs (by contributing on a monthly
basis) and providing access to the Internet that rural populations in northern India
can use to collect information about political issues and election campaigns, is both
an issue of structural injustice and one that an individual can do something about.[6]

Speaking in this way about structural injustices naturally leads to Iris Young's
argument in support of a social connection model of shared responsibility[7] that
we mentioned earlier in this book. Young argues that the notion of individual
responsibility presumed by Singer and others does not adequately explain the
continuing social responsibility every contributing member of global society has
in contributing to the present and future maintenance of structures whose numerous causes cannot be traced to discreet individual agents. Whereas Singer holds
the affluent liable for the poverty endured by the poor, Young counters that it is
both impossible to identify the causal connection between victim and perpetrator
and inappropriate to blame "those connected but removed agents for the harm."[8]
At the same time, she insists that just because unjust structures came about as
the result of aggregate effects of countless actions (innocent and not so innocent)
does not mean that social responsibility for their persistence into the future cannot be assessed.

> The social connection model finds that all those who contribute by their
> actions to structural processes with some unjust outcome share responsibility
> for the injustice. This responsibility is not primarily backward looking, as
> the attribution of guilt or fault is, but rather primarily forward looking. Being
> responsible in relation to structural injustice means that one has an obligation

to join with others in order to transform the structural processes to make the outcome just.[9]

Shared responsibility includes the notion that each individual is personally responsible for the possibility of harmful "outcomes in a partial way, since he or she alone does not produce the outcomes; the specific part that each plays in producing the outcome cannot be isolated and identified, however, and thus the responsibility is essential shared."[10] Simply put, a consumer who purchases clothing from J. C. Penney Corporation, and who becomes aware of the company's contract sweatshops that employ people overseas, is not alone in his/her obligation to do something; on the contrary, this responsibility can only be discharged "by joining with others in collective action."[11] No single customer can change the conditions for employees in a sweatshop overseas, no matter how many items of clothing he/she refuses to buy that were manufactured within sweatshop conditions. However, if we accept Young's theory of shared responsibility, we can distinguish at least four parameters for reasoning about our responsibility for creating a more equitable distribution of shared burdens and benefits. These parameters correlate with one's social positioning. Thus students, social activists, and NGO personnel have a responsibility to raise awareness about and engage the public in issues related to sweatshop conditions; consumers have a responsibility to leverage their purchasing power through boycotts; managers of transnational corporations have a responsibility to enter into non-exploitative relationships with overseas employees that require better working conditions and higher global minimum wages while permitting collective bargaining; and sweatshop employees have a responsibility to organize and advocate for themselves. In accepting our personal share of responsibility, we call on each other to *collectively* change – and not individually assign blame for – the unjust practices and procedures that give rise to structural social injustices.

Case study: aid effectiveness vs. ineffectiveness in development outcomes

Should we maximize our donations by targeting the most effective aid deliverers?

In 2010,[12] approximately one-quarter of the global population was infected with some type of parasite or worm such as schistosomiasis or hookworm. These parasites and worms give rise to a host of medical problems, including various infections that can cause anemia, protein deficiency, and malnutrition. These infections, in turn, have an insidious effect on children – especially young children in kindergarten through third grade – in regard to their attendance in school. At this time, it was discovered in some regions that more than 90% of Kenyan school children falling within these grades were suffering from parasites and worms. In a partnership with the Kenyan Ministry of Health, a Dutch non-governmental organization called International Chistelijk Steunfonds Africa (ICS), which is headquartered in Nunspeet, The Netherlands and raises money from a number of different sources (including individual contributions), began working at the district level to de-worm children in schools.

Researchers found empirical evidence that corroborated the program's effectiveness: absenteeism in the catchment age group fell by 25% or more in schools where the de-worming initiative took place. Absenteeism even decreased in schools located nearby, which were not part of the de-worming program, because the de-worming process led to lowered illness transmission rates. The success of this de-worming program led to its replication and scaling-up in India, with the addition of iron supplements to children who suffered from anemia. Research conducted one year later corroborated not only a decrease in absenteeism by 7% in children ages four to six years old, but also a significant gain in weight and reduction of approximately 50% in moderate to severe anemia.

Summary

Over the course of this book, the authors have tried to clarify moral theory in relation to development practice. In the field of development, we strongly maintain that public *and* private choices reflect moral frameworks. If the implementation of the development program does not work, if it actually hurts people, then it should be discarded or revised in light of the evidence and retooled. So too the theory that gave rise to the program. This is evident to the development practitioner working on the program, and hopefully becomes evident to those students who are fortunate to take part in a social justice immersion trip. Development at best proceeds unevenly and finds itself compromised by realities on the ground. The lack of land and tax reform and the presence of unfair trade policies often means that development helps ruling elites more than the poor who are struggling to climb out of poverty. Neoliberal policies, structural adjustment programs, etc. have maintained the dominance of a worldwide economic system that favors affluent countries and the relatively affluent in all countries. Thus we are led to arguments about economic equity, social justice, human rights, and the preponderance of consequences. Do these arguments make a difference?

This is a textbook in philosophy. As philosophers, we focus on the importance of arguments, their moral and factual premises, and whether these premises are well supported by shared principles and scientific evidence and lead, by some degree of necessity or probability, to sound conclusions. In this chapter, we have reviewed Hardin's and Singer's arguments, as well as Berlin's and Young's, in regard to the debate as to whether or not there is a personal moral responsibility to provide development assistance or aid overseas. We have analyzed the premises and conclusions of these arguments. Can we say with certainty that any one of them is compelling? Perhaps their provoking you to think differently is more important than their convincing you to act in any specific way.

If we think that compassion, fulfilling human capability, reducing disease, providing safe water, adequate nutrition, and a basic education is important for *us*, then we should think that it is important for *others*, however distant from us. We do not live in isolation – the modern world is interconnected in increasingly complex, unanticipated, and variegated ways. This is one good reason why Plato's dictum that "knowledge is virtue" should be kept as a guidepost for all people who feel morally obligated to learn about the historical theory and practice of development in order that they can act ethically in the world.

Questions for discussion

1   Is Hardin correct when he argues that the "ratchet effect" is an unend-ing cycle of misguided altruism and misery, and that we act immor-ally when NGOs or governments provide aid to starving populations in developing countries?

2   Do you think that Singer's position, obligating an individual to pro-vide some sort of assistance to people who are in need overseas, is too demanding?

3   What do you think would be the best way to implement Young's social connection model?

Notes

1   Hardin (1974).
2   Singer (2009).
3   Alan Hochschild (1998). *King Leopold's Ghost.* New York: Houghton Mifflin Harcourt.
4   Fasseur (1986).
5   Berlin (1969).
6   Most people, even those with advanced degrees, let alone development practitioners themselves, are not familiar with the Washington Consensus, Sen's or Nussbaum's theories on human capa-bilities, and perhaps only fleetingly cognizant of what is described as structural injustices related to the history of colonization, neoliberal policies, and globalization. This is where the immersion trip sponsored and hosted by international NGOs is of enormous importance for understanding the conditions of people in developing countries and the impact that the above can have. Such educational immersion trips dispel the persistence of negative myths and are transformative in grasping ethical issues in development.
7   Young (2005, pp. 709–726).
8   Ibid., p. 719.
9   Young (2011, p. 96).
10   Young (op. cit., p. 723).
11   Ibid.
12   Taken from Hassoun (2010).

Suggested reading

Eveline Herfkens and Mandeep Bains (2015). "Reaching Our Development Goals: Why Does Aid Effectiveness Matter." *OECD*. www.oecd.org

Peter Singer's Website: The Life You Can Save. Http:www.thelifeyoucansave.org.

Singer's site spotlights charities that are most effective and impactful in their use of donations and provides an easy way to calculate the impact of monetary donations targeting specific charities.

Joseph D'Urso (2015). "Young, Smart and Want to Save Lives? Become a Banker, Says Philosopher." Thompson Reuters Foundation, at www.reuters.com/article/us-global-charities-altruism/young-smart-and-want-to-save-lives-become-a-banker-says-philosopher-idUSKCNoQ10M220150727.

The interview with Singer and follow-up video link and discussion on philanthropy and "effective altruism" endorse high-earning careerism as one pathway toward increasing life-saving donations.

Pablo Yanguas (2017). "The Role and Responsibility of Foreign Aid in Recipient Political Settlements." *Journal of International Development* 29(2): 211–228.

Iris Young (2011). *Responsibility for Justice*. Oxford: Oxford University Press.

References

Berlin, Isaiah (1969). *Four Essays on Liberty*. Oxford: Oxford University Press.

Fasseur, Cornelius (1986). "The Cultivation System and Its Impact on the Dutch Colonial Economy and the Indigenous Society in Nineteenth-Century Java." In Christopher Bayly and Dirk Kolff (eds.), *Two Colonial Empires: Comparative Studies in Overseas History*, Vol. 6, pp. 137–154. Dordrecht: Springer.

Hardin, Garrett (1974). "Living on a Lifeboat." *Bioscience* 24(10): 561–568.

Hassoun, Nicole (2010). "Empirical Evidence and the Case for Foreign Aid." *Public Affairs Quarterly* 24(1): 14–15.

Singer, Peter (2009). *The Life You Can Save: Acting Now to End World Poverty*. New York: Random House.

Young, Iris Marion (2005). "Responsibility and Global Justice: A Social Connection Model." *Anales de la Catedra Francisco Suarez* 39(2005): 709–726.

Young, Iris Marion (2011). *Responsibility for Justice*. Oxford: Oxford University Press.

Glossary

Capability Approach An approach that measures a society's development in terms of the aggregate development of each of its individual members' capabilities.

Capitalism Any economic system regulated by markets in labor, investment capital, and goods and services in which productive property and investment funds are privately owned.

Communitarianism An ethical theory that gives priority to the good of the community over the freedoms of individuals within and without the community.

Comparative Advantage An economic theory that postulates that nations that specialize in just those industries in which they are the most efficient will increase their wealth by trading products produced in these industries on a global market for goods they are less efficient in producing.

Cosmopolitanism An ethical theory that gives priority to individuals as human rights claimants over the welfare of communities.

Dependency Theory A theory that asserts that poor, undeveloped countries become dependent on developed countries for the purchase of their natural resources in a way which makes them poorer and discourages them from developing their own industries.

Distributive Justice A concept that highlights the justice or injustice in how basic income and other social goods are distributed globally (between nations and selected global populations) and locally (between selected sub-national populations).

Externalities The costs and benefits of an economy that are not directly factored into the costs of production (and do not appear in the way that markets set the prices for goods and services).

Global Economic Multilaterals (GEMs) Institutions, such as the WTO, the WB, and the IMF that coordinate international policies on trade and investment through (multilateral) treaties between two or more nations.

Globalization The growing interdependency linking nations as reflected in global trade, communication, investment, migration, and environmental-security risks.

Greenhouse Effect The heating of the earth's atmosphere due to the atmospheric absorption of CO_2 and other "greenhouse" gases.

Human Development Index (HDI) An index that assesses a nation's development in terms of its Gross Domestic Product (GDP) and its inhabitants' average level of education and life expectancy.

Humanitarian Law International human rights law that specifically concerns war crimes, crimes against humanity, and genocide.

Ideal Moral Theory Moral theory that adduces what rights and duties nations would have toward one another and toward their own inhabitants under realistically achievable, fully acceptable conditions of global well-being and justice for all. Non-ideal theory concerns what rights and duties nations and people should have in order to mitigate current global injustices and shortfalls in acceptable conditions of well-being.

Keynesian Economics An economic approach (proposed by John Maynard Keynes) that endorses government spending to increase consumption and job growth rather than relying exclusively on private investments and markets.

Liberalism In its classical formulation, the political doctrine that defends the supreme value of individual freedom. In the United States, liberalism is also identified with social welfare policies that aim to maximize *equal opportunity* in the exercise of freedom.

Marginal Utility Doctrine The doctrine that asserts a diminishing level of value for additional increments of any good beyond a certain quantity.

Modernization Theory The theory that describes the transition from underdeveloped to developed societies as a transition from pre-modern (agrarian) to modern (industrial) societies.

Negative Duties Duties that prohibit harming others or wrongly interfering with their rights.

Neoliberalism The economic theory that endorses unregulated markets, free trade, and private investment – as distinct from government provision of services – as the best way to promote economic growth.

Non-Refoulement A provision of international law that prohibits the repatriation (return) of anyone seeking asylum to his or her homeland when doing so risks grave harm to that person.

Positive Duties Duties that enjoin positive action to aid another person in need.

Precautionary Principle A principle that states that an action should be avoided if it might cause something very bad.

Primary Goods Socially distributable goods (such as income and basic legal rights) that any person would need in order to pursue a worthwhile life of his or her choosing.

Prioritarianism Principles of reasoning about distributive justice that favor one generation (or category) of humans over others based on considerations of relative need (well-being).

Protectionism A government policy of protecting domestic industry from foreign competition, by levying tariffs on cheaper foreign imports or subsidizing (lowering prices below actual costs) of domestic goods.

Public Morality The duties of domestic and international governing bodies toward each other and toward those they govern.

Purchasing Power Parity   The basket of goods a local currency will buy, expressed in terms of what a US dollar will purchase in the US. Unlike calculating purchasing power through currency exchange rates, PPP accounts for international variations in the cost of living.

Social Contract Theory   An ethical theory that adduces principles of justice regulating cooperation within and between societies. Prudential, libertarian, and welfare egalitarian versions of this theory adduce principles that posit increasingly demanding moral side constraints into what counts as "free and fair" cooperation.

Socialism   Any economic system in which productive assets and investment capital are owned publicly. Historically socialist economies have generally relied on central government planning rather than markets to determine production outputs and prices but existing socialist economies combine markets and planning and may even allow modest levels of private investment and private ownership of small businesses. Democratic management of businesses by workers may also comport with socialism.

Structural Adjustment Programs (SAPs)   Conditions development finance institutions such as the IMF sometimes imposed on borrowing governments. These include devaluation of local currency, tightening of credit, opening up of domestic markets to foreign trade and investment, downsizing of government services to lower debt, deregulation of industry, and restrictions on collective bargaining by unions.

Utilitarianism   An ethical theory that assesses the goodness (and rightness) of any action, policy or rule on the basis of how well it increases overall well-being. Utilitarianism may aim to increases average well-being or total aggregate well-being; its cross-generational application may discount the well-being of present or future generations, depending on additional assumptions.

Index

Note: Page numbers in bold indicate a table on the corresponding page.